# Christian Social Graces

## A guide for the Pentecostal Woman

by
Gayla M. Baughman

**the Baughman group**
MINISTRIES
STOCKTON, CALIFORNIA

# Christian Social Graces

## A guide for the Pentecostal Woman

by Gayla M. Baughman

℘℘

ISBN 0-9710411-0-5

Unless otherwise indicated, all scripture quoted in this writing is taken from the *New King James Version* (NKJV).

Cover art "Lady On The Porch" original painting by Lillie Agnew. Used by permission.

Published by:
**BAUGHMAN GROUP MINISTRIES**
914 Shadow Creek Dr., Stockton, CA 95209
Email: Gayla@baughmangroup.org

Printed by:
**MORRIS PUBLISHING CO.**
Kearney, Nebraska 68847
800.650.7888

# Contents

ॐ

To my beautiful and gracious daughter,
Marenda Jolene.
May you brighten the lives of your guests in your own home
as you have done in your daddy's and mine.

ॐ

# Acknowledgments

I want to say a heart felt "Thank you" to the girls in my Social Graces Classes at Christian Life College for their suggestions and wonderful class discussions. I have learned more from them than all the book learning I have acquired on the subject of etiquette. It is with pride that I share their insights, ideas and perspectives. When I say "we" in this book, I am usually talking about these precious students that have etched a soft place in my heart.

Margie McNall, my inspiration from the "get go." I will never forget our first conversation that germinated the idea for this book. Thank you for your encouragement, timely suggestions and patience. I don't know how you did it, but you found the time to answer all my question-filled e-mails. Those other books are coming!

Judy Segraves, you are not only a great writer but a superb artist! Your illustrations brought my book alive. Thank you for offering your services. You are very special to me!

Mary Lou Myrick, the hours we have spent together have been precious and few. Thank you for editing this book and offering suggestions of form and style. Your wealth of knowledge has given this project a professional touch. You are my friend and mentor. I love you!

Nancy Hunt, my friend and editor. Thank you for the hours of work you have poured over every page, every word and every "comma." You are another example of a gracious lady that I respect and admire.

Lillie Agnew, I have admired your paintings for years. Thank you for letting one of your masterpieces grace the cover of this writing.

My precious husband, Terry. If you did not believe in me I never would have had the confidence to try a mammoth project like writing a book. Thank you honey, you are the love of my life.

My children, Marenda and Terry Robert, thank you for your patience, and sacrifice. You have lived without a mom for several months while I worked diligently at the computer.

Mom Baughman, I appreciate your sacrificing the use of your computer during the Christmas holidays; a working vacation I will never forget. Thank you for taking care of my family while I was prisoner to this project. As I wrote the chapter on *Christian Hospitality*, I thought often of you. I have learned much from your gracious southern hospitality.

Mama, how could I ever write a book on social graces and not think of you. You are one of the finest, most gracious women I have ever known. You were my first mentor and role model in the areas of self and social-image. As a pastor's wife, you taught me how to set a table correctly at a young age and how to entertain guests in our home. As an evangelist's wife, you taught me the importance of giving as a guest, rather than taking. If it were not for you, this book never would have happened. I Love You!

Jesus, I saved the best for last. You are the source of my supply. I am nothing without You. I have referred to Your Word often; yes, even in the subject of social graces. As You walked this earth you were the perfect example of a gracious guest, including the attendance at a wedding. You were a hospitable host, feeding multitudes and caring for their needs. The principles laid down in this book have their foundation in Your Word. Help me learn the lessons as I share with others. Bettering ourselves to serve you gives us the basis from which to strive to be a perfect vessel of honor that You can use.

Gayla M. Baughman
April 2001

# Foreword

At Oklahoma Camp Meeting 2000, Gayla Baughman shared with me her thoughts on writing a book, *Social Graces: A Guide for the Pentecostal Woman.* As she began relating her ideas, I was thrilled. Christian women want to portray Christ in all aspects of their lives, and behaving in the correct manner always reflects a favorable image. I have longed for a book written especially for Pentecostal women to give us guidance for manners and behavior during all types of circumstances we may encounter.

Gayla draws from her six years of teaching experience at Christian Life College. You'll soon see the hours of research and study that have gone into her teaching and writing. She covers the correct behavior for almost any situation, from the most formal wedding to entertaining family in your home. There are special sections for the young minister's wife as well as for a layman's wife. You'll learn just how to answer important phone calls and write a special note or e-mail.

"A wise teacher makes learning a joy," and Gayla has certainly done that. Her writing flows and is easy to read, full of personal examples that help you understand fully what is appropriate.

As Gayla states, "Loving others and serving them are vital to the kingdom of God. God commanded us to care and nurture others as we do ourselves." Read this book and learn how to care for others as well as yourself. I predict this will be your bible for hospitality and entertaining. You will find yourself referring to it often. Read and enjoy!

Margie McNall – *Pentecostal Publishing House*
St. Louis, Missouri

# *Introduction*

While traveling across the United States with my family before I got married and afterward with my husband, I learned there are many more facets to the woman's role in ministry than merely sitting on the pew or playing the piano. The skill and finesse pastors' wives portrayed in their homes fascinated me. Many of these women warmly greeted us at their doors with gracious hospitality, never having laid eyes on us before. They set beautiful tables, cooked delicious meals, and found time to hold my children and entertain us as well.

Where did this education come from? How did they come up with the beautiful way to set a table? Or how did they overcome their fear of having people in their homes? Many of these ladies learned these skills in the "school of hard knocks." In other words, they made mistakes, learned and tried again, eventually perfecting the skill. To some the cooking came easy, but the social aspect was uncomfortable. These ladies had to work on their communication skills. Others could talk a blue streak, but shuddered to think an evangelist would eat the food they cooked, adding their names to the list of endangered species! Some are still in the process of perfecting their skills in various areas of social activities. This is the process of learning social graces.

When I was first asked to teach a course called *Social Graces* at Christian Life College, I began searching for resources. After searching many bookstores and libraries on the subject, I was dismayed to find there was no single source that would serve as a textbook for this class. As I compiled my material from the resources available, I stumbled upon another revelation. From the limited sources put out by Christian companies, many emphasized areas of concern that would not apply to our Pentecostal ladies. When I approached the subject on appearance, I groped for material, refusing to put vain suggestions into the hands of students who were trying to be more Christ-like. The need for a Christian perspective on the subject of beauty and other areas of etiquette inspired this writing. Soon this inspiration blossomed into a desire to put it in the hands of Pentecostal women everywhere.

What does *Social Graces* mean? Webster's Dictionary defines *social* as pertaining to society or companionship, and *graces* as beauty or charm of form, movement or expression. *Social Graces* would mean *beauty or charm of form in the circles of society*. Some people move comfortably in social circles, others find it difficult.

It may seem that the ability to exhibit charm and beauty naturally is a gift. One may say that only extroverts feel comfortable entertaining and interacting with others. Beginning with self-worth, we will walk through the process of preparing you to feel comfortable in the role you play in society. Whether you are shy or outgoing, you can learn to be at ease with social graces.

Social graces is not a gift, it is a skill. A skill can be acquired through education and practice. You can learn to walk, sit, serve, and look gracious; but if you don't feel good about yourself, this will become mechanical and superficial. After we establish the foundation, then we will tackle the social aspect of etiquette. The difference between entertaining etiquette and exhibiting the spirit of hospitality through *social graces* is the difference between putting the skills into practice and a desire to serve others with self-assurance. Whatever areas of social weakness you may suffer, they can be strengthened and overcome.

I hope as you read these pages you will see through research and real-life illustrations that you are one of the most important, beautiful women on earth. You have been chosen by God to exemplify the very bride that He is coming back for. For that reason, it is important to be the best you can be and strive to do your best in all things.

Although this book does not exhaust the subject of etiquette it will help as you begin to nurture your knowledge in this area. Aware of the fact that there is much more information available on the subjects covered in this book, I have included footnotes and a resource list to help you study further if you wish. Along with you, I am still striving to master the skills in social etiquette. The desire to do the right thing the right way is a goal we should always strive for.

My desire for the projected outcome of this book is three-fold:

1. To help you learn basic skills in *Christian* etiquette involving hospitality, communication, and other social concerns.

2. To locate your weaknesses and learn how to rise above them in order to be able to accomplish *Social* skills with *Grace*.

3. To learn how to apply these *Graces* in your everyday life as a Christian woman whether you are single or married and whether you are the wife of a pastor, missionary or layman.

Reading this book will help you gain confidence in yourself. As you accomplish the basic skills in etiquette, learn the value of true hospitality and understand your value in the Kingdom of God, you will be on your way to mastering the best in social graces. You will master ***Christian Social Graces.***

# Part One

# Self Image

# 1
# *God's Design*

You may ask the question, "Why cover self-image in a social graces book?" The answer to that question is, a person with an unhealthy self-image will portray that lack of confidence to others affecting all social interaction. If you do not know who you are and what your purpose is, you cannot help others with the same quest.

Maggie* was one of the biggest girls in my sixth grade class. She was a large-boned, muscle-endowed powerhouse. We weren't close friends, but I meticulously worked on keeping on the good side of her. I had witnessed the black eyes and bruises of classmates who had taunted or teased her about her size, so in my wisdom I smiled at a distance and always nodded my head up and down when she talked. My heart went out to Maggie as I saw her frequently head home alone after school. Maggie didn't have any friends that I can remember. I forgot about Maggie when we moved into Junior High. For more than five years she ceased to exist in my mind.

When I entered High School, it didn't take long to meet one of the most popular girls in school; her friends affectionately called her "Moose." She was a rather large girl with long brown hair and an infectious smile. Moose had tons of friends. She was athletic and could do the splits on the balance beam, her body hanging grotesquely below the

---

* Not her real name

beam. She would roar with laughter at our ashen faces and bounce down explaining she was double-jointed and it really didn't hurt. We were filled with admiration and fascination. She tried out unsuccessfully for cheerleader and ended up Drill Team Captain, a lesser prestigious job but none-the-less coveted by most of the girls in our school. Moose had every reason in the world to succumb to inferiority, but she didn't. It must have been a great disappointment not making the Cheerleader Squad, but she never let it dampen her zeal or school spirit. Thus she was a perfect candidate for Drill Team Captain. Besides that, she was a born leader.

We started a personal evangelism program at church. Our goal was to canvas our entire city spreading the gospel. Saturday outreach became a weekly routine. One day, running late for outreach, I decided to knock doors in the same block as our church. Guess who came to the door only three houses from the church where my father was pastor? I stepped back, that childhood alarm resurfacing when Maggie, the grade school bully answered. Her large image filled the frame of the door.

I braced my shoulders and with the strength of the Lord squeaked out a tentative, "H-H-Hello."

Before I could introduce myself, Maggie wrinkled her brow, waved a large bony finger at my nose and through squinted eyes said, "I remember you." I silently prayed she didn't have me mixed up with someone she had gifted with a black eye. "You're that girl in the sixth grade—the one that always had a smile." I began breathing again, thankful she hadn't mistaken my smiles for sneers or unkind laughter. She interrupted my thoughts with another insight. "I even remember your name; it's Gayla Bibb, right?" (That was my maiden name....really!) I gingerly shook my head affirmatively. "What da ya want?" Her abrupt question brought visions of war, or somewhat lesser battles, so I plunged into a lengthy discourse.

My mouth went dry as I began explaining that our church was just down the street, my dad was the pastor, and I was knocking doors and inviting people to come—and could she come sometime?

As I muttered along, I finally realized with amazement that her big brown eyes were beginning to soften and moisten up with unshed tears. "Gayla, you're different from all the rest. You were always the nicest person in school to me. I don't know why. The other kids teased me, made fun of me and tried to beat me up on my way home, but you were different. If I were going to go to church anywhere, I'd come to yours, but you don't know what you're askin'. I can't come." She cut her eyes to the side and tipped her head toward the room behind her as if signaling something I should understand. "Besides, you wouldn't want my kind in your church anyway." I tried to disagree with her, but she was not to be convinced. Maggie never visited our church and again I lost track of her.

Not long ago I was sorting through some old school pictures and I found Maggie's sixth grade picture. I had forgotten she gave me one, which is not surprising considering it has been thirty years. Her Dutch-boy haircut made her face look large and round. I was awestruck as I looked into the most beautiful brown eyes. She was not ugly at all! She was beautiful! Her face was smooth and unblemished, her eyebrows were thick and naturally arched, and her smile framed perfectly straight white teeth! What happened in Maggie's life to rob her of friends? Where did they all go? Maggie's peers treated her the way she saw herself. Her self-image had affected her social life. Perhaps her home life only added to the disquieting opinion that she was worthless.

By all outward appearances, Moose and Maggie weren't that much different. Their physical attributes were similar, yet how they saw themselves were as opposite as day and night.

Individual characteristics make us unique. We must realize these special attributes are designs of God. Only when we learn to accept ourselves as God's perfect design can He use them to develop us into the person He intends us to be.

There are things about you that cannot be changed. God never intended you to change them. Your freckles, bone structure, skin color or nose size is the way God designed you. He doesn't make mistakes. He didn't slip when he made your nose or hiccup when he made your chin! You are His perfect design!

Let's pretend you are a famous artist, exhibiting your most perfect, recent masterpiece in an art museum. Along comes an amateur and grabbing your masterpiece, he begins to unpack his watercolor paints to "improve" upon your perfection! Globbing black blobs where the sky is and using other auspicious colors, he thoughtlessly begins covering the beauty and natural hues that made the painting a masterpiece. The amateur never once asks your opinion or approval. He plods on, changing things to his own liking. How would you feel about your marred masterpiece? How must God feel when we try to improve upon His perfect design?

# 2

# *What Is Self-image?*

Josh McDowell defines self-image in his book *Building Your Self-Image*, as a mental picture of yourself.[1] Florence Littauer defines it as, "The opinion and value you place on yourself, the reflection of your inner person."[2] Our mental self-portrait plays a very important part in our emotional and spiritual well being. Research has documented that we have a tendency to act according to our mental self-portrait. If we don't like who we are, we don't think anyone else does either. That attitude influences our social life, our job performance, and our relationships with others.

## How Was it Shaped?

The foundation of self-image begins at birth. As a baby, we begin to relate to our parents and other members of the family. By the age of five or six, our self-concept, or self-image (the person we think we are in relationship to others),

---

[1] Josh McDowell, *Building Your Self-Image* (Wheaton, IL: Tyndale House, 1984), 19.

[2] Florence Littauer, *It Takes So Little To Be Above Average* (Eugene, OR: Harvest House, 1984), 27.

is so firmly set that we have difficulty changing it. The concepts that were programmed in us as children many times carry through into our adult lives. A child who was neglected, or consistently told he was worthless, has a very difficult time believing otherwise as an adult.

On the other hand, a child who is secure in his parent's love and told how special he is will be more confident and sure, believing he has value.

### Is My Self-Image Healthy?

Trying to decide if you have a healthy self-image or not can be confusing. Think of some descriptive words that would describe some of your attributes. For instance, when you think of your personality, do you think *drab* or *cheerful*? If the response is negative make a note; if it is positive do the same. List several attributes such as looks, personality, intellect, clothes, self-confidence, conversational ability, leadership skills, spiritual dedication, biblical knowledge, and sensitivity to others. There may be other attributes that also come to your mind. Take your list and write down the descriptive word that comes to your mind when you think of each area. Count how many negative responses you have and how many are positive. If the negative responses outnumber the positive, you have an unhealthy self-image. If the positive responses are more, congratulations! You obviously have a healthier self-image. Look over the list and read it carefully. Think about each item and try to remember when you first formed that opinion of yourself. What caused you to draw this conclusion of yourself? Write down where that description originated.

**Positive Results:**
Hooray for you, if you have more positive responses than negative. Although you may have a healthy self-image,

there are times all of us feel small and insignificant. But, for the most part, you know that these times are just a part of life. You have learned to let God help you conquer each disappointment as it comes.

If you have more negative results and fewer positive ones, keep working through this chapter. You may find in the process, some wonderful things about yourself. The areas you feel are positive are things you don't have to work on. *Accept those positive results!* If you have beautiful hair, admit it and go on. If you have a magnetic personality that everyone seems to like, that would be a positive result. Be honest with yourself as you try to evaluate your traits objectively.

**Negative Results:**

Now start dealing with the negative results. Look your list over again and ask yourself these questions:

*Where did my poor self-image come from?* The most effective way to erase a negative feeling about yourself is to figure out its origin. Did someone tell you that you were skinny, or clumsy? Did the opinion of someone you admire change your view of yourself, or was it just a thoughtless person who could not bridle his or her tongue? You must determine if the original statement came from a valuable source.

*Does it really matter at this point in my life?* Are these negative feelings outdated and irrelevant to your life today? If you have out-grown a bad complexion, why are you still worried about it? Don't worry about things that have been buried in the past. Put a line through every negative feeling you wrote down that is not valid anymore.

*Is this negative opinion actually a problem in my life?* If you have been affected physically by an inferior attitude about yourself, now is the time to do something

13

about it. For instance, if you think you are too tall and you walk with your shoulders slumped, what would happen if you straightened up and walked with your head held high? In just a few moments, you would look and feel better. Your appearance would improve, your confidence would grow and you would enjoy other health benefits of good posture. If your negative attitude causes other problems in your life, it is time to take some action to correct it.

*What do I do when I find some of these evaluations to be true?* Nobody is perfect. You are probably not surprised to find out that some of the negative evaluations are true. So what if you have a long neck. You still don't look like a giraffe, even if the kids in second grade said you did. Before you give up in despair, find out if any of the negative results can be corrected. For instance, crooked teeth can be made straight. Bad habits can be broken, and personality weaknesses can be overcome.

*Is it something I have no control over?* There are some things you will not be able to change. A physical condition that limits your activity can either depress you or improve you. Let me explain. God sees you as a perfect design. Your "imperfectness" may be the very attribute God can use to perfect Himself in you. Ask the Lord to help you accept that part of you as being unique and special, a gift from God for a greater purpose.

We are going to discuss other ways to overcome your negative self-image in the next few chapters. First you must learn to accept yourself just the way God created you. As you realize your value as a person, the concept of your value to God will change. He has accepted you; so why not accept yourself?

# 3

# *Accept Yourself*

Lois was a paraplegic. Injured at the age of sixteen, she learned how to overcome her disability and be a blessing. At twenty-two, she married a wonderful man and about three years later gave miraculous birth to a beautiful baby girl. Lois did everything from a wheelchair. The challenges were great, but with the help of her husband and friends, she loved, disciplined and played with her little girl from a wheelchair or bed.

After twenty-three years of marriage a crushing divorce ripped her family apart, leaving Lois dependent upon her daughter and son-in-law. Lois was diagnosed with cancer later in her life, but she claimed her healing. Finally, a few days before her sixtieth birthday, Lois went to meet the Lord, dying of complications unrelated to cancer. Her dedication was consistent, her sacrifice was courageous, and her faith was contagious. She was my aunt, my mother's oldest sister. For as long as I had known Auntie Lois (my pet name for her), she had been disabled.

One particular time I was suffering from a spasm of self-pity. Trying to justify my own selfish feelings, I asked Auntie Lois how she did it. How could she be so positive about life, not blaming God when she had been dealt such an unfair hand? I will never forget the way she locked eyes with me. Radiating a sincere conviction I hadn't discovered yet, she told me that when she was a teenager, she didn't live for

God as she should have. The accident that bound her to a wheelchair was the wake-up call that released her from sin to live for God. She said she would rather live for God without the use of her legs than have to face life "whole" without Him. He was her sanctuary and her refuge in the time of need. She learned to overcome the obstacles and focus on her value as a child of God.

Lois would overcome the necessary challenges to be in church service; her family heisted her wheelchair up several steps to the sanctuary of our small church. Her beautiful alto voice would fill the small sanctuary as she sang to the glory of God.

Her physical challenges were not an excuse to be uninvolved in other activities in our little home church. She would sit at the grocery store for hours and sell peanut brittle our ladies auxiliary made for a fund-raiser. Offering people a sample of her candy, she would cheerfully encourage them to sit in the vacant chair across from her own chair on wheels. While they chatted she would find a way to witness to them about God, her best Friend.

Lois' positive trust in God would leave many of her customers in tears, and they would usually buy several bags of her candy. More than wanting to do her part selling the candy, I realize now that her primary motive was a chance to share her faith with others.

Although years brought pain from an unhealthy body, a broken marriage, and many other difficult situations, Lois learned how to have a healthy self-image, which carried her through many difficult times. She viewed her handicap a blessing because she believed it opened the door to witness, an opportunity that never would have been, had she been as "normal" as others.

There is always something about yourself you would like to change. Minor improvements here and there are all a part of the process of bettering yourself. Problems come when discontentment causes these little imperfections to grow. A discontented attitude becomes a giant magnifying

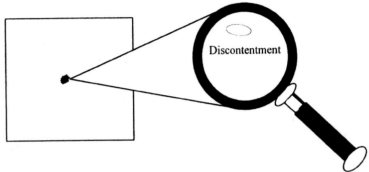

glass zeroed in on a speck. The small speck looks like a big, ugly, black hole, when in fact it is only a speck. The true picture becomes distorted. You may become discontented with your eyes. They are too big, too little, or too far apart—but never perfect. Your hair is too thin or too thick, and your feet are just in-between the right size for sales!

Your personality is *too* loud or *too* quiet; you are *too* fat or too skinny; *too* pale or *too* dark; *too* tall or *too* short. It doesn't matter what area of yourself you are concentrating on, something is wrong with all of it! Throw the magnifying glass of discontent away. What you see now is the true picture. Pray for contentment in the Holy Ghost. You will find that you *can* be content with yourself. The Bible tells us that we should be content if we simply have food and clothing, the basics of survival.

> *And having food and clothing, with these we shall be content (I Timothy 6:8).*

*Not that I speak in regard to need, for I have
learned in whatever state I am, to be content
(Philippians 4:11).*

If only you could see the big picture as God sees it.
Every single thing about you is something He designed to
help propel the purpose He has for your life. As you grow in
His grace and love, realizing the value he has placed on your
life, you will find a quiet contentedness. Now you are able to
accept **you**, the special person Jesus Christ made.

*Accept yourself as you are.*

# 4

# *God's Acceptance*

A distorted view of yourself is a common result of poor self-image. In his book, *Building Your Self Image,* Josh McDowell offers hope for those who suffer from an unhealthy self-image.

> Fortunately, your self-image is not permanently affixed in place like the photo laminated on your driver's license. You CAN develop a more accurate, healthy view of yourself. Sometimes that view will be distorted by weaknesses, blind spots, and natural tendencies, but as you learn to see yourself as God sees you, the picture will begin to fix itself.[3]

Are you concerned about some of your weaknesses? Don't let inferiority become a distorted mountain looming in front of you, challenging your faith to move it. Are your feelings valid? Does the source they came from really matter? Being consumed with one problem could easily escalate out of control and ruin your whole life. Learn Philippians 4:11 and quote it to yourself. **"...I have learned,**

---

[3] Josh McDowell, *Building Your Self-Image* (Wheaton: Tyndale House, 1984), 21.

**in whatsoever state I am, therewith to be content."** Ask the Lord to help you to accept yourself as you are.

McDowell goes on to say that our self-images have definite structures, composed of conclusions we have reached about ourselves. For example, if our parents and grandparents kept saying we were stupid, we began to believe it and to act as if we were. Our grades in school began to reflect our opinions about ourselves.[4] Present actions can be a direct result of the image placed in our minds by someone whose opinion we value.

Fortunately, part of your self-image is changing on a daily basis. That part grows and evolves through different interactions of daily life. Even in your adult life, someone may comment on a job well done or how nice you look, and this will have a lasting affect on your self-image. Positive feedback from friends and family is very important to an adult who lacked positive input in her childhood. Genuine compliments are very valuable. It feels good to receive them, but it is equally rewarding to give them. Remember how positive comments have helped you, and try to reciprocate compliments to others.

A healthy self-worth will make you feel significant. People around you will sense hope, joy and trust. Realizing that you are sinful by nature does not discount the fact that you are an important part of God's creation because you have been redeemed and reconciled to God. This positive attitude helps you see the prospect of becoming all God wants you to be. You no longer have to make excuses for mistakes. You know that you have a forgiving God. You have accepted his forgiveness, moved on and become a better person from the experience. Knowing and admitting

---

[4] McDowell, 22.

your faults and shortcomings is noble, but realizing your value to God in spite of these flaws is essential.

When your self-image is unhealthy, you don't have the ability to relate to others because you are absorbed with your own inadequacies. This is especially true when you are around someone who is constantly belittling you and reminding you of your shortcomings, or when you fall short of the desired acceptance from someone whose opinion you value and want to impress. Consequently, you become so self-conscious that you can't reach out to others because you are blinded by your own needs. As a result you may appear uncaring or proud. The ability for a loving and caring spirit to flow to others is stanched by the tourniquet of your own feelings of inadequacy. You depend on other people's opinions, praise, or criticisms to determine how you feel about yourself at that particular moment.

> Unfortunately, many people see themselves according to the picture formed early in life rather than by their accomplishments as adults. These people expect to be cheated, rejected in life. Expecting the worst, they often create what they fear. They constantly struggle with trying to be accepted while at the same time believing they are not.[5]

When someone constantly thinks she is worthless, her actions will eventually convince others around her that this opinion is the true one. She will mirror the exact image she has of herself. Yet on the other hand, if that self-image is healthy, if she feels good about what is in her heart and her self-worth is based on who she is in Christ, her actions will

---

[5] McDowell, 26.

manifest the same. This is not a new concept. The Bible has been declaring the importance of self-image for centuries.

> *As a man thinks in his heart, so is he (Proverbs 23:7).*

What words of wisdom! And how true it is that what we think of ourselves will be manifest in our actions and appearance.

How can you know your worth? You may be asking, "Am I really worth anything to anyone?" Yes! Yes! Yes! You are worth more than you could ever imagine! Your value is priceless. You are special to the most important One of all, Jesus Christ.

Jesus Christ knows your worth. He is the One who bought you with a price. How could He die for you if He thought you were worthless? God's view of your worth is the true one. Through His grace, He has shown you that even when you were a sinner, He considered you valuable enough to be purchased back by His precious blood. When you were unlovable, undesirable, and worthless, He loved you, desired you, and counted you worthy enough to die for you. As you meditate on God's acceptance of you, watch the distorted mountain of inferiority begin to shrink into the small speck that it truly is. With the mountain gone, you look much better. Now you will see yourself differently; you see yourself as God sees you. You are a beautiful person. You are a perfect creation. You are uniquely made in His image; loved, accepted, and forgiven. You are now set free from the preoccupation of self to be a blessing to others and care for them.

Let me share with you a very special thought that comes from one of my favorite devotional writers, Marie Chapian:

### *Seeing Yourself Through the Eyes of God*

*Speak of yourself as though it was I,*
*the Father, describing you.*
*The new life I have given you*
*does not make room for self-hate,*
*self-derision or self-inflicted insults.*
*You are my own handiwork*
*My workmanship,*
*Recreated in Christ Jesus,*
*born anew that you may do those good works*
*for which I predestined you,*
*taking paths which I prepared ahead of time*
*that you should walk in them*
*Living the good life*
*which I prearranged and made ready for you to live.*
*Do not be rash to utter harsh words against yourself.*
*Be careful with your mouth*
*And stop your heart before it is hasty to utter*
*Negative, demeaning words before God.*
*I Love You!*
*I call you with an everlasting love*
*Constantly,*
*Constantly.*
*If you were to think of yourself as I think of you,*
*How different you would be.*[6]
                                        ---Marie Chapian

---

[6] Marie Chapian, *His Thoughts Toward Me* (Minneapolis: Bethany House, 1987), 37-38.

23

## Notes

# 5

# *May I Serve You?*

Loving others and serving them is vital to the kingdom of God. God commanded us to care and nurture others as we do ourselves. Servitude comes as naturally as blood flowing in the veins to someone with a healthy self-image. An unhealthy self-image can be mistaken for a selfish attitude. Pray for a healing of the internal bleeding of unhealthy self-image. The implosion of self-pity and destruction will begin to dissipate as you realize your value in Christ. Gradually, as your self-image begins to heal, the natural flow will be to look for others to help.  Implosion turns to explosion – an explosion of vitality, encouragement and excitement about the new revelation of who you really are!

The term "self-sacrifice" means to sacrifice yourself for someone or something else. It is giving your time to someone who needs a listening ear. Giving a smile at the counter of a frustrated clerk, lifting a child to the water fountain to get a drink, or letting the other car get the best parking space can be examples of self-sacrifice. When was the last time you put yourself at a disadvantage to make someone else's life easier?

25

It is impossible to love others if you have never learned to love yourself. Matthew 19:19, Mark 12:31, Luke 10:27, and Romans 13:9 all say, "Love your neighbor as you love yourself." Josh McDowell states that in these passages, the act of loving yourself was understood. The commandment to love your neighbor was given with the assumption that normal self-love should be natural to a Christian.[7] Learning to love yourself as Christ does is the first step in serving others. This healthy self-image is, in fact, a measure to help you know how much to love your neighbor. As your understanding of normal self-love grows through God's Word, so will the natural desire to share the same depth of love with those around you. You will no longer be only concerned with your well being, but will experience the virtue of self-sacrifice.

In your effort to balance a healthy self-image, there is a note of warning worthy to be mentioned. An imbalance of *over-love* for self can be as destructive as *under-love*. We have talked a lot about low self-esteem and unhealthy self-image, but the flip side of the coin is a matter of pride. Be careful not to become so involved in evaluating yourself, that **self** becomes your priority of life. You can become so preoccupied with the pursuit of self-esteem, that the purpose of your journey is forgotten. The importance of balance when pursuing a healthy self worth cannot be over stated at this point. The pursuit of understanding who you are in Christ will result in self-acceptance rather than continual self-evaluation. Continue to pursue the worthiest goal of all—knowing Christ in all His fullness.

---

[7] McDowell, 48-49.

# Part Two

# Social Image

# 6

# *What Is Social-Image?*

Now that we have covered self-image, which is the opinion and value you place on yourself, it is time to look at your social-image. Social image is how others perceive you. The gestures and actions that characterize you as an individual are outward expressions of your inner self. Once you have established a healthy self-image you are ready to move on to how others perceive you. "First impressions are lasting impressions," my mom used to always say, which is probably more true than I would like to admit. But unfortunately, first impressions are usually poor introductions to the real person you get to know over time and experience. The people who know you for who you are will be the ones that have spent some time with you, learning what you like and dislike. They are the ones that can tell when you are "in one of those moods again," because they have seen you through the process of time swing from one to the other.

You don't have to fear the image people get from "first impressions" if you are prepared to be yourself at all times. We are all misunderstood once in a while during our lifetime. If you have a phobia of people knowing the real you, it will manifest itself as insecure actions wherever they meet you down the road.

Have you ever said, "If people really got to know me, they wouldn't like me?" Would you rather be someone else?

Or would you like to be what you **think** someone else is like? If you really got to know that person, perhaps you would change your mind. Perhaps you would find that she is having her own set of troubles similar to yours. The safest and simplest way to assure a healthy social life is just to be yourself.

# 7

# *Shoes That Don't Fit*

We tend to idolize those we see as "perfect" and try to use them for patterns, mimicking their actions, gestures, and tastes in style.

When Reverend J.T. Pugh was President of Christian Life College, in Stockton, California, he was admired and loved by many of the students. During that time several of the young men could mimic the characteristic gestures that made Brother Pugh different from other preachers. The way he said "Hallelujah," enunciating each of the syllables, and the way he forced a small "tnch" of air through his nose was just "Brother Pugh." We all loved him for it. He was my husband, T.R.'s favorite preacher. T.R. could sound so much like Brother Pugh, that when he was preaching revivals people would come to him afterward and tell him he reminded them of...guess who? Brother Pugh! T.R. had mimicked him for so long that he acquired some of his actions without thinking about it. I can't think of a better person he could have patterned his life (or speech?) after.

Several years later we ended up pastoring in the Texico District where J.T. Pugh was Superintendent. At a district minister's retreat, one of our dear friends told Brother Pugh that Terry Baughman could mimic him to a "T." With no way of escape, T.R. had to perform for the man he loved and admired, hoping he would not offend him. Brother Pugh

31

was so intrigued he asked him to do it again! I think that broke my husband of the Pugh habit.

Seriously, I have watched preachers try to preach like the newest "big-time evangelist" or another favorite preacher. I have often wondered what great sermons they could deliver if they would just relax and be themselves.

There is nothing wrong with admiring someone and emulating her strengths. But to go so far as to think that you would be more successful or more popular if you were someone else rather than yourself is a trick of the devil to feed on your insecurity.

## Reasons We Act Like Others

There are various reasons we try to act like other people. Usually, it begins with a problem with self-image. You may feel that, "If they got to know the *real* me, they wouldn't like me." Feelings of insecurity and inferiority cause you to decide you have nothing worthwhile to offer a friendship. So, you may look around to see the ones who are popular, evaluate their success and try to mimic their actions for the desired result in your own life. The thought, "She is popular, I want to be popular, so I have to act, dress, and be like her to be popular" is a common assessment of someone who is struggling with an unhealthy sense of self-worth.

## Premature Expectancy

There is a famous painting of a little girl in the attic standing in front of a disheveled trunk, looking in a large oval mirror. The little girl has on an oversized Victorian hat, precariously perched on her head, covering half her face. A delicate lace dress hangs in huge folds around her waist and drags the ground spilling out on the floor several feet. Peeking from beneath this mountain of fabric is a small fragile foot swallowed up in a black, leather high heel with six sizes and twelve years yet to grow.

Sometimes we put pressure on ourselves that is premature for where we are right now. If you are a newly wed, you may want a house full of beautiful furniture, just like mom. The problem is, your mother has had several more years than you to accumulate the things she has. The desire for nice things is a good one, but it is premature. You must give yourself time to acquire the things you want to make your home the perfect place. For some, this is a lifetime project. It is never wise to go out and "charge" all your furniture when you set up housekeeping for the first time. It is better to settle for a few second-hand items so you will have a place to sit and save your money for your first "new" item. This way, you will not deprive yourself of a chair in the living room and at the same time be working on that dream couch you saw in the mail-order catalog.

When you expect things to happen prematurely, you are depriving yourself of some wonderful lessons from God that come with waiting patiently for His timing. You put on

those proverbial shoes that don't fit. They are not bad things, you are just not ready for them yet. Give yourself some time; grow a little in that area. After you have waited for the appropriate time and matured a little, the shoe will fit perfectly.

## Problems That Arise

➤ People don't really know who **you** are.

➤ Frustration and stress mount as you respond to situations out of character and try to "keep up" with a personality that is not YOU.

➤ After trying to act like different people over the years, you won't be able to remember who you were trying to be like and who saw you try to be like what person. You will have a real mess on your hands!

➤ You can't gain friends who are "real" because "real" people are drawn to each other. People who are not themselves tend to be less desirable. You may find yourself surrounded by people who are deceitful in other ways. This sometimes results in getting involved with the "wrong crowd" and heading down the wrong road with the wrong friends.

## Why Not Try To Act Like Others?

The first and most important reason to avoid acting like someone else is because the Bible warns us of judging ourselves among ourselves.

> *For we dare not class ourselves or compare ourselves with those who commend themselves. But they, measuring themselves by themselves, and comparing themselves among themselves, are not wise (2 Corinthians 10:12).*

When we were newly married, my husband and I were privileged to attend a Shepherd's Camp in Louisiana. To my delight, several of the speakers in the ladies' session were well-known ministers' wives. I was amazed to discover the diversity of personalities among the ladies I had admired so much.

First, Thetus Tenney spoke on the importance of studying the Word of God for ourselves. She spoke with such conviction and perfect articulation, I wanted to be just like her.

The next speaker was Ima Jean Kilgore. She was beautiful, graceful and spoke with such a sweet feminine spirit I thought, "I'd really like to be like her, too."

Later, the last speaker Bessie Pugh came to the front. She spoke on "Being yourself." She shared the struggles and insecurities she encountered as a young bride being married to a fabulous, popular preacher. She said she felt like a country bumpkin next to the exquisite wives of her husband's evangelist friends. She began to question Brother Pugh's choice in selecting her as his bride. She said he could have chosen any other more beautiful, more talented, more secure girl to marry. Why did he settle for her? As she spoke, I could see myself struggling with the same feelings of inferiority. I wanted to be anyone but myself. The Lord began to deal with me. I was not content with being just plain ol' Gayla Baughman. I felt the Lord saying the words to me that Sister Pugh's husband said to her many years earlier, "I love you for being you and no one else."

Another good reason to avoid trying to be like someone else is if you do, you are cheating yourself of a perfect example. If we could really see each other as God sees us, none of us would want to be like the other. We all have areas that God has to work on and we are not proud of these weak spots. The truth is, not many see the weaknesses that are so successfully hidden. How do you know that the person you are trying to be like is not really struggling to be like someone else? Perhaps she is trying to find the perfect person to be like. Why not save yourself the trouble and be like the only perfect person who ever lived, Jesus Christ? Besides, using someone other than Jesus Christ for your measure is lowering your ideal. Jesus Christ himself became our example. That is the perfect ideal!

> *For I have given you an example, that you*
> *should do as I have done to you (John 13:15).*

# *8*

# *Inner Beauty versus Outer Beauty*

**The world's perspective** of beauty and God's idea of beauty are two different things. Nowhere is the faulty concept of beauty more apparent than in the mass advertising media. There is an overwhelming amount of advertising agencies, which use a woman seductively leaning on a car or doing some other activity to lure the consumer. Now the entourage includes male models (i.e. Cigarette ads). With this influence plastered on billboards and magazines, it becomes more difficult to counteract the world's concept of beauty with that which God sees as beautiful.

It is easy to get caught up in the snare of the world's "beauty yardstick." Peer pressure can cause people who are insecure with themselves to wish to be like someone they think has "the perfect body." Many women feel they are less than perfect if they look different than what they see—the images of slender, tall, beautiful women with perfect complexions constantly sported on magazines, billboards, and other advertising propaganda.

Severe health problems may develop from the dissatisfaction with the size of a person's body resulting in *bulimia* and *anorexia nervosa*. Both diseases result from an uncharacterized fear of becoming fat. People suffering *bulimia* may have bouts of gross overeating usually followed by self-induced vomiting. *Anorexia nervosa* is also an eating disorder characterized by the intense fear of being fat, resulting in severe weight loss. Many people with anorexia are basically starving themselves to death. No matter how thin they are, they still have the concept that they are fat.

According to the American Medical Association people with these eating disorders see themselves as fat even though their weight is normal or less. These pathological conditions can lead to severe physical conditions and, if not treated, could lead to complications that cause death.[1]

**Who** said a size six is prettier than a size fourteen? A doctor gave my teenage daughter and me a small pep talk fearful that she was not eating properly. She said some models in the fashion magazines have removed teeth to make their faces look slimmer. Others have had ribs removed to obtain that coveted 'hourglass' look, and their skin is stretched and removed to slim them down here and tighten them up there! After this self-mutilation in early years, what kind of monster will await them in the mirror when they are older?

Have you ever seen a movie star in person? They look just as human and plain as the next person walking down the street. In the magazines and on the screen, the film experts are shooting the best side, and weeding out the flaws for a perfect picture. Computer graphics add color and perfection to achieve the finished product. What many people desire to look like is a myth of perfection that cannot be achieved in reality.

---

[1] *The American Medical Association New Family Medical Guide*, Charles B. Clayman, MD. Ed., (Random House, New York: 1994), 758, 759.

**God's idea of beauty** says nothing about the outward appearance. He accentuates inner character qualities. Real beauty is the beauty that comes from fearing the Lord.

> *Charm is deceitful and beauty is passing, But a woman who fears the LORD, she shall be praised (Proverbs 31:30).*

Far too long we have emphasized the outward appearance. The image we ought to portray to others is first the inner person, and then the outer person. For example, have you ever met someone whom you thought to be rather homely, then after getting to know that person, found her to be very attractive? Why? Because the *inner* person was not homely, but beautiful. We often judge others by the outward person, but God judges by the inner condition of the heart.

> *For the Lord does not see as man sees; for man looks at the outward appearance, but the LORD looks at the heart (1 Samuel 16:7).*

This biblical concept does not give us an excuse to neglect our outward appearance altogether. God knows that it is our carnal nature to look on the outward appearance. That is why it is important to look like a Christian because that is the first thing others see. We must remember that we are ambassadors of Christ and want to represent Him to the best of our ability.

There is a difference between keeping ourselves groomed and practicing vanity. When the king sent for Esther, she had accepted some of the beautifying process, but she did not lavish herself with the things the other women obviously did to attract the favor of their prospective husband. Esther attracted him with her natural beauty rather than resorting to the things that stir lustful feelings in a man.

> *Now when the turn came for Esther the daughter of Abihail the uncle of Mordecai, who had taken her as his daughter, to go in to the king, she requested nothing but what Hegai the king's eunuch, the custodian of the women, advised. And Esther obtained favor in the sight of all who saw her (Esther 2:15).*

Esther must have looked natural, clean and pure, a fresh change for the royal court to witness. Accentuated lips, suggestive clothing, and dances with immoral gyrations no longer impressed the court nor gained the attentions of the king. Esther obtained favor in the sight of *all who saw her.* On the other hand, if she would have looked like a poor, ragged, orphan, she would not have been considered for the position in the first place. She smelled good, she had purpose, and must have held herself with that bearing, but she also had a beauty of innocence that attracted the king. Her self-image as well as her social image was healthy.

Taking care of your body, keeping your hair clean, smelling good, and wanting to look your best are important to being a gracious woman. You don't have to add anything to the beautiful creation God made, but you do need to take good care of it.

Your body is the temple of the Holy Ghost. It belongs to God and He has loaned it to you. Someday you will trade in your body for a glorified one, but I hope you take the best of care to keep it in tiptop shape until then.

> *Or do you not know that your body is the temple of the Holy Spirit who is in you, whom you have from God, and you are not your own? For you were bought at a price; therefore glorify God in your body and in*

40

*your spirit, which are God's (1 Corinthians 6:19-20).*

How can you glorify God in your body? It is easy to think of glorifying God in your spirit. When you worship, you are giving Him glory. When you share your testimony, you are glorifying Him in the spirit. Glorifying God in your body is presenting it to him as an offering, just as you do your spirit. When you submit your spirit to His Spirit, you are glorifying Him. By the same measure, when you submit your body to Him, you are glorifying Him in your body. This means to reserve every part of your body for His glory; from the first strand of your beautiful hair on top of your head to the last toenail on your little toe.

Each day you face the world, you should have a routine "house cleaning" of the temple of God. You will glorify God in your body when you keep it clean and free from odor.

First, a daily shower will help you feel good about yourself. There are some wonderful fragranced shower gels on the market at a reasonable price to compliment your cologne so you smell good too! If you are rushed and have to skip your shower one day, wash your face to keep it clean and free from dirt that could irritate the skin or cause blemishes.

Next, a beautiful smile should expose clean, white teeth. Brushing your teeth first thing in the morning will leave your mouth feeling fresh and your breath smelling good. If you plan to go somewhere in the evening, a few moments to brush again will help you feel "freshened up" and ready to meet the public.

Then, fix your hair in a nice arrangement that is becoming to your face. Clean hair is always more acceptable than dirty or greasy-looking hair. You should wash your hair at least once a week. Some women with oily hair must wash it every day to keep it looking clean and fresh. Now find a clean fresh outfit to wear and you are ready to go.

*A gracious woman is a well-groomed woman.* It doesn't cost much to be clean. Every time you leave the house to appear in public, you should check this "temple" to see if it is presentable. Are you representing Christ the way He would want His temple presented?

Keeping this temple healthy is another way to glorify God in your body. This is done with a balance of good nutrition and exercise. Being conscious of what foods you are eating will help to keep a healthy body. You should eat a balanced diet daily from each of the food groups. Eating the right foods will help your complexion, your energy level and keep your weight within normal range. You will feel better physically when you eat the proper foods, getting the vitamins you need naturally.

| Food Groups and Recommended Daily Servings[2] | |
| --- | --- |
| Based on a daily recommended diet of 1600 to 2800 Calories | |
| Milk Group<br>Milk, yogurt, cheese, dairy products | 2-3 servings per day |
| Meat/Protein Group<br>Meat, poultry, fish, beans, eggs & nuts | 2-3 servings per day |
| Bread and Cereal Group<br>Bread, cereal, rice & pasta | 6-11 servings per day |
| Fruit Group | 2-4 servings per day |
| Vegetable Group | 3-5 servings per day |

---

[2] *The American Medical Association New Family Medical Guide*, Charles B. Clayman, MD. Ed., (Random House, New York: 1994), 28, 29.

Some people act like they are going into cardiac arrest whenever exercise is mentioned, but simply remember to keep active. A regime of strict exercise is usually the result of a dedicated, made-up-my-mind strong willed person. If that is not you, just becoming more active is better than nothing. Walk the length of the parking lot rather than finding a parking space near the entrance of your favorite store. Walk to the mailbox rather than drive. Vacuum the house vigorously and rapidly. Sweep with vigor and mop with large sweeping motions. Who said exercise was hard? You can do it while you work! Taking a twenty-minute walk three times a week is good exercise. What a great excuse to go to the mall!

*A gracious woman retains honor (Proverbs 11:16).*

It is good to want to look your best. Outward appearance is what others judge us by, but honor comes from within. Retaining your honor and integrity will do more for your social-image than a "make-over" ever could.

I once met a beautiful girl. She had all the makings for the "perfect" woman. Her hair was clean and shiny, her clothes fit her perfectly, and her complexion was a peachy cream. I asked a companion, "Isn't she just gorgeous?" My friend looked at me as if I had lost my marbles. "Have you been listening to her talk?" With that reprimand, I studied my subject with a little more scrutiny. As I listened to her conversation with a few people, I realized how the inner person flawed the image of the outer appearance. The venom that spewed out of her mouth was disheartening. She was a bitter, angry young woman who had talent and looks but also had a very ugly spirit. That night I learned a great lesson in life. When people learn who you really are, they will look past the outward appearance to what you have to offer from the heart.

The old adage holds true,

> *"Beauty is only skin deep.*
> *Ugly is to the bone.*
> *Beauty finally fades away*
> *but ugly holds its own."*

What do you want the outcome to be when you are old and your youthful beauty is gone? A gracious woman that exudes a beautiful spirit from within or an ugly old grouch?

# 9

# *Character versus Reputation*

Character is what you are. Reputation is what people think you are. Good character develops a good reputation over a period of time. A flaw in character can ruin a good reputation quickly. You may have heard the saying, "A moment of pleasure can result in a life-time of regrets." A good reputation destroyed is not easily restored.

Those aspiring for the ministry and currently involved in it have to be very careful to protect their reputation. Others may be able to participate in situations that a minister or minister's wife, cannot. Just as insulation in the home helps save energy, an unmarked character must be insulated with caution. An evil word from a disgruntled "aint" (used to be "saint"), reaching the wrong ears, could ruin an otherwise flawless character.

One time a very wise pastor was driving alone when he saw one of his saints stranded beside the road with a flat tire. He weighed the situation and decided the chance of ruining his reputation was not worth the price of stopping to help this sister out. As soon as he was near a phone, he sent someone else to help her.

Why do I say he was wise? I remember a story about a similar situation where the pastor did stop, and that was the beginning of a nightmare of false accusations. He was accused of spending hours alone with this woman (**not** fixing a tire), and taking her to a destination other than the gas station and back. There was no one to verify his innocence; it was his word against hers. He lost a great deal in that situation trying to be a Good Samaritan. He learned a great lesson, but was the price worth it? A seed of doubt was planted and his marriage struggled. The media blew things out of proportion. He was asked to leave the pastorate and eventually was forced to leave the community. No one would believe his innocence. Years later, this woman confessed that she had made up everything. It was all a lie. But it was too late. She destroyed a man's integrity, his career and almost destroyed his life. Although the truth eventually came out, it was years before this preacher could get back on his feet, and he never preached again.

Careful thought must precede every action. Paul was very clear about appearances.

> *Abstain from every form of evil. Now may the God of peace Himself sanctify you completely; and may your whole spirit, soul, and body be preserved blameless at the coming of our Lord Jesus Christ (1 Thessalonians 5:22-23).*

It is important to remember that appearances are important to your witness. Someone in the world is watching you. What they see you do may help them make the decision to follow or reject what you represent. It doesn't take much for appearances to be misunderstood. Pray to be sensitive enough to recognize when a warning is going off. Pray it is like a red light flashing "ALERT! ALERT! ALERT!" in your spirit.

If you have any reservation in a situation, don't do it. Many times the first instincts are strangely correct. Maybe this is the Holy Ghost checking you. Give a lot of thought to what you do and where you go on a daily basis. If you feel that participating in a certain activity will compromise your character, you have every right to refrain. Making right choices is a privileged part of life. Ten years down the road, you will be able to look back on your past, with no regrets.

*The safe road is when in doubt, don't.*

# Notes

# *10*

# *I Am Made in His Image*

One of the most wonderful things about being a Christian is the opportunity to learn first hand what God thinks about you. After your conversion there comes an increasing desire to know God better by the reading of His Word. As you begin to study the Bible, it will not be long before you see how important you are to Him.

You were created in His image. He took the time to mold and make you in your mother's womb. You were a perfect design that was under way long before your mother felt your first "butterfly kick."

*I was cast upon You from birth. From My mother's womb You have been My God (Psalms 22:10).*

*For You formed my inward parts; You covered me in my mother's womb. I will praise You, for I am fearfully and wonderfully made; Marvelous are Your works, And that my soul knows very well. My frame was not hidden from You, When I was made in secret, And skillfully wrought in the lowest parts of the earth. Your eyes saw my substance, being yet unformed. And in Your book they all were written, The days fashioned for me, When as yet there were none of them (Psa. 139:13-16).*

49

As you begin to understand God's perspective, soon you will be looking at yourself through His eyes. Personalize these verses by placing yourself in the truth of the Word.

### I Am Made New

*Therefore, if anyone is in Christ, he is a new creation; old things have passed away; behold, all things have become new (2 Corinthians 5:17).*

### I Am Holy

*...in the body of His flesh through death, to present you holy, and blameless, and above reproach in His sight (Colossians 1:22).*

### I Am Precious

*Since you were precious in My sight, You have been honored, And I have loved you (Isaiah 43:4).*

### I Am loved

*For the Father Himself loves you, because you have loved Me, and have believed that I came forth from God (John 16:27).*

*And walk in love, as Christ also has loved us and given Himself for us (Ephesians 5:2).*

### I Am Accepted

*To the praise of the glory of His grace, by which He has made us accepted in the Beloved (Ephesians 1:6).*

### I Am God's Child

*For you are all sons of God through faith in Christ Jesus (Galatians 3:26).*

### I Am Chosen

*Just as He chose us in Him before the foundation of the world, that we should be holy and without blame before Him in love (Ephesians 1:4).*

*But you are a chosen generation, a royal priesthood, a holy nation, His own special people, that you may proclaim the praises of Him who called you out of darkness into His marvelous light (1 Peter 2:9).*

### I Am Righteous and Holy

*"and that you put on the new man which was created according to God, in true righteousness and holiness (Ephesians 4:24).*

Isn't it amazing that God's perspective of us is based on our relationship with Him rather than the outward appearance? Not one of these scriptures accentuates the outer person. God does not judge on the merits of the outward person, He judges you by the heart.

> *Do not let your adornment be* merely *outward; arranging the hair, wearing gold, or putting on* fine *apparel; rather* let it be *the hidden person of the heart, with the incorruptible* beauty *of a gentle and quiet spirit, which is very precious in the sight of God (1 Peter 3:3-4).*

When you received the Holy Spirit, you were clothed in Christ's righteousness. He is now the reflection everyone should see. As you grow and mature in the spirit, you will also grow in dignity and purpose.

If you find that you are not growing in these areas, go back to the One who gives dignity and purpose to life—Jesus Christ. Start at Calvary and accept His penalty for your sins, repent of them and ask him to renew His touch in your heart. If you have not received the Holy Spirit, ask Him for it. The Holy Spirit is the greatest therapy for mending a fractured, disfigured social image.

*Spiritual growth involves
a growing awareness of one's personal
dignity and purpose.*

# Part Three

# A Gracious Woman

# *11*

# *A Gracious Attitude*

Others can sense your attitude before you say a word. That is why is it so important to develop an attitude that is gracious. People can tell if you are proud, haughty or critical. They can tell if you are being real or if you are hiding your true feelings. They can also tell if you genuinely love people and care about how they feel.[1]

It is normal to experience a change in your attitude due to changes in your physical cycle. Certain times of the month, you may feel a bit more "edgy" than at other times. Many women experience similar feelings and would categorize this as basically normal. But, if you notice a great change in your attitude that makes you wonder what in the world is going on, you may need to visit your doctor. When female chemicals and hormones begin to change, many women experience emotional imbalances. Please, go see a doctor before you leave a wake of wounded souls behind your outbursts and mood swings!

## Servitude Attitude

Have you given much thought to cultivating a *servitude attitude*? This attitude is essential if you plan to minister to others. I am not talking about dropping your

---

[1] Florence Littauer, *It Takes So Little To Be Above Average* (Eugene, OR : Harvest House, 1983), 104.

household chores like the disciples did their fishing nets, and following Christ to the next town. You can minister to people in need within your reach. I'm talking about the people who live in your circle, the ones you rub shoulders with in the midst of your daily routines. If you desire to **MINISTER** to them, you must have an *attitude of servitude*. You are at their disposal, waiting for an opportunity to make their lives easier, happier, and more fulfilled. If you will digest the *servitude attitude* concept and practice it, you will be a true "minister," one who ministers to the needs of others.

Another interesting benefit of a servant's attitude, is respect. It is impossible to gain respect from others by demanding it. I'm sure you have witnessed this attitude among your acquaintances, but when you begin serving others, and showing humility, respect will come. It will be earned by the simple act of serving.

### Accepting Compliments

A meek and humble spirit is a characteristic worth striving for. But, sometimes it is a challenge to know yourself, if you are showing humility or false pride. You may have to cope with the balance between humility and pride the rest of your life, but this doesn't mean you cannot accept a compliment when one is given.

Accepting compliments can reveal your true nature. The way you respond to another's praises can reveal whether you are humble or proud. You can graciously accept a compliment and not be guilty of pride, or you can exhibit false humility, *acting* humble, which in truth manifests great pride to others.

Negative responses to positive compliments are not an assurance of humility. Sometimes in an effort to be humble, we insult the intelligence of the person giving the compliment. It is much more gracious to express gratitude for their comments. A simple "Thank You" is sufficient, unless you wish to respond with something positive.

A positive response to: "Your hair always looks nice." would be, "Thank you, I'm really pleased with the girl who does my hair."

"Your outfit is really classy!" You might say, "Thank you! Coming from someone with your taste, I especially appreciate your comment."

A number of years ago, my husband and I were at a camp meeting where Murrell Ewing was the guest speaker. Before the preaching, he sang one of those soul-gripping songs his wife wrote. After service I had the opportunity to compliment his singing. With a man that talented, I wasn't sure how he would respond to a stranger's compliment, but I wanted to let him know how much I had been blessed. I told him that I always enjoyed hearing him sing and I felt the Lord in his songs. His response was, "Thank you, you are so kind to say so." I was impressed with his warm response and prayed that I could develop the same graciousness when I received a compliment on my singing.

*"Accept each compliment as a present, words wrapped up in a box with a bow on top. Say thank you and you'll receive more; reject the praise and you'll soon receive none."*[2]

---

[2] Littauer , 38.

## Giving Compliments

It would be very difficult to have a gracious attitude if all you ever thought about was yourself. Selfishness has never been a godly trait. God himself loved the world so much that He *gave* His only begotten son as our example. As Christ gave, so should we be willing to have an attitude of giving. I am reminded of a woman in the Bible who learned the lesson of her life through giving.

A drought in the land had caused food to become scarce. The widow at Zarephath had stretched her small supply of flour and oil to feed her and her son. The food was almost gone. She was now gathering sticks to build a fire and fix a small cake for her and her son to share. After they ate, they had no choice but to wait to die of starvation. Even as she probably pondered their fate, the prophet Elijah came walking up the road. He stopped and asked her to bring him a drink of water. As she turned to get it, he asked her to bring back a piece of bread also.

She was very polite but answered that there was only a handful of flour left in the bin and a little oil in the jar. She was preparing to make what little she had left and then she and her son would die.

> *And Elijah said to her, "Do not fear; go and do as you have said, but make me a small cake from it first, and bring it to me; and afterward make some for yourself and your son. For thus says the LORD God of Israel: 'The bin of flour shall not be used up, nor shall the jar of oil run dry, until the day the LORD sends rain on the earth.'" So she went away and did according to the word of Elijah; and she and he and her household ate for many days. The bin of flour was not used up,*

*nor did the jar of oil run dry, according to the*
*word of the LORD which He spoke by Elijah*
*(I Kings 17: 13-16).*

When the opportunity comes to give of yourself to someone in need, or compliment a well-deserving person, you are allowing a place to be emptied so that in return a blessing can come to you. This is called replacing or *replenishing virtue.* If you never give of yourself unselfishly, your self-centeredness will begin to implode upon itself, but as you freely give of yourself to others, the flow of emptying and filling begins and cleanses the *virtue* channel.

The more you give, the more space you have to receive from others. As you receive from others and feel overflowing with gratitude, the need to empty the virtue channel becomes so great that you begin looking for opportunities to pour yourself into others. You begin to find excuses to compliment each other. You look for ways to make your sister feel better, to build up the morale of a discouraged young person, or to spend some time in the altar with someone in need.

The woman in this passage was about to learn the lesson of replacing virtue. At first, she was afraid to give Elijah what he asked. This would mean she and her son would starve. After his reassurance, she did as she was asked, giving the last of her provisions to the prophet. When she went back to make a cake for herself and her son, there was a sufficient supply. As time passed, the bin of flour was never used up and the jar of oil never ran dry. As she was willing to take out of the bin and the jar, it was replenished to meet her needs and also sustain the guest lodging with her. What would have happened if she had refused? She and her son surely would have starved, but that is not the end of the story.

This widow woman had an extra room for travelers probably as an income to support her and her son. When she offered her home as "bed and breakfast" to the traveling prophet, she probably never realized what lay in store as a result of her unselfishness to give in a time of need. God had another lesson for her to learn, showing her the value of trusting the One who is the giver of good gifts.

This woman's son became very sick. She told the prophet about it. Wondering if her suffering was a result of sin, she became very fearful of losing her one blessed child.

> *And he said to her, "Give me your son." So he took him out of her arms and carried him to the upper room where he was staying, and laid him on his own bed. Then he cried out to the LORD and said, "O LORD my God, have You also brought tragedy on the widow with whom I lodge, by killing her son?" And he stretched himself out on the child three times, and cried out to the LORD and said, "O LORD my God, I pray, let this child's soul come back to him." Then the LORD heard the voice of Elijah; and the soul of the child came back to him, and he revived. And Elijah took the child and brought him down from the upper room into the house, and gave him to his mother. And Elijah said, "See, your son lives!" Then the woman said to Elijah, "Now by this I know that you are a man of God, and that the word of the LORD in your mouth is the truth (I Kings 17:19-24).*

Once again God used the replenishing virtue principle when the prophet asked her to give him her son. She had to release him from her arms into the hands of the prophet. The loss of her son was great. Asking her to release him from her arms may have seemed another callous request of the prophet. But she trusted him because of his track record. One time before he had asked her to sacrifice, and in doing so, she was blessed beyond measure. God would not fail her now and neither would His prophet. This demonstration of giving once again was rewarded amply. She was not only blessed as God brought her child back to life, but her faith in a living God was rewarded with great abundance.

After a Sunday evening service, a college student came and shared something with me that had changed her life. She thanked me for my part in this drama of change, and sincerely poured her heart out to me as she expressed her appreciation. I was very touched by her sincerity. I immediately thought of the class I was planning on the subject of *Replenishing Virtue*. I briefly explained the principle to her and told her she had blessed me by making herself vulnerable to me and I was filled with virtue from her. Then, I stepped out by faith to test this principle, and told her to look for that virtue to be replaced by someone else in a compliment or other good word. Little did I know what was in store for her. She shared the rest of the story the following week with the class.

Unknown to me, it took all this girl's nerve to express how much this situation had changed her life. It was a delicate situation involving the termination of an engagement to be married. When she was finished talking with me she said it felt like a heavy weight had been lifted from her. As I told her this would be replenished, she thought to herself, "There's no way a simple compliment will replace the huge void I left behind with Sister Baughman." A phone call awaited her as she returned from eating out after church. It was her fourteen–year-old sister who had been a backslider.

She just called to thank her for the time they spent together during the summer. She told her that she appreciated the influence she had on her life and her example as a big sister. She had gone to church that night and wanted to let her know that she had made a decision to live for God, no matter what anyone else was going to do.

As she related the story to our class, we wiped tears of joy from our faces, realizing the test was a success! This was replenishing virtue at its best!

**What do you have to give?**

*...For out of the abundance of the heart the mouth speaks. A good man out of the good treasure of his heart brings forth good things, and an evil man out of the evil treasure brings forth evil things. But I say to you that for every idle word men may speak, they will give account of it in the day of judgment. For by your words you will be justified, and by your words you will be condemned (Matt 12:34-37).*

Do you give good gifts? What kinds of things are abundant in your heart? If you have good gifts, then you will see good results now and on the day you are judged by God. If your heart is full of evil gossip, backbiting, and ugly attitudes, that is all you will have to give. If you can only spew evil gossip to a neighbor or complain daily about things that don't go your way, you will not only be reckoned with in the judgment; but you can expect the same in return while you live here on earth. Wouldn't you rather have virtue flow from you to others with the reward of the replenishing virtue principle? Not only will you be rewarded here on earth, but at the same time, you are storing up treasures in

Heaven because your heart is full of virtue ready to be shared.

ᔌᔌ Grace Notes ᔌᔌ

*For one week speak a compliment when you think it. Every person you come in contact with should be rewarded with a kind word from you. As you pour out of yourself, be prepared for God to use others to replace that virtue you are willing to give to others.*

### Accepting Criticism

This may be one of the most challenging areas in developing a gracious attitude—accepting criticism. Let's think about this for a moment. Have you ever witnessed someone on the receiving end of criticism accept it graciously? What was your opinion of that person? Did you remember the criticism over the attitude they exemplified? You may have heard that "actions speak louder than words." I believe that **attitudes** speak louder than words. When someone criticizes you, your response will either prove them wrong or confirm their accusations. Perhaps you feel there is no gracious way to accept criticism. I hope I can change your mind.

There is a *right* way to accept criticism, just as there is a *right* way to accept compliments. No one likes to hear it! It is not a sin to dread criticism. We all would like to be perfect, but none of us are, at least not to my knowledge.

*The way of a fool is right in his own eyes, But he who heeds counsel is wise (Proverbs 12:15).*

63

There is a fine line between counsel and criticism. The person receiving either will make the call in her heart. Believe it or not, criticism can be a blessing. This sounds strange when it hurts so much, but if it is from someone who loves you, it can be as this scripture suggests, counsel. First of all, remember who is telling you this gem of information. Is it someone who loves you and is your friend? Sometimes standing up and telling someone they are wrong is an act of love rather than criticism. When you make decisions that will hurt you physically or spiritually, it is your friends that will be honest enough with you to try to save you from your own destruction.

Dealing with criticism can be very challenging. You must overcome your natural responses and learn to accept the criticism with the right spirit. When someone blatantly criticizes you she **is** expecting:

➤ You to become defensive.

➤ You to lose your cool – which will validate her opinion that you have a problem and you are not acting like a Christian.

A response she is **not** expecting is for you to accept her advice cheerfully and thankfully. This usually stops the criticism immediately, and sometimes this will turn the situation about face saving you from further embarrassment! Here are some possible responses to this kind of criticism:

➤ "Thank you for caring enough to mention that"

➤ "I'm sorry if I offended you, I will try to be more sensitive"

➤ "I appreciate you pointing that out. Perhaps I could put a little more work into this project"

It may take some practice to accept criticism cheerfully, but it can be done. The important thing is to keep your anger in control. If you lose your temper, it will only complicate the matter and make the other person feel superior. Keep your cool, check your anger level and always stay in control. This is not easy to do, and it may take some practice. That's okay, at least you are working on it.

After you have learned to keep your cool, the next step is to **graduate** to being able to *ask* for constructive criticism.

## WAIT A MINUTE!!!
### Did I say "ask" for criticism?

You read that right. **ASK** for constructive criticism. You don't want to approach the person you know has it in for you. Ask someone that you know will be honest and caring. I would not suggest you find the coldest heart in town to try to beat you up with venomous remarks just so you can crawl away saying "I asked for it!" Please be careful *whom* you ask for constructive criticism.

Constructive criticism is criticism that will improve your character. You don't want destructive criticism that destroys your self-confidence. It may be hard to find someone who believes you really want their constructive criticism, but with a little convincing you may reassure them that yes, this is what you really want. You want to **graduate** in the area of accepting your faults and working on them.

The three steps in the school of accepting criticism are:

1. Being willing to *accept* criticism at all,

2. Being willing to take it *cheerfully,* and

3. Finally, being willing to *ask* for it.

What if the criticism is untrue, or you are not sure whether it is true or not? When someone acts in jealousy, many times things will be said that are untrue but hurtful just the same. When this happens, the best thing you can do for yourself is evaluate the facts. Walking through the "Fact Flow Chart" will be helpful. *(See page 68.)*

First, ask yourself if the statement **true**. If it is true, move to the next question.

Is it **relevant**? Does it apply to your life and functions today, or is it outdated? Have you already taken care of the problem or taken steps to improve in this area? If it is not relevant you need to forget it! If so, move to the third question.

Is it **vital**; something that needs your immediate attention? If it is not vital, but will take time to change, be aware of the prospect for the future.

If this problem is true, relevant and vital, then take some ***action now.*** Ask yourself, "Can I make some improvements? Is my attitude bad? Do I have a problem in this area? If so, what can I do to fix the problem?"

If you are not sure a statement is true, follow-up with a second opinion. Watch for signs of this being true. Get more data, more input, then ask the question again and complete the process with the information gained. If it is true, but you never gave much thought to how relevant the problem is, you may consider evaluating it more closely. Does it hinder your productivity? Has it offended friends that you were not aware of until now? As you take a closer look at some negative actions and responses in your life, you will be in a better position to improve upon them.

If the statement said about you is untrue, just **forget it!** Bury it and refuse to worry about a ridiculous accusation that has no concrete basis.

Don't believe everything you hear and believe only half of what you see (especially if it is about you). Sometimes you are your worst critic. Be honest with yourself. If what has been said about you is untrue, just forget it and get on with life. You have better things to do than try to figure out how someone came up with a ridiculous criticism.

ৡৄ৵   Grace Notes   ৡৄ৵

*Think of some areas where you have been criticized. Begin working to improve yourself in the areas that are true. Take time to prepare yourself for the next time someone points out your short comings and practice accepting it with a gracious, cheerful response. Practice some possible responses ahead of time in the mirror. Note the response of your accuser when you are cheerful. Don't forget what to do if the accusation is untrue!*

# *Fact Flow Chart*

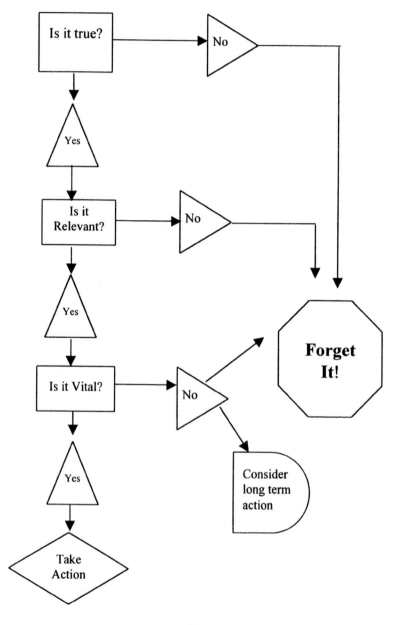

# *12*

# *Gracious Poise*

My favorite pastime while waiting for a flight at the airport or resting my feet in the mall is to "people watch." I have seen the most peculiar oddities while resting my feet. In fact, I can almost come up with life stories of the people just by looking at the way they carry themselves. Some meander down the hall, half stooped over looking like they are carrying the burden of the world on their backs. Others whiz by with the speed of light, trying to be different with rings in their nose, purple hair and leather coats. Most of them have a certain bearing. Some look confident no matter what the quality of clothing, and others look scared and unsure.

### The Esther Attitude

What makes the difference in each person's inner poise? A lot depends on how people feel about themselves. Florence Littauer calls the inner poise that exudes confidence, *bearing*.[3] I call this the *Esther attitude*. Esther had the bearing of a queen before she ever became one. There was something about her that convinced her uncle, Mordecai she was palace material (See Esther 1:7,8). There was an air about Esther from the moment King Ahasuerus

---

[3] Littauer , 107.

saw her that made him feel comfortable, inviting her to remain in the palace as his queen. *Bearing graciousness* is having the poise of a queen. People love royalty. They love the pomp and glory that goes with royal protocol. They love observing the way the royal family is treated; they admire the way royalty carry themselves and act in public.

Princess Diana won the world's admiration by her self-assured actions, her classy fashion, and her public compassion for the less privileged. She had the demeanor of a princess. Fashions followed her lead. Suits, hats and matching pumps came back in style. Princess Diana's short hairstyle was the latest fashion on young women. It seemed that women all over the world were trying to look and act like the princess. In fact, her sinful lifestyle was over-looked and even justified by men and women alike after her death because she won the heart of the common people by her princess-realness.

Although Princess Diana didn't do all the right things and live the virtuous lifestyle, she did have a gracious bearing. She was an excellent example of gracious poise. You can *look* like you have it all together, even before you do! Stand up straight, walk with confidence, and speak with conviction. If you are "tall and gangly," stand erect and be proud that you have a gracious height! If you are "short and stubby," remember valuable things come in small packages! Your social image will exude confidence when you look confident, and you will feel more confident when you practice poise.

**Improving your poise**

Here are a few tips to improve your poise.

1. Place a medium sized book (preferably hardback) on top of your head. Walk from one end of the room to the other. If the book stays balanced on

your head, then you have good balance. If the book keeps sliding off, keep practicing until you can walk the length of the room with the book on your head.

2. When walking in a straight line, tuck in your derrière (your rear-end) and point your toes ahead. Be careful not to point them outward, like a duck, or inward like a pigeon. A good way to practice this is to find a seam in the carpet or put down some masking tape in a straight line. Now position your feet on each side of the line, walking as consistent as possible with the line between your feet. Practice until this becomes easy for you without losing your balance.

3. When in the process of sitting in a chair or pew (at church) make sure you refrain from smoothing your skirt over your derrière. It is more graceful if you sit on the edge of your chair, keeping your spine straight as possible, and then gently move backward until your back is lined up with the back of the chair. A good rule-of-thumb is to remember that our derrière (which unfortunately, is the larger portion of most women's bodies) is not to be sticking out or protruding as the leader

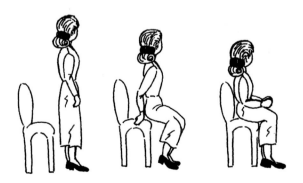

of this parade! Keep it tucked in while walking and as unnoticeable as possible while in the process of sitting.

4.  After you are seated, keep your knees together and your feet on the floor with one foot just in front of the other one. With the various lengths of skirts, it is easier to refrain from crossing your legs than remembering to keep yourself modest in a shorter style skirt. Straight skirts are very difficult to keep down with your legs crossed even if they are within about two to three inches below your knee. It is better not to cross your legs. If you feel the urge to cross your legs, you may cross one ankle over the other one. This way, when sitting for long periods of time, it will be easier to shift to a more comfortable position.

5.  Keep in mind when sitting on the platform or in the choir loft, that dress lengths look shorter when you are elevated above the congregation. It is better to sit with your knees pointing to one side rather than straight ahead. If you have trouble keeping your knees together while sitting at an angle, crossing your ankles and scooting them behind the front border of your chair or pew will help.

ᛒ᷎ᴗ    Grace Notes   ᛒ᷎ᴗ

*Find a friend to practice sitting and walking gracefully with. Critique each other and try to apply what you have learned the next time you are in public.*

# *13*

# *Gracious Clothing*

Clothes may or may not be at the top of your list of priorities. You may ask, "What does clothing have to do with being gracious?" Frankly, the way you dress has an affect on your social image. If you are a pastor's wife or supervisor, what are you saying to those who are under you? If you are a Christian, what do your clothes say to the sinner? How does the way you dress affect your effectiveness?

When you are choosing a wardrobe, there are a few details to consider before spending valuable cash.

1. Try it on, then look in the mirror at all sides. Does it cling? Is it too tight, too low or too suggestive? If you can't tell, or if you are a new convert and you're just not sure, take a friend, preferably someone who will be honest with you.

2. Is it made of good fabric? Can it be washed or are you willing to pay for dry-cleaning?

3. Lift your arms and jump around just like you would in church. Would this outfit stay modest when you are shouting in front of the entire congregation?

4. Is the color right for you?

5. Even if it is a bargain price, do you really like it or will it hang in the closet? No matter how cheap, it's not a bargain if you won't wear it.

If you want to be a leader, wear the clothing of a leader. Step out of the norm and **be** the example you have always wished for in your life.

If you are a minister, minister's wife, or leader of any kind, those you are over will tend to live just under your standards. If you wear your dresses just below the knee, those under you will wear them in the middle. If you wear three-quarter-length sleeves, they may keep theirs closer to the elbow; if you wear your sleeves to the elbow, they will wear them above. Set the standard in others by going *beyond it* to achieve the desired length and modesty.

It is a courtesy to respect the wishes of the pastor in the church where you are presently worshipping or ministering. It is always in order to ask when in doubt. Preventive medicine wards off disease just as preventive questions ward off embarrassing situations.

It is true that beauty should not depend upon outward adornment, yet the virtuous woman in Proverbs was clothed in tapestries and fine fabrics.

> *She is not afraid of snow for her household,*
> *For all her household is clothed with scarlet.*
> *She makes tapestry for herself; Her clothing*
> *is fine linen and purple (Proverbs 31:21,22).*

This woman also dressed her family and servants in good quality clothing. She did this not only to keep them warm but also to represent the status of her husband who was known in the gates and sat among the elders of the land.

You may not feel you know how to dress well but "to care is halfway there." Go to your closet and try on each outfit. What do you see when you look in the mirror. If all you can see are stripes or flowers, the fabric may be too loud. If you see a lot of flesh, it may be too revealing. If you see the lines of your underclothing, it is too tight. Whatever you see in the mirror will be magnified when others look at you.

It is important to take note of the culture and social status of the people who surround you. In other words, if you attend a church where the people do not wear expensive clothing, you would feel out of place if you were over-dressed. Wearing your new name brand, fully lined suit and the matching hat with a feather may also make the people around you uncomfortable.

Whether we like it or not, we are categorized by our social image. If you dress too nice all the time, you will be branded as rich or spoiled. If you never dress up and always wear casual clothing, you may be categorized as a *tomboy* or poor. It just depends on how the majority of the women dress in the area of the country you are in.

There is a time and place for each style from dressy clothing to casual clothing. You would not be expected to paint the bedroom in a suit you wear to church. Neither would you want to wear your paint clothes to church or to the grocery store.

You can dress nice and yet not stick out like a sore thumb. It is true some areas of the country could use a pacesetter, but to push fashion changes too soon could cause problems that you would never be able to fix. It takes time to help some women understand that they can dress very nicely for the same amount of money they spend on denim skirts and sweatshirts.

I have a dear friend that came with her husband from the big city to pastor a church in a small rural community. It was a culture shock for the women in the small congregation to have a pastor's wife with big city class. Every service she dressed as if she were going to conference. Her clothes were always clean and neatly pressed. Every outfit was accessorized with matching shoes and a small evening purse. It wasn't immediately obvious, but changes slowly began to take place. One woman and then another began dressing up more for other services besides Sunday morning. After a while, the majority became very classy looking ladies. They did not have to buy complete new wardrobes, they just gathered a few new ideas from the visual teacher of their pastor's wife, an excellent example.

Aaron was a priest in the Temple. God commanded special clothing to be made for him for two important reasons. First, for glory, to signify his separation from the other people, and second, for beauty.

> *And you shall make holy garments for Aaron your brother, for glory and for beauty. So you shall speak to all who are gifted artisans, whom I have filled with the spirit of wisdom, that they may make Aaron's garments, to consecrate him, that he may minister to Me as priest (Exodus 28:2,3).*

The Living Bible paraphrases this passage. "Make special clothes for Aaron to indicate his separation: beautiful garments that will lend dignity to his work." Aaron had a very important job; he was the high priest in the Temple. His clothes were intended to represent the importance of his position. It also identified him with God, as a consecration of separation.

Your clothes make a statement to those around you. If you were given an important job and you dressed in a wrinkled, dirty rag, how would you convince anyone to listen to you or accept your work? Your work would be questionable because your appearance is questionable. On the other hand, if you dressed in nice, beautiful clothes, your clothes would add dignity to your job, just as it did with Aaron. Whatever your position is in the Kingdom of God, it is important. Wear clothes that **Add dignity** to your work.[4]

### Clothes that fit your shape

Wearing clothes that add dignity to your work starts with clothes that fit correctly. Clothes that are too small or too large take away from a well-groomed look. There are several different considerations when choosing fashion styles. Facial features, height and bone structures are some of the things to consider when trying to determine which style suits you best.

Study your features in a full-length mirror. Is your face round, square, or rectangular? Do you have a short neck or a long one? Are you tall and slender, or short and thick? Do you have a thick waist or a very thin one? Are your hips

round or flat? Are your legs long, short or average? Try to determine the shape of your face and body.

*Necklines* - A contrasting neckline balances your face. For example, if you have a round face, avoid round necklines. If you have a square jaw, avoid square necklines and so on.

---

[4] Littauer , 110.

If you have a long neck, a V neckline will make it look longer. Scarves and turtle necks or cowl collars are better for long necks.

A short neck needs an open collar, V-neck, or a scoop neck (Not too scooped; bend over and make sure it is modest).

*Height* - A short, stout person would want to avoid horizontal lines because they cut the image in half and make her appear shorter. If a short woman wants to wear skirts and blouses or suits, the high-waisted clothes and shorter-length jackets and vests look best. Long vertical lines make a person look taller and slimmer. A tall, slender person can wear more variety in fashion than the shorter person. Low-waists and fuller styles look fine on this body shape, but if

she is very tall (5'7" or taller), she needs to avoid the short-waisted jackets and high-waisted lines.

*Weight* - Tight fitting clothes don't flatter either large or thin-framed bodies. Stretchy or thin fabrics cause an outfit to cling more than other fabrics would. Showing a panty line is a ***no-no!*** The poorest of taste is exhibiting your underclothing. If the skirt is not too tight, this can be remedied simply with control-top pantyhose or a slip. A slip

is a wonderful little invention. It will smooth out unwanted lines, it will keep your clothes from looking transparent and it will aid in fighting against static cling. With the exception of some denim fabrics, skirts that do not have a lining need a slip. Usually, skirts designed from heavier fabric such as wool or linen will have a lining, so a slip is not needed.

Seeing through your clothing is another ***no-no!*** Flowing fabrics that are double layered but still thin, need a slip. If you are unsure about wearing a slip, step to a window and allow a friend to tell you if she can see through your skirt or if your panty line is showing. It is not only embarrassing for other girls to see "straight through you," it is also embarrassing for the guys as well.

A tight skirt or dress will make a thin woman look underweight. Rather than

flattering the thinness she does have, she will highlight the lack of curves she does not have. Extremely thin bodies can soften the angles with fullness in the sleeves and by wearing prints and detail. Larger women can enhance their frames with vertical lines. Be careful these lines are not too far apart though, this will make you appear wide rather than slim and vice-versa for the thin frame. The large woman should wear accessories that draw the eye away from her middle.

### Ten Ways to Look Thinner:

1. Practice good posture. Stand up straight, square your shoulders, tuck in your tummy and hold your head erect.

2. Monochromatic colors create the illusion of height and slimness.

3. Darker colors are more minimizing than lighter shades.

4. Keep a closer fit rather than baggy clothes. Large, loose fitting clothes tend to add pounds, but keep in mind that tight fitting clothes show the excess pounds too!

5. Avoid drop shoulder styles that make you appear shorter and wider.

6. Choose lighter weight fabrics to slim your silhouette rather than adding bulk with heavier garments.

7. Straight skirts are great for a slenderizing effect.

8. Be careful not to overdo heavy embroidery, sequins, and lots of pockets and pleats. These add bulk to your figure.

9. Balance fuller pieces with narrow ones. For example, wear a loose fitting jacket with a straight skirt.

10. Choose pumps over ankle-strap shoes which make your legs look chunky. Also, if you are wearing boots, your skirt hem should cover the top of the boot. A space between the boot and the skirt make your legs look shorter.

***Wide hips wear:***

&#x6273; Dark solid colors on the bottom and lighter colors on top

&#x6273; Shoulder pads to balance large hips with small shoulders

&#x6273; Narrow belts rather than wide ones

***Thick waists wear:***

&#x6273; Tops that end below the waist

&#x6273; Single-breasted jackets with defined waists

&#x6273; Wrap or flat front skirts

&#x6273; Shirts untucked and jackets open over tops

***Thick thighs wear:***

&#x6273; Trouser-skirts or straight skirts with narrow pinstripes

&#x6273; Extra thigh-control panty hose

&#x6273; Fingertip-length jackets

***Large bust wear:***

&#x6273; High necklines to offset curves

&#x6273; Wide straps on dresses and tops

&#x6273; Darker colors on top

&#x6273;Open jackets or cardigans with skirts

***Small bust wear:***

&#x6273; Bright colors on top

&#x6273; Shoulder pads to give balance

&#x6273; Tops with vertical stripes[5]

---

[5] "McCall's guide to dressing 10 Lbs. Thinner," *McCall's Magazine*, Sept. 2000 Extra.

Broadens

Slims

Broadens

Slims

## Clothes that fit Your Personality

Personality states your style. Many times it depends on your personality as to what type of clothes you pick out at your favorite store.

The quiet, easy-going type of person rarely likes to wear large fluffy sleeves and bright colors with sequins. You will notice that the woman with more extravagant taste in clothing is probably the most outgoing in nature. This does not mean that shy people don't like bright clothes or that they never fall into the "paid too much" bracket. It is the style of clothes we are talking about, not the price.

Everyone is different, and we all like to have our own style. The personality of each person plays a big part in what type of clothing she will wear. The introvert is the quiet, shy person that does not want to be embarrassed by undue attention, whereas the extrovert is the opposite. A person that is outgoing, sometimes loud, and the center of attention is the extrovert. No matter what style of clothing these two basic personalities have, they will dress to either blend with the crowd (introvert) or make a statement (extrovert).

*The tailored person* - This person likes straight lines rather than puffy sleeves and peplums at the waist. Whether she chooses more subdued colors and conservative fabrics or bright, bold exotic cloth, she tends to lean more toward straight sleeves and skirts. This person often chooses solid colors over prints. A fabric that can be worn year-round suits her fine. This is not to say she wouldn't like a jungle print, but she may choose to put it with a jacket or vest of a coordinating color. It is all right if she is not the "lacey" type of person. She can still look very feminine in tailored clothing.

*The frilly person* – Ruffles and lace are the signature of the person who likes a more frilly style of clothing. Puffed sleeves lend a softer touch to an outfit. Put this person in an outfit with sheer overlays and flowing soft fabric and she will feel right at home. She tends to pick out the lightweight material with prints over the heavier solids.

Whether she is small, medium, or large-sized, there are frilly styles that look good on her. The larger woman may want to steer clear of an abundance of large ruffles in the wrong places, but moderate ruffles and lace can be very feminine.

*The combination person* – It just depends on the mood. Sometimes a tailored suit with a shirt or turtleneck fits the occasion and other times a soft frilly dress with lace at the neck will feel more suitable. The combination person experiences more versatility dressing either tailored or frilly.

Perhaps we all should try some variety, but just as there is a time and season for many other things, there are times and seasons for certain types of clothing. Formal wear should be reserved for evenings or special occasions. In the workplace suits have been more acceptable in the office of an executive, but are rising in popularity for other occasions.

Although personality has a bearing on the clothes we prefer to wear, there is a call for moderation as a leader. Business executives wear a conservative "uniform" that directs attention *away* from appearance *toward* the content of their position. The same should apply to Christians, being careful to wear clothing that exemplifies Christ. Personality, intelligence, charm and ability can shine when someone is dressed in proper attire.[6]

---

[6] Linda Phillips and Wayne Phillips, *The Concise Guide to Executive Etiquette* (New York: Doubleday, 1990), 7.

### Clothes that fit Your Budget

Believe it or not you can be on the lowest of budgets and still find clothing that is nice and gracious. *Quality* and *style* are the two key factors to look for when shopping on a budget.

If you find something of good quality but it is out of style, you have not found a bargain, unless you hold on to it until it comes back into style (only about 20 years or so). If you find something that is in style but of poor quality, you may look great in it at first, but you won't get the wear you bargained for.

Here are a few things to remember to get the best quality clothing for the best price.

1. Look for quality in fabric and construction. For example, cheaper quality clothing will have larger stitches in the seams, patterns will not be matched at the seams and the fabric may be lighter weight than other outfits of similar design.

2. Look for care instructions. "Dry clean only," does not mean it is a better garment. Some inferior dry-clean garments will shrink in spite of the utmost care even when professionally done.

3. Look on the label for blends. One hundred percent cotton will last a long time, but many times it must be pressed after each washing (and sometimes between). Wool should feel heavier than a blend of wool and polyester. Some linen can be hand-washed, but acetate rarely comes through liquid unscathed. A blend of polyester

and cotton is very sturdy fabric. If you get a larger percentage of polyester than cotton, it will be permanent press. (I love it because I hate to iron.)

In the next chapter, we will discuss how to shop smart when dealing with a limited budget. We all love bargains! It is very rewarding to be able to find something of superior quality at a reasonable price.

# *Notes*

_____
_____
_____
_____
_____
_____
_____
_____
_____
_____
_____
_____
_____
_____
_____
_____
_____
_____
_____
_____
_____
_____
_____
_____
_____
_____
_____
_____
_____

# *14*

# *Shopping Smart*

When she walked into the room, we all turned our heads. Not because her clothes were loud or flashy, but because we knew that when Rona dressed, it would be the best. I always admired the way her clothes fit. "She must shop at the most expensive places," I confided to my mother.

Rona never looked frumpy or disheveled. Her clothes were always pressed and neat, and her hair was always perfect. I, among others was a distant admirer, allowing her to be a pacesetter for my own style.

When we got a little better acquainted, I found out her secret. Keep reading and you will too.

### On-sale Items

On-sale items can be great money savers if you time your shopping right. On the other hand, if you buy something simply because it is on sale at a great price and never wear it, you have thrown away valuable cash. The money you save resisting something you would never wear could be applied to something you will wear even if it is a little more expensive.

## Outlet Shopping

Outlet shopping is very popular. Sometimes you can find real bargains at these stores, but you have to be careful not to expect department store prices. The outlets will have items at approximately a thirty percent discount. If you are expecting fifty percent or more, you may be better off going to the department store when they are running a sale. Finding a sale at an outlet is my favorite thing. Hooray! Now that's a bargain!

When you shop the outlets the clothes will be off-season. You may find sweaters and wool blazers during the summer and short-sleeved tops and linen blazers in the winter. If you plan ahead, this will not be an inconvenience for you. When it is ninety degrees outside it may be more difficult to purchase a wool sweater, even if it is on sale. Remember, a warm sweater will feel good a few months later.

## Thrift Store Shopping

If you don't mind spending hours thumbing through racks and racks of used clothing to find something that has been worn, this is the place for you. Many times you can find name brand clothes that are fairly used. It is great when you find something that someone has either out grown or no longer fits because she lost weight, with many seasons of wear left. Thoroughly check the clothes for holes that cannot be fixed, such as in the fabric rather than at the seam. Look for fading and fabric wear. Then take the time to try it on. If it doesn't fit put it back. Buying something for "when I lose weight" is not smart shopping.

## Consignment Shopping

Well, here it is – Rona's secret. Yes, believe it or not she was a consignment shopper. She was also a seamstress. She would buy clothes at these elite shops, and then adjust them to fit her to a "T." Take heart if you can't sew. There are plenty of wonderful things out there that will fit you without taking in a seam here or adding a piece there.

Consignment shops have different policies. Usually they will have to sell clothes you bring to them before you receive your part of the price. This would be a great place to take those clothes you bought for "when I lose weight," but are still hanging in your closet.

Some shops will give you cash for your clothes and you may shop anywhere with the money. Others will give you a voucher to spend only in their store. At any rate, the clothes in a consignment shop are usually less worn and of higher quality. However, you may pay a little more than at a thrift store.

Some consignment shops are conscious of the seasons, so you can find things to wear immediately. I shop at a nice consignment shop in my hometown. After cleaning out my closet, I take my nicer clothing to this exclusive second-hand shop. They sell the clothing and put the money on my account. I can either get cash or shop in the store. I like to shop there because I can find the nicest things for less than half the price I would find in the department stores. Many of the things I have purchased there are almost new. The clothes that don't sell at this consignment shop, are donated to a worthy cause. Try it. This way you can't lose!

### Discount Shopping

Discount stores buy merchandise in bulk, which makes it cheaper for the consumer. Consequently, you may see fifteen blouses just like yours at the next camp meeting or youth convention. If you are the type of person that doesn't like to see yourself coming down the street, you may want to use discount shopping for your lingerie, shells to wear under blazers, or other accessories that blend with your primary outfit which was purchased elsewhere.

Although a discount store will carry a more casual line of inventory, the quality of clothing is usually just as nice as at a department store. The main advantage to shopping discount stores is that the price is right.

*There is nothing more beautiful*
*than a godly woman.*

# Part Four

# Communication Graces

# 15
# *Introductions*

Every year we made it a point to attend the United Pentecostal Church General Conference. My husband and I met hundreds of people because we traveled as evangelists for many years. My only apprehension was meeting people I should know and not being able to remember their names. If I saw a couple at a distance I couldn't quite remember, I would start quizzing myself under my breath immediately. "What is their name? Where are they from? Do they have kids and how old are they? Think! Think! Think!"

Finally, when I had tortured myself long enough, I would lean over coyly and ask my husband, "Dear, do you recall that couple's name?" To my frustration he could always remember their name, not to mention their phone number, street address and car license number! I would smile sweetly, pretending this was a first and lean back with steam shooting out of my ears. I sure wish I had a memory like that! But I don't. So, I have to work with what I've got!

Have you ever felt that way? A wave of panic rushes through your body as you realize you are expected to make an introduction or remember someone's name for some other reason and you know good and well that the name is as elusive as the proverbial butterfly. Panic! Now the flying nuisance is in the pit of your stomach! Maybe we could just wipe introductions out of our lives. Sorry, that won't work. Whether you are good at it or not, introductions are a necessary part of our society. Okay, come on, quit digging in your heels. If you have to do introductions, take a minute and learn how to do them right.

Introductions are in order when two strangers meet in the company of a mutual friend. Whether you remember their name or not, put them in the wrong order or make some other mistake, some form of introduction is better than avoiding one. It is rude to chat with a friend and leave the new comer out of the conversation.

Generally speaking, you say the name of the person to whom the other is being introduced first: "Mrs. Brown, may I introduce Mrs. Smith." Otherwise, proper introductions start with the person according to gender, age, and social status.

### Three Rules:

1.  A ***man*** is always introduced to a ***woman***.

    "Mrs. Brown, I'd like you to meet Mr. Matthews"

    *Or* "Karen, this is my cousin, Andrew Matthews. Andrew, this is Karen Brown."

    *Or* "Dr. Shine, may I introduce you to my teacher, Mrs. Anderson?"

2.  A ***young*** person is always introduced to an ***older*** person.

"Professor Johnston, I'd like you to meet my niece, Mary Cooper."

"Aunt Ruth, this is my roommate, Carol Sims."

3. A *less important* or prominent person is always introduced to a *more important* person. A good way to determine who is more important is use the rule of thumb, a woman is never introduced to a man unless:

> ❧ The head of a country
> ❧ A member of a royal family
> ❧ A church official
> ❧ An older man in high position, such as a governor

## Don'ts for Introductions:

1. Never phrase your introduction as a command. "Mr. Jones, shake hands with Mr. Brown."

2. When introducing two acquaintances, don't call one of the people you are introducing "my friend." You may say "my aunt" or "my sister," but to pick out one person as "my friend" implies that the other person is not.

3. Do not repeat —"Mrs. Jones–Mrs. Smith. Mrs. Smith–Mrs. Jones." Saying each name once is enough.

4. Do not introduce your spouse as Mr. or Mrs. unless you are speaking to a child. To another adult, refer to him or her as "my husband, George" or "my wife, Carol."

5. When introducing a pastor, always refer to him in his professional title, as "Pastor Brown," or "Bishop Johnson," or you may say, "This is my pastor, Brother John Brown." "Reverend" is a proper form, much more formal than "Pastor" and is used frequently in traditional denominations. If you are introducing your pastor in an

environment that this term is considered protocol, it is correct to do so. It is becoming more acceptable for the pastor to be referred to by his first name as in Pastor John or Pastor Rick, but this is a personal preference and ultimately up to the pastor.

6. If the pastor is your husband, and you are introducing him at church to a new convert or visitor, it is acceptable to identify him as your husband along with the desired title he wishes the congregation to call him.

## Help! I Forgot Their Name!

We've all done it! Someone we should know stands before us and we draw a blank when it comes to recalling his name. If the person whom you are desperately trying to remember does not detect the glassy glaze coming into your eyes and fails to come to your rescue, the best thing to do is confess! Of course there are gentle ways of letting him know you have forgotten his name. If you don't want him to get the impression that he is not important enough to remember, perhaps you could say, "I'm sorry, but for some reason I cannot recall your name," or "I remember meeting you, but I'm afraid my memory fails me when trying to remember your name." "I forgot your name," sounds rather abrupt.[1]

When you are talking with someone whose name you are struggling to remember and a friend joins you and looks inquiringly from you to the nameless person, it is tempting to ignore her to save embarrassment. Of course, you can't do that because it would be rather rude to ignore the friend that has walked up. There is nothing you can do but introduce

---

[1]Linda Phillips and Wayne Phillips, *The Concise Guide to Executive Etiquette* (New York: Doubleday, 1990), 83.

your friend to the stranger. You may save some face by saying to the latter, "Oh, haven't you met Mandy Wills?"

Hopefully, the stranger will be tactful and understanding enough to announce his name. If he says nothing, however, and Mandy Wills makes matters worse by saying, "You didn't tell me your friend's name," the situation reaches the height of embarrassment. The only solution then is to be completely frank, admit you do not remember the name, and ask them to complete the introduction themselves.

On the other hand, when you are meeting someone who obviously does not remember your name (or even someone who *might not* remember), it is perfectly fine, in fact it is merciful, to offer it at once. *Never* say, "You don't remember me, do you?" and then stop. Start right out with "Hello, I'm Sheila Smart, I met you at the church bazaar last summer." Also it is quite rude to say something like, "It starts with an *S*." This is a name game and is not appropriate to be played during formal introductions. [2]

I have been accused of looking like a pastor's wife in the Arkansas District, my good friend, Debbie Dean. Since we do not live there, and are rarely seen together, it is understandable to see the likeness.

Several years ago, soon after the birth of one of her children, we attended the Arkansas Camp Meeting. My husband and I were asked to sing. My first child was due in five weeks so, to put it mildly, I was quite large. After service someone introduced me to a fellow minister's wife. With wide eyes and a very relieved expression, she confessed. She thought I was Sister Dean, pregnant again – and so soon (Judging from my size, it was obviously

---

[2] Peggy Post, *Emily Post's Etiquette*, 16th ed. (New York: Harper Collins, 1997), 286-290.

impossible!). What really confused her was that I was singing with a strange man!

Debbie and I had a good laugh. Thankfully I am not the sensitive type. I'm not sure if this woman knows to this day who I am. She may still think I am Debbie Dean when she sees me. I do believe that introduction was a total failure!

# *16*

# *Conversation Graces*

Once you have met a new friend, you begin talking to each other, learning what things you have in common and other details to help the relationship along. It is imperative to have a balance of listening and talking to accomplish the ideal conversation. It is amazing how many people can make conversation but have difficulty communicating. Conversation graces include the ability to communicate as you interact with another person. For some, this takes discipline, especially if they like to do all the talking. Frankly, if you do all the talking, you need to learn to stop and listen. Give the other person a chance to say something. You may find that the people you talk to every day are really quite interesting.

Conversation is a two-way connection. When one person dominates the conversation, it is like cutting the phone piece in half and holding just the mouthpiece. It is obvious that the person dominating the conversation is not in the least interested in what you have to say if she never gives you a chance to say it. What would happen if she cut the phone piece in half? She  would end up with no one to talk to because the communication device has been broken. The same misfortune happens when someone breaks the device of two-way communication. They may end up talking to themselves.

## Tactless Blunders

There are some people who talk before they think. A moment of thoughtful speculation can save an enormous amount of embarrassment when a tactless blunder is on the way out of the mouth. There are some things that should never be asked. Questions such as, "Why aren't you married?" "Are you getting a divorce?" or "What's wrong with your baby?" when the child is disabled are like rubbing salt into an open wound. It is also tactless to ask a one-armed person what happened to his arm, or question the details when you hear someone is having a "minor surgery." There is no need to comment at all about many things, especially if they are extremely personal. If the person wants to talk about it, they will initiate the subject. It is **never** up to you to do so. Take a moment to think before you speak. It could save great embarrassment not only for you, but also for the person with whom you are speaking.

## Undesirable Traits

### Bragging

Bragging is easy to do and hard to listen to. Peggy Post pointed out, "There is a big difference between sharing the accomplishments of ourselves or our loved ones with close family members and extolling their virtues to anyone we happen to meet."[3] Family members will be as proud as we are of accomplishments done because it affects them

---

[3] Post, 8.

also, not so with others outside the immediate family. You may be bursting with pride and want to share it with the whole world, but frankly, the whole world has little interest because it does not affect them.

When I was young, a new acquaintance went with a group of us to a theme park. In an effort to impress a young lady, we were subjected to great, sensational feats this young man had accomplished during his lifetime the entire day. Every time a new story was coming, we would hear, "I'm not bragging or anything, but..." By the end of the day, we were exasperated, reverting to laughter as a healing balm to soothe the chaffing irritation of this braggart. "I'm not bragging or anything, but..." became an inside joke as we remembered this incident.

Statements like this are a sure indication that you are about to brag. If you are not bragging, your listener will know. You need not preface your remarks with a disclaimer.

It can be a delicate situation if you are excited about a recent revival or some real up-beat things going on in your church and you try to share that with someone from a neighboring church. My suggestion is to enter a conversation like this with great sensitivity. If the person you are talking to is from a struggling church, or a smaller youth group than yours, it may sound like you are bragging. Even if she seems to be rejoicing with you, it is important to show genuine interest when the conversation turns toward her church and what they are doing at present.

When a braggart captivates you, the best escape is to comment politely about her remarks, then try to turn the conversation to a new subject. If another bloated story is on the way, the best you can do is politely excuse yourself.

**Boring**

Being held captive in the presence of a boring person is miserable. Boring people are avoided and our fervent hope is that we are not among them! Listen to yourself talk. Are you bullying or monopolizing the conversation? Do you give the other person a chance to respond? Check frequently to see if you hear only your voice during your conversations with others. Make sure the feedback is two-way! Also, watch the other person's reactions to your conversation. If they are frantically looking around the room, they may be in search of a better conversationalist. If they are looking blankly into your face, unfocused, you may be putting them to sleep. An animated expression and balanced feedback are the most invigorating conversation signs you could ask for. Watch for them.

**Whispering**

Whispering to a single person while in a group is a subtle way of saying you wish you were alone rather than with your other friends. This makes the group uncomfortable, not to mention the person to which you are telling the secrets. Others cannot fail to feel that either the person whispering is talking about them or that they are missing some especially juicy tidbit. This also applies to speaking a foreign language which most of the group does not know. It is exactly like telling a secret and equally as rude.

**Interrupting**

The interrupter has an undesirable habit of finishing a sentence when the speaker is slower at expressing it, or breaking in and changing the subject altogether. This rude action makes the other speaker feel inadequate. It also makes you look like you are stealing the show. When someone is genuinely grasping for a word, not just slow in uttering it, it is acceptable to offer a suggestion or single word to help him or her along; but be careful not to take over and instate yourself as the speaker at that point.

It is good to teach children not to interrupt when two people are engaged in conversation. This does not mean children should be ignored in the case of an emergency or expected to wait for a half-hour while you reminisce childhood memories with a friend. A good balance is necessary, considering what is important enough to ask the person with whom you are speaking to, "Please excuse me, my child needs to tell me something." A gentle reminder to the child should be enough to let them know that they should not interrupt. Respond to the child with something like, "Just one moment, honey, I am talking. Please wait." Lay your hand on the child's arm. This will remind you they are waiting for your attention, and it will remind them that you know they are there. Do not delay in giving them your attention as soon as you find a proper break in your conversation with the other person.

*The story snatcher* is another vice of the interrupter. She is always jumping in half way because she knows the story also. This is an inconsiderate action that makes the original storyteller feel cut-off and insignificant. What the story snatcher is saying by her actions is, "You are not telling this as well as I can, so you may be excused."

This is very common among family members but should be avoided the same as among friends. Even if a child is telling a story, it shows a great deal of respect to allow him or her to finish the story with as much attentiveness as possible. This not only gives the child a sense of importance, but it is a great way to teach him or her how to hold a conversation with an adult. Respectful manners between siblings, spouses, or parents and children should be the goal of each family unit. Patient practice will cause manners to become an everyday occurrence.

Often a joke can be told so many times that the entire audience could recite it. As tempting as it may be to cut the joke off short, it is still better to let the person finish. There may be someone in the group that has not heard it yet. It is a kind gesture to laugh at someone's joke, provided it is a clean one, than to remain sober-faced because you have heard this one a million times. I have heard people say, "She even laughs at my jokes," as a compliment to someone being a gracious listener. I have never heard, "She is so honest, she won't even laugh at my jokes," as a compliment. Do you remember your mom saying, "Treat others the way you would want to be treated?" Being polite to others will never go out of style.

**Gross Detail**

Most of us don't want the gory details. Gross detail is exactly that...gross. Some may say this is a problem more among men than women, but I hesitate to say this is a gender-related habit. I have heard women as well as men launch into a detailed tirade of gory description with no regard to the comfort of their listeners. Keeping the conversation agreeable and interesting is a fundamental and common sense rule of all conversation. Dwelling on misfortune and sicknesses may be interesting to your family and dearest friends, but your general audience is not interested in the record number of times you have survived the operating room, unless of course, you have a miracle to share.

Another thing to avoid is inappropriate conversation at the dinner table. If the subject matter cannot be discussed without the person across from you turning green, it is probably better left unsaid. Our society has become so free and undisciplined regarding public subject matter, that it almost seems old-fashioned to curb our tongues, but

Christians should always remember they are exemplifying Christ.

*For by your words you will be justified, and by your words you will be condemned (Matthew 12:37).*

**Wandering Eyes**

Even if you are listening, and you let your eyes wander, it gives the appearance of being quite bored! When you are at a large conference with many friends in attendance, it can be quite challenging to give your full attention to one person. Put yourself in his or her position and think how you would feel, it will help you know how to deal with the situation.[4]

I have left conferences with the elated feeling of being special to someone I highly esteemed. Cleveland M. Becton had the gift of making his acquaintances feel like close friends. He was never too busy to stop and share a greeting and smile. I remember many General Conferences where Brother Becton took the time to stop and spend a few moments, giving his undivided attention to my husband and me. It was not the quantity of time that made an impression, but the quality.

Eye contact is very important. I have learned this attending Christian Life Center in Stockton, California (one of the largest Pentecostal churches in the nation). Joy Haney, the pastor's wife, doesn't have the time to spend thirty minutes with each saint after Sunday services. Somehow in our brief encounters, she has made me feel important and loved. We don't spend a lot of time together, but she is always affirming and genuinely caring. I know if I have a need, she will stop and take the time to help. She has reached

---

[4] Post, 8-13.

out in passing, taken my hand in both of hers, looked me in the eyes, expressed how she loves me, and then she is on her way. She has spotted me across a busy conference floor in a different district where she was speaking, and with a wave of her hand, a smile and wink, she singled me out as someone special. I felt like she was saying "You are one of mine! And I'm glad to have you here for prayerful support." She got it! Although much of our communication is eye contact, I have never felt slighted or ignored by Joy Haney. I am not vain enough to presume that she only treats me this way, but each lady in the church is special and loved by this great pastor's wife.

It may be impossible to break someone of the habit of the wandering eye, especially if it is a first-time introduction. Years ago, a mutual friend introduced me to a well-known singer in our movement. I was so excited to meet this person and hustled halfway across the conference floor to be introduced. When we approached the singer, however, the introductions went well, but as the conversation progressed, I noticed him raising his head and looking above mine as if in search of someone else. I was humiliated and felt degraded. I was obviously not the caliber of person he wished to be associated with. I left feeling hurt and disappointed. Consequently, after that I had great difficulty getting through my hurt feelings to feel the presence of the Lord when he sang. It was not until years later, when I had the opportunity to meet him again, that I realized he meant nothing by this gesture. He was actually a very likable person. I wish I would have had the nerve to bring it to his attention at the time, but I was too intimidated and self-conscious.

If you are speaking with someone and their eyes begin to wander, you may want to stop talking and look with them as though curious about what he or she finds so fascinating. If he asks what you are doing, you could say

"Oh! I was just interested to see what you were looking at," and continue your conversation. They may get the hint! This may seem a little rash, but there is no excuse for rudeness. If they don't get the hint, don't hesitate to find someone else who appreciates your company enough to look you in the eye and hold a conversation.

# Notes

# *17*

# *Telephone Etiquette*

Alexander Graham Bell invented the telephone for the purpose of enabling people to communicate efficiently and effectively when they don't happen to be in the same place. Unfortunately, efficiency and effectiveness doesn't always happen during telephone interactions.

Ideally, telephones help us make short communications and get questions answered quickly. But realistically, telephones also cause a great deal of frustration. Emily Post said, "With the frequency of the telephone's use also comes the frequency of its abuse."[5] If someone were to interrupt you while talking, working, or with some other pressing business, it would be labeled rude and over-bearing. But when the telephone rings, it can be just as intrusive and frustrating. Because of the widespread use of the telephone, its interruptions are not considered rude.

Sales, and obscene or inconsiderate calls have caused some to use the filtering of answering machines as an endeavor to gain control of their privacy. This seems to have helped a little but has not gone without being highly criticized by others. Being held captive on the phone can be frustrating, even between friends. The solution to telephone hassles is as simple as good manners.

---

[5]Post, 57.

### Personal Calls

When you are talking on the telephone, the person on the other end cannot see your expressions or gestures. Your message depends entirely on the clarity of your voice and your ability to communicate over the telephone. It is important to speak clearly and give some thought to what you are about to say so you won't be misunderstood. "Yes," and "No," are better than "*uh-huh*" or "*unh-unh,*" which is difficult to understand over the phone.

You do not need to raise your voice when speaking into the receiver. The telephone is an amazing machine that has been designed to carry your voice at its natural volume. 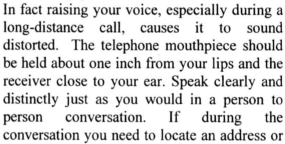 In fact raising your voice, especially during a long-distance call, causes it to sound distorted. The telephone mouthpiece should be held about one inch from your lips and the receiver close to your ear. Speak clearly and distinctly just as you would in a person to person conversation. If during the conversation you need to locate an address or phone number in another room, put the phone down carefully. When you are finished, gently hang up, being careful not to slam the receiver down.[6] Slamming the receiver can be interpreted as an expression of uncontrolled anger and should be avoided. There are times when the receiver may slip from your fingers and fall in its rightful place. You may wish to call the person with whom you were speaking and explain that you were not angry nor did you intentionally slam the phone down. If you let it go, this small mishap could grow into a problem that takes much longer to solve than a simple phone call to clarify your true intentions.

---

[6] Ibid., 70.

**Answering Your Telephone**

When you hear the familiar ring of the telephone, it is best to pick it up as soon as possible. It is not good to keep someone waiting while you finish a task that could wait. If you are in the middle of a conversation, you may say "Excuse me, let me get that," and finish your conversation when the call has been terminated. If the conversation is an urgent matter that cannot wait, answer the phone asking the caller if you can return the call later because an emergency has come up. Then respond with a return call as soon as you can.

Although it may seem simple, the best way to answer your telephone is still "Hello." Answering, "Yes," is abrupt and may sound a bit rude. "This is Mrs. Jones' house" gives too much personal information, and "Mrs. Jones speaking" leaves you without a chance to retreat.

It is best to answer the telephone in your own home rather than asking a guest to answer it for you. It is not advisable for a woman to answer the phone in a single male's home even if the couple is engaged. There are several reasons for this. The first one is to avoid seed for idle gossip. Even though she may be there with several other people, the person on the other end of the telephone line cannot see that. It may appear that she is alone in the apartment with her fiancée. Secondly, she is still a guest in the privacy of his home, and will be, until she moves her things in at the time of the marriage. Thirdly, when a young lady answers her boyfriend's phone, this gives the appearance of filtering his phone calls which could lead to feelings of distrust. No one wants to feel his or her privacy has been violated, even when it comes to personal phone calls. Answering someone else's phone is as unacceptable as listening in on a party line! (Do we even have those any more?)

While we are on the subject of personal calls, there is something that came up in one of our *Social Graces* classes. Consider what happens when a guy and a girl talk on the phone, late at night. The students in our class observed that when a couple indulges in conversation late at night it has an adverse affect on their relationship. This is especially true with new relationships. Talking to each other in the dark makes one feel more liberty to speak openly about his or her feelings. It seems the cloak of darkness would hide the results of speaking candidly about things they would not mention in the light. It puts the relationship at a disadvantage because it rushes conversations that should be reserved for a more mature level that only comes with a time-nurtured commitment.

There is a distinct difference in the quality of the conversation if the young lady or man is lying in the bed, under the covers. I agreed as the class came to the conclusion that talking to each other in bed is inappropriate behavior for two Christian young people engaging in conversation, whether on the phone or in person. The only difference on the phone is the absence of physical sight. The knowledge of such a setting is much more detailed in the mind. Knowing a young lady is lying in bed could be a very difficult image for a man to try to purge from his mind. The Bible reminds us of the things we should think about in Philippians 4:8.

> *Finally, brethren, whatsoever things are true, whatsoever things are honest, whatsoever things are just, whatsoever things are **pure**, whatsoever things are lovely, whatsoever things are of good report; if there be any **virtue**, and if there be any praise, think on these things.*

It would be easy to say the young man should have a pure mind and if he thinks bad thoughts it is his problem.

However, when a young lady understands the power of visual impact on a man, she will go out of her way to deter any mental image that would not be pleasing to God in the mind of the young man. If she has feelings for him at all, the responsibility of helping him guard his mind will draw them closer in the right way, crushing any lustful thought that could eventually drive a wedge between them. If she does not have romantic feelings for him, she should refrain from intimate conversation for the pure propriety of the matter and to preserve her reputation.

By the same principle, it is very disturbing to announce that your roommate is in the shower, or getting dressed when her boyfriend calls. These mental images are hard enough for young Christian men to deal with. It would not be easy to deal with feelings of guilt if you learned that you were partly responsible for one's moral failure.

**The Caller**

It is courteous to give one's name as soon as the person at the other end answers your call. *What* name you give depends on how well you know, or are known, to the person who answers. If your call is legitimate, then you have no reason to hide your identity. Give your name at once. Here are some of the most common forms:

- To a secretary: "This is Mrs. Franklin. Is Mrs. Harvey available?"

- To a child who answers: "This is Mrs. Franklin. Is your mother available?"

- When you recognize the voice answering: "Hello, John. This is Helen. Is Sue there?"

- When the person you are calling answers: "Hi, Sue, this is Helen," or "Hello, Mrs. Brooks. This is Mrs. Franklin."

115

ಲ An older person calling a younger one: "This is Mrs. [or Ms.] Bailey."

ಲ A young person calling an older one: "Hello, Mrs. [or Mr.] Knox. This is Janet Frost."

**The Person Receiving the Call**

Unfortunately, not everyone gives his or her name when calling. They may respond to your "Hello" by saying, "May I speak to Mrs. Franklin?" or "Is Mrs. Franklin in?" If you recognize the voice you may say, "Just a moment please," or "This is she," or "This is Mrs. Franklin."

Most people prefer the person who answers to ask the caller to identify themselves, before they take the call. It used to be considered rather "snoopy" if someone answering the phone said, "May I ask who is calling?" or a child said, "Who is this, please?" but today it is becoming more acceptable. This is not only a convenience but also a common courtesy. If someone calls and does not immediately identify himself or herself, it is perfectly logical to find out who it is before passing along the call. It may seem a little rude to ask the caller's identity, but it stems from the rudeness of the caller not identifying himself.[7]

## Children and Telephones

Having children answer the phone can be a great learning experience, but if they are too young, they may give personal information to a stranger, opening themselves and others to unnecessary danger. You can never be too careful about securing your privacy. A few minutes a day with a toy phone can be a wonderful teaching tool, preparing the child for "the real thing" when the parents decide they are ready.

---

[7]Post, 59.

There are also educational toy phones available that make this job quite easy and fun. Here are a few tips to help a child learn how to safely answer the telephone.

1. Say "Hello" loud and clear and listen carefully to who the caller is.

2. If the caller does not give his/her name say, "May I ask who is calling?" If they still will not tell you who they are, they are being rude. You may hang up on rude people. ☺

3. Never *ever* say you are home alone, even if you are. If someone asks if Mommy and Daddy are home and they aren't, say, "They are not available right now, may I have them return your call?"

4. Never give your name and address over the phone. Mommy and Daddy will do that.

5. When you go get the person being asked for, lay the receiver down softly beside the phone. Do not call them while the phone is in your hand close to your mouth.

Safety plays an important role when a child is alone in the house. There is the chance that someone may call expressly to find out if an adult is there or the house is empty. Role-play is a good way for the child to practice what he/she will say when the real time comes. If an older child answers the phone and does not recognize the voice of the caller, he or she *must* say, "Who is this please?" Then if the name is still unfamiliar and the caller still does not identify him or herself, the child does **not** say "She is not at home." But rather "She is not available right now, may she return your call?" This way, the child is not lying, but does not have to reveal personal details to a stranger.

117

It is unprofessional to have a young child answer a business phone. If the phone in your home is doubling as a business or church phone, it is unwise to have a child answer no matter how cute or smart they are. Older children may be given permission at the discretion of the pastor or someone in charge. I have heard of very important calls being missed because a child took the wrong information. It would be unfortunate if a pastor missed a call regarding someone being rushed to the hopsital and needing prayer because his child took the call and failed to relay the message. Utmost discretion is required on home phones used for business.

### Four Important Don'ts

1. When you get a wrong number don't ask, "What number is this?" Ask instead, "Is this 555-3456?" so you can look it up again or dial more carefully the next time.

2. Don't answer and then say, "Wait a minute," keeping the caller waiting while you go do an errand. If the doorbell is ringing, tell them you will call them right back, then do it!

3. Don't let children who are too young answer the telephone. A caller's valuable time may be wasted trying to make a child understand a message and relay it to the right person. If there is a long silence, it is impossible to know if the child is hunting for Mom or playing with the dog.

4. Don't hang up before letting the telephone ring at least **SIX** times. Give the person you are calling time to get from the bathtub, garage, or other extremity of the house to the phone.

## Guys and Girls—Who Calls First?

In the past, there was no question about the opposite sexes calling each other. It was understood that girls didn't call boys. Now, with pagers, call waiting, e-mail and other communication devices the hard and fast rule has been rapidly left behind. There are some basic principles that will help the Christian woman understand what is proper for her.

It is still proper for the man to be the aggressive one in a relationship. Unless the gentleman requests the woman to call, she should let him make the first call. When a woman calls a man *without invitation*, it puts him at a disadvantage. It robs him of the opportunity to be the pursuer and could possibly portray a leading role in the woman that may not be intended. This is not to say that the woman must sit around and wait for the man to call even if he "begs her to do so." The key words here are *"without invitation."*

The scenario is completely different if the gentleman has requested the lady to call. Then, she may do so as a courtesy to his wishes, or she may deem it necessary to refrain if she feels the relationship is unhealthy or does not desire the pursuit.

It is unusual for a man to revel in the continual, aggressive pursuit of a woman. Yes, it is nice to know you are worth a little "running after" but after being chased awhile, a man will miss the pursuit role that feeds his natural ego. A woman can make a man feel important when she expresses her desire for more of his time and affection, but a continual diet of this behavior results in the high risk of misinterpretation. He may misunderstand her pursuit as a sign of ungodly aggression contrary to a godly woman's role. *The risk is not worth the price.* These principles can be applied to every part of the relationship rather than just the communication skills between a man and a woman.

My low opinion of a man who will not take the lead in areas of relationship is usually affirmed after the marriage vows. This type of a man usually will not take the leadership in the home, leaving the woman to be the natural and spiritual leader. What a shame she didn't see the "writing on the wall" before the wedding. There are ways to test the waters to see if your suspect will *cop out* of his leadership role.

What would happen if a woman *insisted* on letting the man take the lead, even if he insists he doesn't want to? Doing this will reveal several things.

1. The woman is willing to practice submissive behavior even though she is not required to do so.

2. It gives the guy the opportunity to practice being a leader.

3. If the guy **won't** take the lead he is either, not interested in her, so she should leave him alone, or lacking backbone as a leader. Who would want a husband like that?

Some general rules of "who calls first" depend on where the couple is in their relationship. Obviously, when a couple has been dating for several years, there has been time to come to some understanding about the woman returning his calls or what his desires are. This needs to be taken into consideration when trying to apply these principles to your own life.

It is a little more acceptable for a woman to page a man. Although I do not propagate un-responded pages, at least the male has the option to return the page or not.

## Terminating Telephone Calls

Normally, the person originating the call is the one who terminates it. This bit of information is nice to know if the conversation is dragging on and getting nowhere. The caller may simply say, "I'm so glad I reached you—we look forward to seeing you on the seventh. Good-bye," or some other appropriate remark. The person who places the call is also the one who calls again when you are cut off in the middle of a conversation.

What about being trapped on the phone with a long-winded caller, a determined salesman, or perhaps a talkative friend? If you have made several tentative efforts to end the conversation and they don't seem to work, more aggressive measures may need to be taken. At the first pause, or even interrupting if necessary, you may say, "I'm terribly sorry, but I simply must hang up," or a truthful excuse like, "I'm in the middle of my housework."

Another occasion when a quickly terminated phone conversation is in order is when the person who receives it has a visitor step in. This can be either in a business office or at home. It is inconsiderate to continue talking on the phone when you have someone trying not to listen to your conversation. If the conversation is one that you know needs some time involvement, you may need to postpone it until another time. You may say, "Joan just dropped in for a visit, so may I call you back in a little while?" Then you should return the call as soon as you can.

On the other hand, if you make a call which you know will be time-consuming, it is polite to ask, "Is this a good time to call?" or "Do you have a few minutes to chat?"

## Obscene Calls

The best way to handle obscene phone calls is to hang up immediately. Don't give the caller the satisfaction of upsetting you. If the caller immediately calls you back, leave the phone off the hook for a while. If the caller is a prankster, or random-number-picking pervert, he will soon give up when he keeps hearing the busy signal. If you find this is happening on a regular basis, notify the Phone Company. In serious cases, they can trace the call.

Another effective remedy that discourages the occasional obscene caller is a whistle. As soon as you hear the first obscene word, blow with all your might right into the speaker (which will be his ear)! The caller will drop you from his list of victims then and there!

## Business Calls

Occasionally, the church phone and the pastor's home phone are the same number. In this case, their home phone is considered a business phone and should be answered as such. The proper addressing should include the church's full name. "United Pentecostal Church," would be appropriate if the phone is an extension of the actual building of worship. If there is a phone in a public location in the church building that several saints are in the habit of answering, it is a good idea to make them aware of the fact that the phone is a business phone and should be answered as such.

# *18*

# *Electronic Communications*

In our fast-paced society, it has proven to be a blessing to be able to communicate by the move of a mouse and the click of a button. Electronic devices such as fax machines, computers, pagers and cellular telephones used for communication purposes have been instrumental in the radical transformation of quick mass communication. Never before has it been so easy to drop a line to someone in a matter of seconds, whether halfway around the world or across the street, and to receive an immediate reply.

This computerized generation has become more and more sophisticated. The wide use of e-mail, on-line chat sessions, and interactive websites has introduced new opportunities and problems to the field of communication.

Unfortunately, the law cannot monitor unacceptable behavior such as brazen conversation, pornographic and violent websites, or prevent personal danger from sleazy predators. A result of these problems has caused the computer literate to call for some guidelines of cyberspace etiquette. People using these conveniences see the need to implement some code of conduct to preserve manners and respect for each other. When electronic convenience began its rapid growth, it seemed in many cases, that etiquette was being left behind. Like the telephone, we have learned the frequency of its use brings about the frequency of its abuse. Now that we have experienced some severe disadvantages, the cry for some form of manners is being heard. This *hail for help* has resulted in a term called "netiquette," or cyberspace etiquette.

It came as quite a surprise to me how close netiquette is to just plain etiquette. No matter what the setting, it has always been rude to bore people, to hog the floor, and to conduct a private conversation in front of others. Some computer users may feel they can ignore plain good manners while they surf the web, send inappropriate e-mails, and dominate chat rooms; but these are the same people who consequently exhibit the same behavior in off-line manners. They are the ones who lose in the end. If these people are blatant and uncaring on-line, that character trait will surface somewhere else in their lives. This may go on for a while, but sooner or later it will catch up with them. Judith Martin warns, "Cyberspace society may not be able to identify its miscreants, but it can trace their origins and warn the innocent to stay away from their advances."[8]

## Cell Phones

Cellular phones have become almost as common as carrying a purse. Many women are carrying one for safety purposes as well as communication convenience. With the use of cell phones, being stranded by the road on a dark night, is no longer the fearful ordeal it once was. Of course, there are a few common courtesies and safety rules that should be observed.

---

[8] Judith Martin, *Miss Manners Basic Training: Communication* (New York: Crown Publishers, 1997), 24.

If your cell phone rings in a public place or private meeting, answer it immediately. It is better to turn it off during the few hours you are in social gatherings such as funerals, weddings, graduations and church services. The annoying sound of "Old McDonald," or "The Charge," coming from a cell phone in the middle of a sermon is most distracting.

There are times when an emergency arises and you expect a call during church or another private meeting. If possible, change the setting to "vibrate." If you must, remove it from your purse and hold it. You should excuse yourself from the room before speaking into the phone.

It is easy to forget when using a cell phone in public that everyone within earshot can hear your private conversation. Be careful not to infringe upon others rights. The people around you do not want to hear a private conversation between you and the person on the other end of the line. It makes others uncomfortable trying not to eavesdrop on your conversation.

Some states have passed laws concerning the use of portable phones while driving in your vehicle. It is understandable that your attention is divided as you talk on the phone and try to drive safely. It is better to wait until you are stopped to dial a number. There is a device available that makes it possible to talk on the phone with your hands free. This is a nice alternative to subjecting yourself to danger while driving.

### E-mail

Although e-mail is one of the most popular forms of quick communication, regulations are a must because of the technological ability to expose the public to the danger of uncensored frankness. With hasty "snail-mail" (a letter going through the postal service), the author has some "buffer time" of practical preparations. During this time of putting the letter in an envelope, finding a stamp, and then delivering it to the post office, the contents can be thought over. If for some reason there is something in it that should not have been said, or some statements were made in haste, this grace period is essential so that the letter can be either re-written or disposed of—not so with hasty e-mails.

Once those words are clicked out feverishly in an e-mail on the keyboard, suddenly CLICK! the "send" key is touched. The mail is gone...not to be explained, re-thought or retrieved. Misunderstandings are many and feelings can be hurt when the mail has been sent with no forethought. For this reason, we come to the conclusion that new tools need new rules.

Let's start with a general rule: Heavy emotions should not be communicated through e-mail or bulletin boards. *Miss Manners* calls statements like, "Will you marry me?" "I'm leaving," "I'm pregnant," and "You're fired," emotional bombs that should not be dropped by e-mail.[9]

A wedding invitation that is in the mail could be preceded by e-mail but not take the place of it. It is understandable that there are some friends you just can't wait to tell, but it would be the height of rudeness to delete them from your guest list. Your guest list is the data with which you draw from to decide who receives a wedding invitation. To delete one from the other would be to exclude them as a guest to your wedding. E-mail attempts at intimacy are equivalent to the lowest of street remarks and should be reported immediately.

---

[9] Martin, 18.

There are various opinions on sending thank you notes by e-mail. Although it may be more convenient to e-mail a *thank you* to the person who sent you a lovely gift or some thoughtful action, there is nothing like receiving a handwritten note to convey your sincere gratitude. Of course, a *thank you* by e-mail is a better option than none at all. A good general rule for e-mail *thank you* notes is: Informal thank you notes are acceptable by e-mail, but formal thank-you notes are usually hand-written. Wedding thank-you notes are *always* handwritten.

**Here are a few basic *No-No's* to remember:**

1. You should never use E-mail for condolences. At a time when a friend or close acquaintance is mourning the loss of a loved one, the more personal touch would be a handwritten note either at the end of a purchased "sympathy" card, or a nice paragraph on stationery.

2. Wedding Invitations should not be sent by e-mail. For a less casual occasion, invitations may be made by telephone, which is a little more personal than electronic mail.

3. Never, ask for the first date through e-mail. Subsequent meeting arrangements may be made **after** the first one is asked, either by written invitation, over the telephone or in person, using a sequence of formality.

Peggy Post shares the following "Ten Commandments for Computer Ethics," provided by the Computer Ethics Institute:[10]

---

[10] Post, 55.

1. Thou shalt not use a computer to harm other people.
2. Thou shalt not interfere with other people's computer work.
3. Thou shalt not snoop around in other people's files.
4. Thou shalt not use a computer to steal.
5. Thou shalt not use a computer to bear false witness.
6. Thou shalt not use or copy software for which you have not paid.
7. Thou shalt not use other people's computer resources without authorization.
8. Thou shalt not appropriate other people's intellectual output.
9. Thou shalt think about the social consequences of the program you write.
10. Thou shalt use a computer in ways that show consideration and respect.

# *19*

# *Note Writing and Correspondence*

In this fast-paced world, it seems the handwritten note is rapidly vanishing. Unfortunately, the fountain pen has been set aside for more sophisticated gadgets introduced by our advancing technology. It may be easier to drop a line over the Internet, or call at the last minute but the simple pleasure of receiving a handwritten note in the mail is never lost on a loved one. There is just something about knowing someone took the time to sit down and pen a few special thoughts to you. The written note is still more personal and warm than a typewritten or computer generated one. Getting a note in the mail is like receiving a gift. Alexandra Stoddard captured my feelings when she wrote,

> What a treat to receive a letter from a friend! When I do find one, I hold my treasure tightly and wait until I have a quiet moment alone before I open it. I hate to dilute the anticipation and appreciation of someone's thoughts and feelings by facing them when I'm distracted. Someone has taken time to focus on me, even if only for a moment. I feel

touched and want to savor the all-too-rare experience.[11]

When I am shuffling through our mail, most of the time I absent-mindedly categorize each piece. Who is it for and where is it from? When I come to one that is handwritten, it captures my attention. I also savor the moment, finding a soft chair and time alone to read a dear friend's thoughts. The gift of a letter is priceless. I hope the art is not a lost one. When I think about how I feel when I receive correspondence from a friend, it makes me want to share the gift with them also.

Letter or note writing is thinking out loud on paper. Being able to communicate deep truths and loving thoughts to someone else is one of the virtues of letter writing. It is easier to be uninhibited in a letter. Letters are a powerful form of expression because they have a tendency to reveal the vulnerability of the soul. Sometimes it takes a little practice to write heart and soul on paper, but the effort is well worth it.

Why are handwritten letters so rare? Less than six percent of all first-class mail is personal and half of all household-to-household mail is greeting cards.[12] Some of the  reasons we hesitate are: we don't really know where to start, we are afraid to make mistakes in spelling or grammar, or perhaps we are just too busy to take the time to pen a long letter.

---

[11] Alexandra Stoddard, *Gift Of A Letter* (New York: Doubleday, 1990), 25.

[12] Ibid., 57.

## Finding the Right Words

If you have problems knowing where to start, follow these simple guidelines to help inspire you. Finding the right words is surprisingly accessible when you know how to look for them.

**Target the recipient.**

A good note reflects the person you are writing to. Who is this person and what is the nature of your relationship? The degree of distance or intimacy depends on the relationship.

**Identify your feelings about the person.**

Good notes also reflect you. How do you feel about this person? What are the qualities that make this person important to you? The answers to these questions will affect what you say and how you say it.

**Focus on the occasion.**

What does the event mean to the person? What does it mean to you? Many people feel a twenty-fifth wedding anniversary is a great achievement in this society where fifty percent of our marriages end in divorce. The birth of a miracle baby is cause for extraordinary rejoicing. Most mothers consider Mother's Day a *very* special occasion and would be crushed if they were overlooked or forgotten. These and other ideas can inspire ideas for note and letter contents.

**Decide on the message.**

What do you want to say? This can be the tough one. Many times the answer to this question is, "I don't know." Fortunately, there are ways to find out. Slow down and think about the points above. Try not to censor yourself by thinking your words are not original or good enough. Write what you feel, no matter how silly it sounds. You can always go back and edit your work later, but try to be unbiased. As you relax and stop worrying about the grammar and creativity, important feelings will probably surface naturally. Perhaps the feelings that normally would be kept to yourself, like, "I care about you" or "you are important to me" will be easier to write on paper than speaking them aloud. Write your thoughts on scrap paper first. That way you can feel less pressured to make it right the first time. Then you can copy it to a card or stationery.

You don't have to compose something long to be effective. Sometimes the most touching letters are short notes that took only a moment of time to compose.

## Helpful Devices

One of the secrets of effective note writing is to be able to write in such as way to show you have the recipient in mind. A meaningful note will identify with the person reflecting a special connection.

You can personalize your note by using the name of the person to whom you are writing. The basic "***Dear*** Maria" or, "***To*** Mr. And Mrs. Jones," can be used. Other identifying information like, "To the sharpest lawyer I know" is also proper for personalizing, but adding specific details of a mutual experience or shared memory goes a step farther. This type of note writing is good for the widest variety of occasions from an anniversary to a successful ball game.

You can refer to events in people's personal lives if you are on an intimate level with them. Consider their hobbies and interests. These can help give you some ideas to write about. Do they like crafts, skiing, music or recipes? Does the person have special interests like quilting or speaking? This relevant and effective subject material can be a tool to help achieve a personal message.

Relate the message to the gift, if there is one. This is exceptionally helpful when a response is difficult to put into words. Florence Isaacs shared an example in her book, *Just a Note To Say,* about someone who sent a new bride a wooden duck. She did not know the distant relative of her new husband, but found a creative way to thank them by saying, "Marriage is ducky--just like your gift. We've found the perfect place for it on the shelf in the den."[13] This is a great example of creatively connecting the gift with the message.

Sometimes you can say something significant with a favorite quote. It is important to choose one that fits the occasion and reflects you, as well as the person you are writing. For a young graduate, you might write:

> *Shoot for the moon. Even if you miss it you*
> *will land among the stars.*
> > *—Les (Lester Louis) Brown*

You could then add a few personalized lines. You may want to clip and save anecdotes in a file folder. *Reader's Digest* is my favorite source for quotes. Also available are an assortment of books of quotations categorized by subject for ease of use.

You may want to write down some starters and keep them on file. By "starters," I mean sentence beginnings that will help you get rolling. A few of these are:

> *I hope you know how special you are to me.*

---

[13] Florence Isaacs, *Just a Note to Say* (New York: Clarkson Potter/Publishers, 1995), 21.

*I was thinking about you today...*
*We miss you.*
*I was praying for you today.*
*The Lord has placed you on my heart.*
*It is warm and I am sitting by the window...*
*I remember when...*
*I realized today how long it has been since I've heard from you.*
*I'll never forget the time...* (This is good for writing a condolence note).
*What a...* (to precede many different beginnings).
*What a delicious dinner we had at your home last evening.*
*What a lovely gift you sent.*
*What a wonderful time we had at the barbecue.*
*What a thoughtful gift. You remembered how I love roses.*

Try to keep your writing in the same style as you talk. After writing, read it aloud and picture yourself saying it to the person face to face. If the words aren't you, adjust them to be more real. Would you use the words "I was ecstatic to see you" when you speak? Would "happy to see you" be more your style of conversation?

## Tools of the Trade

You don't have to be a professional to write good notes and personal letters. Spelling, grammar, form and style are skills that can be sharpened, but don't let the lack of perfect penned notes discourage you from sending a warm heart-felt note to someone who deserves it.

When I was in college, my mother sent many cards and letters. They were received with great jubilation and excitement. I treasured each one as I read about the things going on at home with my family and friends. Those little excerpts on life at home helped me make it through some very difficult times, when I missed being there so much. I remember my first visit home when Mom voiced her fear, and I realized the love that had gone into those letters. She feared I would laugh if she wrote a letter with several misspelled words in it. She kept telling herself that someone who loved her as much as I did would never berate her. She set her fear aside and penned some of the most beautiful words I had ever received. I was surprised to hear of her fears. I enjoyed her letters so much that I never noticed whether she was a poor speller or not.

Keeping a dictionary handy will help you with spelling. There are small pocket-sized dictionaries for your convenience.

If you have a question on the spelling of a word, typing it on the computer, running the spell check and then hand writing the final copy may help put your mind at ease. Remember to read your note before copying it, because the spell check will only catch words that are not in its dictionary. If "sinning" is spelled correctly, but used incorrectly, where you should have used "singing," *spell check* will not catch this mistake. It would be embarrassing if you congratulated someone on their wonderful sinning! Proofreading is very important to good note writing.

A thesaurus is a helpful tool, giving you a variety of words that mean the same thing. It is a book of synonyms  that not only will help you find a more colorful word for the one you chose, but will also help build your own personal vocabulary. For example, the word "response" also means: acknowledgment, answer, comeback, counter blast, feedback, reaction, rejoinder, reply, respond, retort, return, and riposte.[14]

Venture out with some new words, but remember to keep your writing you. Writing is an expression of your personality. Adding humor, poetry, or some other "signature writing" will enhance an already welcome letter to a friend.

## Occasions to Write

When you want to drop a note to someone it is always a welcome gesture. There are many other occasions you would write a note that are not the casual "how are you" type of correspondence.

### Birthdays

When sending someone a birthday wish, it is nice to send a card but make it special with a small reminder of how important that person is to you. People like to feel they are a one-of-a-kind person. Sentences that start with, "You are the most..." can be a springboard to help give personalized character to that special birthday note.

---

[14] *Websters New Dictionary and Thesaurus*, s.v. "response."

## Anniversaries, Weddings and Engagements

An anniversary is a great milestone in this day of divorce, and those who are married for several years should be commended. It is a thoughtful gesture to send a note of congratulation even if you do not plan to send a wedding gift. Newlyweds are usually grateful to those who take the time to wish them happiness. In the past, engagements were celebrated on a larger social scale. Today a special acknowledgment can be an unexpected joy to the couple who is up to their ears in wedding plans.

## Births and Adoptions

Sometimes the birth of a child will be instrumental in drawing young parents to God as they ponder the miracle of new life. A timely card could be an important instrument in God's hands. Couples who were not able to have children naturally, and are finally working through the red tape of adoption deserve congratulations as well. This is a great opportunity to show Christian love and concern through a card or note.

## Promotions and Graduations

Times of special achievement and discipline are important occasions to remember. Use the three C's for achievement notes: Consider, Congratulate, and Compliment.

1. **Consider** the level of achievement. Is it graduate school, college, high school, middle school or kindergarten? Is it a job or perhaps a political, church, or district promotion? Consider the age of the recipient. If it is someone returning to school after years of dreams, your congratulations will sound a lot different than for a six-year old graduating from kindergarten. A note to someone starting his first job is vastly different than the retirement of an older person.

137

2. **Congratulate** them on their achievement. Although a person may not be the valedictorian or salutatorian, his accomplishment is worthy of mention. Any awards or special accomplishments should be included, even if it is an after-school job.

3. **Compliment** the person in some way. Let him know how much you appreciate his friendship and how proud you are of his determination. It may seem to be a small thing to send a note to someone who has just graduated from the eighth grade, or received his first driver's license. It means a lot to the person experiencing the joy that you have shared in his jubilation. A moment taken to write small notes at opportune times can cultivate a lifetime friendship.

## Condolences

Letters of sympathy sent to the family of a person who has passed away are called *condolences*. They should always be handwritten unless you have a handicap and must use a word processor or typewriter. They should be brief and positive, including an uplifting and encouraging message to those who have lost their loved one. A fond memory of the deceased can supply a moment of precious reprieve to the saddened recipient. "I'm praying for you" when used alone can seem overused and redundant, especially when the recipient knows you are praying for him. If however, the memory of a cherished moment with his or her deceased loved one is added you have shared a common feeling with the grieving person. It is a comfort to know that friends are experiencing the loss of this loved one also.

## Thank You Notes

Traditionally, a thank-you note was always hand-written. Most authorities on etiquette will agree that a handwritten thank you note is still preferred. They are much more personal and warm than a typewritten note or quick e-mail. Gabrielle Goodwin, author of *Writing Thank-You Notes,* makes an exception. She agrees that thank you notes should be handwritten with the exception of e-mail.[15] Goodwin's philosophy seems to be that a note of thanks sent through the Internet is better than no thanks at all. *(See page 125 for more information concerning thank-you notes and e-mail etiquette.)*

If a thank you note is part of a longer letter, it may be typewritten. You may find a card with a beautiful poem or verse that says just what you want, but it is still necessary to write a personal note that is comparable to the verse and the situation.

A thank you note for a **gift** should be sent within two to three days. Three points to consider when writing a thank you note for a gift are:

1. The item should be mentioned. It makes the giver of the gift feel good if they find out they have chosen a special item that you "always wanted" or "will be put to good use."

2. Add a personal touch such as your fondness for the sender or something special you have been doing that would interest him or her.

3. Remember a shared experience from the past or a mutual friendship.

A hand-written thank you for a wedding gift should be sent as soon as possible and at least within the first three weeks of marriage. A written note to acknowledge a thank-

---

[15] Gabrielle Goodwin & David Macfarlane, *Writing Thank-You Notes* (New York: Sterling Publishing, 1999), 11.

you gift received in the mail is proper. It is common courtesy to let the sender know that the gift arrived safely. Thank you notes for gifts received for birthdays, Christmas, and graduations should be sent within two to three days. It is not mandatory to send a note to someone who hosted a dinner party, but if you choose to do so, it will almost guarantee another invitation. It is nice to receive a note from a traveling evangelist when he was your dinner guest or stayed in your home. A note of appreciation for help in a time of illness or special gifts during convalescence should be sent when you are feeling well enough to respond to the kindness. Upon receipt of notes or flowers of condolences, an expression of appreciation is always in order.[16]

## Get Well Wishes

Get well wishes should be encouraging and light. When someone is confined to bed for a few days, it is wonderful to receive a card or letter from a friend who is missing her and praying for her recovery. A get-well note does not have to be long to lift the spirit of someone who is ill. A funny card or perky note can lift a person from the doldrums who is confined to a hospital room or sick bed. The Bible says in Proverbs 17:22, "A merry heart does good, *like* medicine, But a broken spirit dries the bones." There is a healing affect in laughter.

## Support and Encouragement

Whether someone is moving, changing jobs, or going through a divorce, a friend's understanding can be priceless. Support and encouragement can be valuable tools in times of transition. At its best, a major change is still traumatic. We don't like to experience it, but change is inevitable. Knowing

---

[16] Ibid., 10.

someone understands and is praying for you can help make the transition easier.

## Christmas Letters

With the use of the computer and the technology of scanning pictures, Christmas letters can be a joy to read. To engage however, in a month-by-month rundown of the year's past activities, including each member of the family can be too much even from the most entertaining writer. Catch-up newsletters should include highlights only, such as graduations, birthdays and weddings and should not be more than one page long. Of course I need not remind you that mass mailings (no pun intended!) are not suitable for those who are close enough to your family to know events as they happen.

The larger circle of friends and family should be informed of births, marriages, and deaths as they happen. Close friends and relatives may be told of vacations, promotions, children's triumphs, health problems and philosophical insights.[17]

The recipient will be delighted with a short, informative note rather than a lengthy newsletter. Pictures add a visual dimension of interest available through the technology of scanning and digital photography. There is another advantage to keeping these informative letters shorter; the writer is relieved of the stressful drudgery of endless hours journalizing family activities throughout the year.

---

[17] Judith Martin, *Miss Manners Basic Training: Communication* (New York: Crown Publishers, 1997), 38.

## Chain Letters

*Chain letters are never acceptable!* Not only are they against the law for the inconvenience they cause the United States Postal Service, but they can be hurtful to those receiving them. One dear lady wrote *Miss Manners* about receiving countless chain letters during her fight against cancer. These people may have meant well by telling her to copy them and receive good fortune, but to use her energy to do such silly running around was taking unfair advantage of her as a friend. Her response to these letters was one of disappointment, which resulted in her wondering if these "friends" perhaps didn't like her. The best way to handle chain letters whether by "snail-mail" or over the Internet is to promptly put them in the waste basket or delete them.

## Proper Form for the Personal Letter

### The Address and Date

If your stationery does not have your return address on it, it is a good idea to include it in your correspondence even though it will be on the envelope. This way if the envelope gets thrown away, your address is still available for a reply. It is usually placed in the upper right-hand corner of the first page, with the date below it. If your stationery includes your address, the date only should appear at the upper right hand corner of the first page. Writing out the date *May 17, 2001* is preferable to *5-17-2001*.

### The Salutation

The way you open a letter or note depends on your relationship with the recipient and the formality of the situation. Your first name or nickname is appropriate when the letter is informal and written to close friends and family. Dear *Miss, Mrs., Ms., Madam, Mr.,* or their professional title may be used when addressing your letter in a more formal manner. Traditionally, the husband's name appears first when addressing couples. The appropriate form for addressing an unmarried couple (which unfortunately is very common) is using both of their names, such as: *Dear Mr. Thornton and Ms. Riley.* If you do not know the gender of the person to whom you are writing, you may use *Ladies and Gentlemen* or *Dear Madam or Sir.*

**The Body**

When writing a shorter letter, the first and third pages should be used if the stationery has a side-fold. The fourth, or outside page is left blank so it will not show through the envelope. For longer letters the first, second, third and fourth pages may be written on in regular order or the center may be opened as you would a book, and written on as a full sheet.

Letters may be written on both sides providing the paper is not so thin that the writing shows through. This makes the letter difficult to read. Sometimes you will find extra paper in stationery sets with no design. This paper is intended for the second sheet or for the third sheet if you are writing on both sides of the first one.

If the stationery has a top-fold with no design or embossing on the first page, you may write on that page starting from the fold. The note will begin on the first page and continue onto the second page starting at the upper edge. The page is opened flat and written as if it were a single sheet. If the note is short, begin the writing on the lower half of the page.

If the writing continues it should be turned over and written from the edge of the paper. This may seem up- side down, but the letter should be read in a continuous manner for the convenience of the recipient.

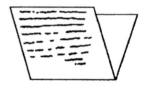

When using embossed stationery with an initial or design in the center of the first page, a full page of writing should begin at the top of the opened page. If the letter will not take the entire sheet, it may be started at the fold or the lower half of the opened page. I was thrilled

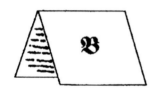

to find that when the letter is too long, it may be continued on the backside. (I always seem to find more to say than room in which to say it!) In this case, the writing should start from the cut side and finish toward the fold.[18]

**The Closing**

When writing to government officials in a formal setting, the closing should be *Respectfully yours*, or *Respectfully*. Business letters that are less formal but are still on a professional level use closings that include: *Very truly*

---

[18] Peggy Post, *Emily Post's Etiquette,* 16th ed. (Harper Collins: New York, 1997), 20-21.

*yours, Yours truly, Very cordially yours*, or *Very sincerely yours*.

*Sincerely, Sincerely yours, Best Wishes, Cordially, Kindest regards*, and *Your friend* are informal signatures that would be appropriate for friends and family. *Love* is probably the most used closing and the most misunderstood. It is true that when you are writing to someone you care about you will naturally sign it with an affectionate ending. *With love, With all my love*, and a more casual *Love ya, Always*, or *Much love* are all appropriate closings and convey warmth. *Love* should not be used when you are not on an intimate level with the recipient. An ending such as *Warmly, Affectionately* or *Fondly* can be used as an option. Many Christians enjoy signing with a spiritual note such as *Yours in Christ*, or *Together in His Service* for formal letters. If these do not feel natural perhaps you might try *Regards* or *Looking forward*. Simply signing your name is always acceptable. Whatever ending you choose, keep it friendly and natural sounding to the person you are addressing. Be careful to convey the true nature of your relationship with the recipient in the closing.

For formal closings, sign your entire name. For informal situations, sign it as you prefer the recipient to call you.

### Envelope Insertion

With the popularity of semi-formal and informal correspondence the importance of insertion etiquette has become more relaxed. For convenience sake, rather than protocol, here are a few suggestions.

Your correspondence should be inserted into the envelope so that a right-handed person would be able to read it as it is removed.

Cards with a side-fold are placed with the fold entering the envelope first and with the straight edges lined up just below the outer flap.

When two envelopes are used as in formal or wedding invitations, the inner envelope should face toward the back of the outer envelope. If a small RSVP card is used, place it in the inner envelope in front of the invitation. The names written on the inner envelope should be right side up when removed from the envelope.[19]

If you are sending a top-fold greeting card or engraved note, it is inserted into the envelope with the straight edge first. The front of the card should be facing the back of the envelope. Proper insertion of a personal letter is not quite as crucial as the formal invitation or announcement. It should be folded to consume as much of the space in the envelope as possible. This varies with the size of the envelope. Note cards are designed to fit envelopes that come with them, but once in a while you will have extra envelopes on hand and want to send a note on paper that did not

---

[19] Steven L. Feinberg, ed., *Crane's Blue Book of Stationery; The Styles and Etiquette of Letters, Notes, and Invitations* (New York: Doubleday, 1989), 140.

originally come with it. At our house, extra envelopes produce like rabbits. I'm not sure how this happens, perhaps because I keep them in a dark tin. I have recently acquired the habit of measuring the envelope with the card in the store before purchasing it. I'm sure this will slow down the over population of envelopes.

A good rule of thumb when stuffing an envelope is that the person opening the letter should be able to begin reading immediately as it falls open naturally.

### Addressing Envelopes

There really aren't many options when it comes to addressing envelopes. The United States Postal Service prefers the return address in the upper left-hand corner. Since this is not possible with engraved or printed envelopes, one

usually puts it on the back flap. Printed address labels come in very handy and meet the requirements of the Postal Service. If the envelope is small and the label is rather large, you may put it on the back flap.

The recipient's correct name and address should be written as legibly as possible. If your writing is poor, printing may be easier to read. Include the city, state, and zip code. If available, use the full nine-digit zip code (ZIP +4) for more efficient delivery. If not, the five-digit code will get it to the right place. Either way, the zip code should appear on the same line as the city and state. Traditionally, the use of address labels was reserved for informal letters. This hard and fast rule has relaxed some since the wide use of computer labels has come into existence. It used to be "taboo" to use labels on wedding invitations, but convenience has won out and it is becoming more popular.

The clear address labels seem to be the most popular for wedding invitations. Whether the letter is formal or informal, the recipient's full name should be on the envelope preceded with *Mr., Mrs., Ms., Miss., Rev., Dr.,* etc. You may use the first and last name when it is preferred. Although you may not see this practiced much, there is a correct way to address young people. A young girl is usually addressed as *Miss* with her first and last names following. Until the age of seven, a boy is addressed as *Master* with his full name following. As he gets older, a boy is addressed without a title until he is approximately eighteen, then he may take the adult title of *Mr.*[20] This may seem trivial, but when time is taken out to address a child in formal structure, it really makes them feel important and will not soon be forgotten.

### Finding the Time to Write

Not everyone is an avid letter writer. In fact there are a great many people who feel they just don't have the time to sit down and write a heart-felt letter. It is not that they wouldn't like to. On the contrary, they would very much like to write more and usually admire those who can. It may be a comfort if you fall under the category of "too busy," to know that a few lines at the end of a card or post card are better than receiving nothing at all. You may want to put a few in your purse and carry some stamps (which are cheaper for post cards!) When you have a moment in the doctor's office, at the courthouse, awaiting jury duty, or any other 'dead time,' you can drop a friend a line. Carry addresses of friends and family with you, either in your purse or an organizer, with a pen handy. When inspiration comes, you will be ready.

---

[20]Post, 27.

I have a friend in Arizona, Margie Staten, who writes beautiful cards and letters. I have received several timely notes from Margie just when I needed encouragement the most. I asked her one time where she found the time. She was a very busy lady, juggling between being a pastor's wife and mother with a full-time professional position. She shared with me her writing secret (printed with permission, of course!) Margie has a writing table, a small desk with all her writing utensils handy. This special writing desk is stocked with pens, stationery, cards, stamps and addresses. Margie sets aside a special time each week for writing. She schedules it in! What a wonderful idea!

### ❧❧ *Grace Notes* ❧❧

❧ *Save a few of the "love" stamps from the postal service for use after they are discontinued. Write a Valentine love letter to your beloved or a special "I love you" to the special lady who raised you and gave you so many happy memories.*

❧ *Sprinkle some potpourri in the envelope or spray a letter with your favorite perfume.*

❧ *Buy some calligraphy pens and try your hand at fancy lettering to make it look special.*

❧ *Put some beautiful stationery, a pen, and stamps in a basket. Give it as a gift to the college student who is far from home.*

❧ *Put an English Tea bag and a small package of sugar in a card to encourage someone to pamper herself for ten minutes and "have a cup of tea on me."*

> *Tucked inside this card*
> *Just for you to see,*
> *Is a special moment*
> *With a prospective cup of tea.*
> *Put it in a cup,*
> *Sit in your best chair,*
> *And as you drink your cup of tea*
> *Pretend that I am there!*
> *--Gayla M. Baughman*

ఎ Write a special letter to your child on important mile-marker birthdays:

>    <u>five</u> – starting school, leaving home for the first time

>    <u>thirteen</u> – new life as a teenager

>    <u>sixteen</u> – now an adult and can drive the car? (**Scary** thought!)

>    <u>eighteen</u> – graduating from High School, going to college and leaving home for the second time!

>    <u>twenty-one</u> – getting married or a special promotion at work

>    There may be other special years that stand out to you. These letters will be saved and cherished by your children for years to come.

# Part Five

# Showers & Gifts

# *20*

# *Who Gives the Shower?*

Traditionally, a friend gives the shower. Whether it is a wedding shower for the bride or a baby shower for the mother-to-be, normally, it is not the immediate family (mothers, mothers-in-law or sisters) unless there are extraordinary circumstances. For a wedding shower, this may be the case when the bride is from a foreign country, or the shower is being held in the groom's hometown and the bride knows no one outside her future in-laws. For the mother-to-be, anyone except her mother or sister may host a shower. It is fine for a sister-in-law, cousin, or close friend to initiate the invitation, but direct relatives should never do so at any gift-giving event. This would include a house-warming event also.

In Pentecostal churches, it is customary for the church to throw a wedding shower for the bride or a baby shower for the mother-to-be. This is a tradition that has been practiced for many years. This practice would fall under the category of "Pentecostal Etiquette," because we have customized traditional protocol to meet our needs. Appointing someone in the congregation to oversee showers is an excellent idea. In the event that one of her family should need a shower, someone else should be appointed to fill the position for that time. I am sure a great deal of appreciation would be extended to the one responsible for being sensitive enough not to overlook the person organizing showers or her close relatives.

A shower does not have to be given by only one person. Two or three friends can get together and give a "joint" shower for the guest or guests of honor. This can be a great relief financially on one single pocketbook. If your church is in a position to host all showers, pay for the decorations, and provide a facility, this is a service that may be offered to the members. If someone in particular wants to host a shower and shoulder the costs, a note of appreciation would be sufficient coming from the leaders of the church and a special "thank you" from the guest or guests of honor.

An occasion may arise when a new convert's family or friends want to put on a shower, including the new friends the guest of honor has made at church. For what could be an awkward situation for all involved, it would be better to abandon the traditional approach rather than causing problems for the new convert and her family. A compromise agreement could be made with the person or persons planning the shower. For instance, it would be possible to offer the services of the church facilities. Allowing them to host the event would not only show Christian kindness, but perhaps win them to the Lord in the process.

If you find yourself in a situation where a sister or mother, unaware of traditional etiquette, insists on giving a shower, the best thing to do is to work with them, showing kindness and willingness to be a part of their plans. It is very selfish to refuse to attend a shower just because you were not the hostess. Neither is it acceptable to bully your way into educating them just for the sake of keeping the rules.

Manners are an integral part of etiquette. To forsake good manners for the purpose of propagating etiquette is unwise and defeats your purpose.

# *Notes*

# *21*

# *Wedding Showers*

Emily Post defines a wedding shower as, "a gathering of friends in honor of a forthcoming marriage."[1] Having a shower too close to the wedding could prove to be very inconvenient for the bride, who is busy with the wedding preparations. Neither do you want it too early; there could be a change in wedding plans.

Wedding showers should be held anywhere from two weeks to two months prior to the wedding. In the event there is no time for a shower before the wedding, there have been occasions when the shower was given after the honeymoon.

There are several types of wedding showers. A second marriage, an older woman or a bride already in living accommodations would not necessarily need many gifts that a household shower would provide because she is already set up. Likewise, if the groom has been living in an apartment, he probably has some things the couple would not need duplicated. Check with the bride

---

[1] Peggy Post, *Emily Post's Etiquette,* 16th ed. (New York: Harper Collins Publishers, 1997), 762.

to see what she will need. If the couple does not need any household items, there are some other options to the household bridal shower that could continue the fun tradition of giving a shower.

It is perfectly fine if more than one shower is held for a new couple. As long as the bride has the time for several showers, and she agrees, there are limitless ideas. Keep in mind that if the church is a small one, the guests may have limited budgets, so multiple showers including the same guests each time may be out of the question.

If the church is a larger one and the guests can be distributed between several showers, consult the bride for suggestions on who should be invited to which shower. However, it may be interesting as well as fun to let the guests decide which shower they would like to attend.

**The Wedding Shower (Household Shower)**

Traditionally, only the bride and her female family and friends were in attendance at the wedding shower, but modern ideas have changed the original protocol. Very often the groom is now invited along with husbands and boyfriends of the female guests. It is usually a "couple" festivity, but not necessarily limited to such.

A morning coffee, luncheon, or buffet dinner are all suitable for serving at a shower. Wedding showers can be held any day of the week that is convenient for the guest of honor, the hostess and the majority of the guests. Originally, this shower was in *lieu* of bringing gifts to the wedding reception.

Gifts such as towels, kitchen utensils, centerpieces, serving bowls, china, appliances and other useful household items

are given at a wedding shower. Many times, if the bride is from another part of the country, the church she is from will give her a shower while she and her groom-to-be are in town. This is perfectly acceptable even though the wedding will be held elsewhere. If the miles are many, it may be that only the family will be able to attend the wedding, so this gives the hometown friends a chance to be part of the celebration.

**Bridal Shower (Lingerie Shower)**

The bridal shower is a personal lingerie shower for the bride-to-be. Friends and family usually give her under-garments that can be added to her trousseau (the bride's wardrobe). Since only girls and women are present, there is more freedom to indulge in giving a negligée or other personal items that would be impossible with men present.

It is fun to buy "gag" gifts and "bedroom" lingerie, but to embarrass the bride or other guests with crude remarks or inappropriate behavior is uncalled for. Keep in mind that moderation is a virtue and Christian showers have a different emphasis than worldly ones.

**Combination Shower**

This shower is the combination of lingerie and household gifts. The guests are welcome to bring either or both to this shower. Consequently, this is usually a ladies-only shower.

**Round the Clock Shower**

Bring a gift that is appropriate for that hour. For example, a 6:00 p.m. shower would reveal gifts that would be used at dinnertime. These gifts would revolve around the kitchen and dining room such as kitchen utensils, cookbooks, table linens and centerpieces. Wall décor such as mirrors, or framed prints, and other useful items such as magazine racks, bookends, and photo albums are just a few suggestions.

**Recipe Shower**

The recipe shower would be a perfect personalized party for the bride who loves to cook. Each guest brings an inexpensive gift accompanied by a recipe. As examples, a blender with a salsa recipe or a crystal bowl with a *Jell-O* salad recipe would be excellent ideas for this shower.

**The Wishing Well**

If the invitation includes a note that a wishing well will be at the shower, this suggests that each guest should bring a small additional gift for the wishing well (such as a small bottle of detergent). Each gift is put into a cardboard replica of a wishing well which can be made either by the hostess or rented. Gifts may be wrapped or unwrapped depending on how much time is allotted for the shower.

Remember that the bride will be opening the regular gifts also. A poem in the form of a riddle could be attached to each gift. When the bride "fishes" out the items from the well, she will try to figure out who brought each one.[2]

## Wedding Shower Themes

Decorating and selecting a theme for a wedding shower can be fun and full of variety. Although decorations are not required, there are things you can do in moderation and still carry a theme. You may use the colors the bride has chosen for her wedding, but it is not necessary. There may be a favorite line of collectibles that will help in the area of decoration. For instance, if the bride-to-be is collecting Victorian dolls, you may want to decorate with pictures of classic porcelain dolls. If she collects figurines of children depicting couples in love, you may want to use the color scheme and décor that has pictures of children on them. Many showers are decorated in a general fashion with no particular theme except wedding items. This is fine and can be very beautiful. If you are in need of original ideas, try some of the ingenious ones suggested by students in my *Social Graces* college classes.

### Victorian

A Victorian Shower is decorated with hats, tea sets and lace doilies. Victorian roses attached to pins or magnets could be prizes. The guests dress up in Victorian era costume. This would be great for a shower set as an afternoon tea shower.

---

[2]Ibid., 765-766.

## Money Shower

Decorate this shower with dollar bills (which the bride keeps). For the bride who has everything, you could do

this instead of bringing gifts. Set a minimum monetary gift without the bride's knowledge. A money tree could be part of the décor (tying rolled bills to a silk tree). Make the cake look like a dollar bill. This theme might be good for an older couple getting married.

### Hawaiian Luau

Decorations in bright, festive colors would be expected at a Luau shower. Hawaiian punch, a pineapple centerpiece and sliced ham remind us of Hawaii. The table could be dressed in a grass skirt (unless you want the bride-to-be to wear one).

## Games

## Pin the Lips on the Fiancée

Have a snapshot of the lucky guy enlarged and backed with thick cardboard. Make over-sized red lips to cover the blocked out ones on the picture. Play like you would *Pin the Tail on the Donkey.*

**Piñata**

A Mexican tradition that is filled with fun is the *Piñata*. This is a large, hollow *papier-mâché* object in a shape related to the occasion such as a wedding bell. A hole on the top is left for putting candy or other small objects inside. As the *Piñata* is suspended from a rope, each person is blindfolded and handed a stick, or other hard object (such as a baseball bat) and instructed to take a swing in an effort to break the *piñata* open. After several attempts, a blow lands, the *Piñata* bursts open, and out come the "prizes."

Each guest is given her share of the bounty. Rather than stuffing with candy, you may want to fill it with small lotions, Chap Stick, and other small items for a lingerie shower. Once it is broken open, everyone gets a prize (and the bride gets the underwear in a plastic egg)!

**Design a Wedding Dress**

The guests are divided into three teams. One person is chosen as the model and the others work as a team making a wedding dress out of toilet paper. The bride is the judge— would she really wear that?

## Notes

# 22
# *Baby Showers*

Baby showers can be given before or after the baby arrives. It is good to ask the mother-to-be which she would prefer. When the shower is scheduled before the baby arrives, gifts are more tailored for either boy or girl, unless the couple know what the baby will be. Now, with the use of sonograms, more mothers know what to expect, but there is no real guarantee. I've been to showers where they were sure the baby was a little girl and low n' behold, a boy came along! The pink room had to be repainted and all the little girl items returned for little boy things. All the pretty little pink items had to be returned also. For some reason, we won't dress boys in pink—any other color, but not pink!

If the mother-to-be prefers a baby shower after the baby has arrived, this is appropriate. It also gives the family a chance to purchase items of sentimental value or give heirlooms to the baby before a shower is given.

*First baby* showers are very needful. The first baby has nothing new at the start. There are no big brothers or sisters to hand down clothing, furniture or other items. It is a start from scratch shower, which can be very exciting for the new family. If you wish to purchase a large item, you should check with the family to make sure it is not on lay-a-way or another member of the family is not planning to purchase it. The gift selection is large in spectrum from baby beds and strollers to diapers and lotions *(see gift ideas on page 188)*.

*Second baby* showers are acceptable but should be restricted to very close friends and family. This is less common because the baby will have things from past siblings to use. The baby probably already has a crib, changing table, stroller, car seat, some clothes and other things. A second baby shower is more appropriate if the mother has moved to a new town and has a different circle of friends, if the first child was a girl and her second one a boy, or if several years have passed since the birth of the last baby.

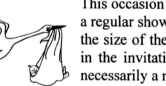

*Adopted baby* - Adopted babies need showers too! This occasion is treated just the same as a regular shower with the exception that the size of the baby should be included in the invitation since the child is not necessarily a newborn.

*Single mothers* – In a church setting, this is a very delicate situation. In an effort to promote virtue, it is tempting to overlook a young lady that has had a baby out of wedlock.

According to etiquette, a shower for a single mother is acceptable, but should be kept small and restricted to close friends and relatives. If a young person from your church gets pregnant and chooses to keep the baby, she has at least made one right choice. An abortion would have been a second wrong choice. Therefore, it is a kind gesture to reach out to such a person with love and compassion as we are commanded to do in Scripture. A shower would definitely be a blessing, but keep it light and less festive.

Another option would be to collect the gifts from the people in the church and have a small get-together after a service, not actually calling it a shower at all. This is something you will have to decide. Check with your pastor and find out his opinion. If it involves the women of the church, it is best to have his permission for the sake of unity. He may have some other good suggestions that will be suited to the needs of the mother.

### Baby Shower Themes

*Winnie the Pooh* – Decorate in yellow and red: Pooh's colors of course. If the mother is decorating the baby's room in *Winnie the Pooh,* the guests could select items she has registered for at a favorite department or specialty store. The mother's corsage would be designed from small baby items such as diaper pins, cotton swabs, pacifiers, etc.

*Noah's Ark* – Decorating with baby animals by two's would give this theme a connection with baby. If watermelon is in season, a centerpiece in the shape of the ark could hold a healthy fruit salad. Animal crackers would be a cute snack for this shower.

### Games

*Diaper the Baby* – Divide guests into two teams. Each person has to diaper a doll blindfolded. When she is finished, she must blindfold the next person who in turn diapers the baby. The first team done wins.

*Feed the Baby* – This game is played the same as the one above, except you feed baby food to the next person in line while blindfolded.

*Guess the Baby's Food* – Take the labels off several small jars of baby food and have each guest taste it (with a fresh spoon, of course). They write down what they think it is. The person with the most correct answers is the winner.

*Dirty Diaper* – Each guest is given a miniature diaper pinned with a small gold safety pin. Just before the mother opens the gifts, the diapers are removed and unfolded. The one with the brown mark (or dirty diaper) wins the door prize.

*Don't say "Baby"* – When each guest arrives she is given a small safety pin. (A clothespin can also be used.) If someone catches her saying the "B" word, she has to give the safety pin up to the person who heard her. The one with the most pins at the end of the game wins a prize.

# *23*

# *Other Showers*

### Housewarming Party

When a couple moves into their first home or builds a new one, they are eager to show off their hard work by inviting friends informally or having a housewarming party. Invitations may be sent on informal or commercial fill-in cards, or a simple telephone call would be appropriate. Be prepared to give a "tour" of your new home whether this is a party-style get together or a come-and-go open house. Make sure you have someone else greeting your guests at the door if you are busy directing the tour. You may want to greet them yourselves, if you don't mind letting them wander through the house without you. A housewarming party is not expected every time someone moves. It is up to you if you want to have a "party" at all. When you host your own housewarming party, it is not proper to ask for gifts.

There may be someone in your church who would like to host a gift-giving housewarming party in honor of a couple's new home. If this is the desire of your group of friends, and the couple approve, the most important thing to remember is to accommodate the convenience of the couple in the new home and ensure their availability. Keep in contact with them at the time of their move and when they are ready for guests, you may proceed with the festivities. Often guests will bring gifts to help subsidize the costs of new appliances, utilities, building and other expenses when they are invited to a housewarming. (*See gift ideas on page 191.*)

### Shower by Proxy

It is perfectly in order to have a shower for someone who is not able to attend. Many times friends from far away places would like to be involved in a shower but cannot. This type of shower gives them a chance to give something. When a shower *by proxy* is being given, the hostess can call the guest of honor when all the friends get together or put a card with the gifts that everyone has signed. One suggestion is to have a gift wrapping party. Each guest brings her gift unwrapped and wraps it with everyone else at the party. This way everyone has an opportunity to see the items. All the gifts are then boxed and shipped to the guest of honor.

# *24*

# *Invitations*

Any shower invitation may be written on commercial fill-in shower invitations, short personal notes, telephoned or issued in person. It is correct etiquette to include the name of the guest of honor and the type of gift expected with every invitation.

In these busy days the listing of places where the bride or new mother has registered is a token of courtesy for the guests' time spent in shopping. These now include more

reasonable shops like *Target* and *Penney's* as well as the more exclusive department stores to accommodate the pocket book of the guests. This does not mean that the guests are required to buy gifts from these stores. It just gives them a guideline to help narrow down their choices.

Colors should be included when the gifts are for decorating or furnishing the house or apartment. Lingerie-shower invitations for the bride should include her sizes.

# Notes

# 25

## Guests

Traditionally, only close friends and relatives were invited to a shower (since the invitation automatically means 'bring a gift'). On wedding showers, Peggy Post quotes her grandmother-in-law as saying, "Huge showers that include almost everyone invited to the wedding are in the *poorest* taste. The entire idea of an intimate party is lost, and they are no more than a demand for more gifts. As such, they are an unforgivable imposition on those invited."[3] In publishing this quote, I get the feeling she feels as strongly about this as did Emily Post.

I don't make it a point to disagree with the authorities on etiquette, but I am not in total agreement with this practice. I do agree that showers were traditionally sentimental occasions, and only those intimate with the guest of honor were included. I would be reluctant to say however, that it is a *breach* of etiquette to have all the ladies of the church come to a shower just because Emily Post said it should be only intimate friends and family.

Time may prove to be altering this traditional view. *Modern Bride* holds the opinion that only those guests being invited to the wedding should be invited to the shower. It does not imply that it should be limited to a certain number

---

[3] Post, 764.

of those guests.[4] The exception is when a wedding is extremely small and restricted to family only, perhaps with no reception, or the wedding is in another part of the country and the friends who are unable to attend because of distance, want to give a shower.

It is a good idea to consult the bride about the guest list unless there is a "surprise" shower given. In that case, a close relative may be of assistance. The hostess wouldn't want to leave out a close friend or someone who is not in her flow of acquaintances but is close to the bride or the new mother. *Pentecostal Etiquette* includes the tradition of inviting all the ladies because we are bonded as sisters through Christ. Many of us are closer to our church family than unsaved blood relatives. The exclusion of anyone in your church family could send the wrong message, thus compromising a spirit of unity.

Etiquette was never intended to complicate life. Emily Post said, "Etiquette is meant to make life easier, not to impose unnecessary or impractical rules."[5] I would venture to say when a question comes up about what is proper, a good rule of thumb is to examine the situation and do that which is most convenient and gracious for all the involved parties.

[4] Bride's Magazine, *Bride's Wedding Planner* (New York: Fawcett Columbine, 1997), 169.

[5]Post, 763.

# *26*

# *Shower Protocol*

### Decorations

Although you may wish to go to great lengths to make a shower look beautiful, decorations are not necessary except a centerpiece for the table. Many times the hostess is on a tight budget and this allows for the most conservative arrangements and yet freedom to do something nice for the future bride,  mother, or new homeowner. The cake, serving-dishes, and place settings make a pretty backdrop for a nice shower. Arranging the gifts in an attractive way also serve as part of the decorations. The hostess may give the bride, mother and future mother-in-law corsages, but this is not obligatory.

### Refreshments

When choosing refreshments for the shower, it is a good idea to keep in mind what would be appropriate to the hour of the day and taste of the guests. A cake is not necessary for every shower, but if that has been the tradition in your area, to leave it out might offend the guest of honor.

If the shower is mid-morning, a drink and small snack would be plenty, especially if you plan to serve cake. A combination of hot and cold drinks makes it easier to accommodate a number of guests. Soft drinks, iced tea, punch or coffee should be offered. A late afternoon shower would call for an afternoon tea menu where sandwiches, cake or cookies, tea, and coffee are served. A dinner party is rare for a shower, but if guests arrive home too late to squeeze in supper, a light dinner is needed.

## Entertainment

Formal entertainment is not necessary for a shower, but games and planned activities can be good entertainment. Playing music in the background is nice for setting a mood. If you plan to play games and give prizes, they should be just that – prizes for the winners of the games. These prizes should **not** be handed over to the guest of honor. Elizabeth Post noted that the guest of honor, "has already received a gift from each guest. It is more fun when everyone has a chance at the prizes."[6]

## Opening the Gifts

Opening the gifts is the highlight of the shower. This should be done after everyone has arrived. The guest of honor opens each package and thanks each giver.

Cards should be enclosed to make this convenient for the recipient. One of the bridesmaids, or friend of the mother-to-be, should sit beside the guest of honor and make a list of gifts and givers. Noting the gift on each card, would prevent confusion if the card is separated from the gift. This would also be handy when writing acknowledgments for gifts received.

---

[6] Elizabeth L. Post. *Emily Post's Etiquette,* 15th ed. (New York: Harper Collins Publishers, 1992), 697.

# 27

# *Canceled! Returning Gifts*

In the event the wedding is canceled, if at all possible, the gifts should be returned. Wedding gifts are given with the intent to be used in the bride and groom's new home. Since that possibility is gone, they should be sent back to the ones who gave them. Monogrammed gifts or used items obviously cannot be returned. A note of thanks should be sent along with the returned gift. If friends or family insist the gifts be kept, it is appropriate to do so.

As the gift giver, in the event the fiancée is killed or tragically removed, it is better to take the gift back and return

it for a refund. To insist the bride-to-be keep the gift may seem insensitive rather than generous. Keeping the gift may be a painful reminder of her loss.

If the bride-to-be becomes engaged again, she should ask friends who insisted on her keeping the gifts not to give another one. The first one may still be unused and if nothing is said, it will appear the bride-to-be is greedy, hoping for more gifts from those who have already given her one.

In the event a baby boy arrived and the mother was expecting a girl, she will need to return gifts that are inappropriate. This is understandable and expected. The situation can be very disheartening if a bereaved mother and father have to return gifts. Although it may not be treated quite the same, a couple planning the adoption of a child and something happening to prevent it can be very devastating also. For these reasons, it is becoming more common to have a baby shower after the happy event.

# *28*

# *Giving Gifts*

One of the most exhilarating things I can think of is finding the perfect gift for someone and watching her eyes dance when she opens it. As I have gotten older, I would rather watch my children open gifts on Christmas than open

my own. I don't want to miss their expressions. Why do I feel this way? Because I love them and I love making them happy. It is the same for anyone you love. Making them happy is the best gift you can give.

Letitia Baldridge, an authority on manners and etiquette, remarked in her book the *New Complete Guide to Executive Manners* that the best gift is:

- ঌ chosen specifically with the recipient in mind
- ঌ unexpected
- ঌ a true gesture of friendship
- ঌ one that shows a sense of humor
- ঌ one that shows great research and thought
- ঌ one that does not exceed your budget [7]

---

[7]Letitia Baldrige, *Letitia Baldrige's New Complete Guide To Executive Manners* (New York: Rawson Associates, 1993), 272-273.

I received a Christmas gift from a friend that included a personalized theme. She knew that I loved to compose songs and play the piano, so she gave me an ornament with a musical instrument on it. Tucked away in the tissue was a treasure. Instead of a traditional Christmas card, I found a mini-book entitled, *Music Lovers: Quotations from the world of music.* The thought that she had taken extra time to find something so personal made the little book even more special to me. It struck a chord of close friendship in my heart.

The best gifts are not always the things you buy. Some gifts can be your time, your space, or something you've made with your hands. Being short of money is not a  good enough reason to refrain from gift giving. I learned this little lesson one February when we were low on cash. My husband had gone to work, driving our only car and I was left with our daughter, who was a toddler at the time. I was distraught when I realized it was Valentine's Day and I had no way to get to the store. Town was too far to walk and I was sinking deeper and deeper into depression. My little girl was busy in her room making Valentine cards for "Daddy and Mommy" when suddenly the light turned on! A homemade Valentine! That's what we'd do. I summoned my little girl from the bedroom and together we created the biggest Valentine cookie ever! It was beautiful! Then we decorated it with all the loving things you say at a time like that. That cookie was probably the best Valentine's Day gift I ever gave my husband. There is no card to remember it by, but the memory is engraved in my mind and my husband's affectionate response is etched on my heart forever.

Lately, I have discovered the art and satisfaction of giving gift baskets. They are fun to put together and you can make them as expensive or as frugal as you please. A basket full of homemade treats is always special, or you could tailor it to a fisherman with hooks, bait, and other items unique to the hobby. The advantage to a gift basket is that it can be personalized for anyone.

Always remove the price tags from the gifts you plan to give. If you feel they may need to exchange an item, keep the receipt and let them know that they are welcome to exchange it. Some stores are printing "gift receipts," which make it very convenient to exchange an item. These receipts have a bar code so the cashier can tell how much the item was, but it is not printed on the receipt. This type of receipt can be included in the wrapping of the gift.

It is a good idea to keep a record of the gifts you have given to various people. Not only is this advantageous for income tax purposes, but it could save some undue embarrassment if the gift is accidentally duplicated several years later.[8]

Listing the person's name, describing the gift, the price, the date you purchased it and the date you gave it as a gift are all important facts that could be useful. Your chart could be drafted on the computer and saved on the hard drive or it could be printed out and kept in a safe, handy place until it is needed. After that, it is as easy as filling in the blanks.

---

[8] Linda Phillips and Wayne Phillips, *The Concise Guide to Executive Etiquette* (New York: Doubleday, 1990), 111.

Following is an example that may be helpful:

## GIFTS GIVEN

| Name | Gift Item | Price | Date Purchased | Date Given |
|------|-----------|-------|----------------|------------|
|      |           |       |                |            |
|      |           |       |                |            |
|      |           |       |                |            |

### Gag gifts

It is fun to give and receive gag gifts, but if things are not kept in moderation these gifts can be hurtful and at the very least, embarrassing. When you plan to give a gag gift, use the following guidelines and you will probably be all right.

1. It should not point out a flaw in character.

2. Be careful not to point out a physical handicap.

3. People who cannot laugh at themselves would not be good candidates for gag gifts.

4. Make sure it does not remind the receiver of something sensitive in nature (like the death of a loved one).

5. Be sure you are doing this in love and not spite. If there is the small chance that you are trying to get even, forget it and discuss the problem with God before you go any further.

When a friend opens a gag gift, a chance is always taken. Take care if you are going to participate in this kind of humor. A friendship damaged over a silly gift is not worth the time you put into finding it. Find something else to laugh about.

### Inappropriate Gifts

There are times when it is inappropriate to give certain things to people. Most of the time these are obvious blunders that would not be made. For safety sake, let me take a moment to review. You don't want to give a box of candy to a diabetic or lingerie at a mixed shower. Be careful giving a gift to someone under you that could be misunderstood as a bribe. Be sensitive to the needs of others and you will give gifts that say the same.

A gift can be the tool to cement a relationship, but when given inappropriately, it can be the very thing that destroys it. Never give gifts as a payback, a bribe or as an apology for a wrong that has been committed.[9] Gifts touch the most obscure part of our emotions. Whether a person is emotional or not has nothing to do with the deep feeling a gift stirs. For this reason, it is impossible to undo a wrong done with a gift. Why do you suppose God chose to call the most precious Holy Ghost a gift? When He offered us this wonderful present, how could we turn it down? How can anyone turn a gift down? It is almost impossible. By the same token, the most horrendous example of gift giving was when Judas gave Jesus a kiss to betray him. There was no taking it back. The damage had been done.

---

[9] Letitia Baldrige, *Letitia Baldrige's New Complete Guide To Executive Manners* (New York: Rawson Associates, 1993), 272.

There are gifts that come with great sacrifice. These are the most touching when the price is known. Sometimes, you will never know the sacrifice someone has made for you to have a nice gift. I am reminded of *O'Henry's Short Story* about a young married couple that loved each other dearly. For Christmas they wanted to get the best gift for each other. The young man had admired a beautiful gold chain for his pocket watch in a store window, but passed it with a sigh for he was too poor to buy his beloved a Christmas present, let alone buy himself something. He knew what he wanted to buy her; it was a beautiful jewel-embedded comb for her long, beautiful, uncut hair. The young lady had watched her sweet new husband admire the chain and wondered how she would be able to afford it for him for Christmas.

Christmas Eve finally came and after a hard day at work in the factories, they came home to a cold house to share their treasures with each other by candlelight. He proudly presented a small box for her to open. When she opened the beautiful comb, she broke into tears. Removing the scarf from her head she revealed a cropped, unprofessional hairdo. "What happened?" he cried. "I sold my hair to have enough money to buy you a present." He cried as he opened his gift, thinking of her sacrifice so he could have this little gift. When he opened it, he was horrified to find the gold chain for the pocket watch he had sold to buy her comb for her hair.

Their sacrifices were greater gifts than the items they could have given. Their true love was exemplified in the price they paid for the pleasure of the other. Even though the gifts became useless with the watch sold and her hair gone, the example of love became a lesson to young lovers for years to come.[10]

Finding the perfect gift can be challenging especially if you don't know the person real well. It is appropriate to ask a friend or family member what a person would like if you are not close enough to them to know yourself.

When we were first married my husband and I had lengthy discussions on what to give on Mother's day. He thought a skillet or mixer was a tremendous idea. When we had our first child and I became a Mother, I got a little more vocal about the whole matter. I dug in my heels with resolve. I wanted something personal like a bottle of perfume or a new nightie, **not** pots and pans. It wasn't that I was ungrateful, but appliances represent work, and the Lord knows we don't have to be reminded of how much work it is to be a mom!

This went on for several years until our daughter, Marenda got big enough to put in her opinion. Of course she has done that since she was able to talk! Thankfully, they went shopping for a personal gift for Mommy. When I unwrapped my "personal" gift, it was the ugliest, most modest nightgown I have ever seen! It was a light blue stretchy polyester (the kind my grandmother used to like) that got caught on my hangnail and wouldn't let loose! The scoop neck had narrow elastic lace that stretched a mile. The sleeves were huge bell-type barrels that hung grotesquely past my elbows and the length hung modestly somewhere between my knees and ankles. Oh yes, did I mention that it was a *large?* I tried to be gracious (really, I did) and thanked my two favorite people for the *thoughtful* gift. But alas, as time went on, the absence of this particular nightwear did not

---

[10] Don Chaffey, dir. *O. Henry, The Gift of Love.* Writ. Caryl Ledner. Monterey Movie Company, 1992. Video.

go unnoticed. My husband began to inquire about it. I responded with the usual excuses.

"Oh my, where could it be?" "You don't suppose we have rats do you?" All talking came to no avail, I finally had to cough up the truth. "Honey, I'm sorry, but I hate that thing. If I accidentally stepped on the hem, the stretch neck would reach my knees. I would have the nastiest black eye on its assent!"

"I hadn't thought of that. I thought it would be modest to run around in front of our little daughter in," he piously replied.

"Modest!" I roared. "If I raised my arms at the same time you would be able to see straight through, from the back door to the front, because the sleeves are as big as our doors!" I was on a roll. There was no stopping. I compounded my exaggeration raved and got my point across to him hours before I stopped. Pots and pans wouldn't be so bad, I decided.

Not long after that I got a beautiful gown and robe set from *Victoria's Secret*. I raved for days about the wonderful gift. I wore it everywhere—well *not* everywhere—just everywhere in the house. Sheepishly my husband confessed, "I let Marenda pick it out this time."

I'm not sure you would call pots and pans inappropriate gifts for Mother's Day, but I don't think I am alone in my opinions. Many women feel the same way. Of course, since I've gotten older, I'm getting less picky. I'm just thankful I'm remembered as "dear ol' Mom."

## Timing

Sending a gift or card and timing it to get there on the appropriate day is a virtue. This is an area in my life that needs work. For some reason, I can't remember anyone's birthday until a few days after. I think it is something emanating from my calendar. When I look at it there is a sedative that radiates from it to put my "birthday radar" to sleep! When this mysterious sedative finally wears off, I go flying out the door and skid into the nearest store to find something "perfect" in ten minutes to send—three days late! At least they get a gift, right? Wrong! I know how I feel when I receive something in the mail on that special day. My mother-in-law (I call her my second Mom) has this gift. I don't know how she does it, but every card or gift I have received from her has either been on the exact day of the celebration or early! I think I will steal her calendar! Seriously, there is something to be said about the person who takes the time and effort to think ahead, timing it just right to get it in the mail to arrive on or before that special day. I'm working on it—not the theft of my mother-in-law's calendar, but the planned timing.

## Anniversary Gifts

Traditional gift giving is practiced more some places than others but it is fun to know what things you give on the anniversary of each year of marriage. Although this is not obligatory, it is still practiced to a great extent on the twenty-fifth, fiftieth and seventieth anniversaries.

## Traditional Gifts

| | | | |
|---|---|---|---|
| 1 | Paper or plastics | 12 | Linen (table, bed etc.) |
| 2 | Calico or cotton | 13 | Lace |
| 3 | Leather or simulated | 14 | Ivory |
| 4 | Silk or synthetic | 15 | Crystal or glass |
| 5 | Wood | 20 | China |
| 6 | Iron | 25 | Silver |
| 7 | Copper or wool | 30 | Pearls |
| 8 | Electrical | 35 | Coral and Jade |
| 9 | Pottery | 40 | Ruby |
| 10 | Tin | 45 | Sapphire |
| 11 | Steel | 50 | Gold |
| | | 60, 70 & 75 | Diamond |

Besides the gifts listed above, other anniversary gifts could include photo albums, framed family portraits and books related to hobbies or a favorite author. An edited video of family members over the years is priceless for the parents or grandparents.

## Baby Shower Gifts

When looking for the perfect baby shower gift, it is very helpful if the mother will register at her favorite store. This is not only convenient for the guests, but it is also convenient for the new mother. She can register for large items such as strollers, car seats, and high chairs with the understanding some friends may want to go together to purchase one of the items. Smaller items may also be selected for those who like to purchase gifts the baby will need. Some of these items are diapers, bottles, bibs, bath lotions, gels, and clothing. When buying clothing for a newborn, it is a good idea to ask someone close to the new mother what size she prefers. Many times she will receive a lot of newborn size clothes at first, so she may prefer larger sizes of twelve-months or more. If all she has received are larger sizes, she may request a few newborn outfits or a smaller one if the baby is premature.

## Birthday Gifts

Birthday gifts tailored to match the age of the recipient may or may not be a good idea. General guidelines for children, young people and adults are easy to remember. A five-year old boy wouldn't appreciate a tie any more than a grandpa jump with delight over a push toy. It is easier to buy for someone in the age bracket of those you have living in your home.

For children, toys usually have the suggested age they are designed for printed on the package. The challenge may come when buying for a teenager the first few times or you need a gift for a girl and all you have are boys. Be observant, watch what she likes when you shop or browse through a magazine together. You can learn what people like if your ears are perked up and you listen to them talk. Does a co-worker play golf? Is that teenager a bookworm or an outdoor biker? Find out if he has a collection. A coin holder for the person who collects coins is a nice gift; include a few rare coins he has not yet found. Whatever the choice, a few extra moments spent on finding something the recipient really wants can be ultimately rewarded with the acknowledgment that "This is exactly what I wanted!" It is wonderful to hear a delightful "How did you know I wanted this?" when you have taken the care to be extra observant.

It may be fun to remind someone how they are aging, keeping in mind that it beats the alternative, however, you may find that some people are a little more sensitive about their age than others. Give some thought before purchasing an age-reminder gift to a person fifty-five or older. Some senior friends may receive a gift certificate for twenty bottles of *Ensure* more favorably than others. The same consideration would go into a gift such as tickets to the nearest theme park.

General gifts are probably the safest route. Articles of clothing, stationery, electronic devices, (radios, CD players, etc.) books, games and toys are among the large variety of items great for birthdays.

### Bon Voyage

Giving a gift to someone traveling on a lengthy trip or overseas is very special. Something to help pass the time is always appreciated. Books, games, a trip diary and sunglasses are a few suggestions. I always liked to pack "traveling bags" for my children when we were going on a trip. I would put little surprises in small gift bags and present it to them somewhere along the long drive or flight when the children became bored. I would include miniature color books, crayons (or markers if you're traveling in the hot summer), small games, cards, and puzzles. A special snack of hard candy, animal cookies, nuts, dried or fresh fruit were included. In fact, teenagers like it too! I was surprised to find out that my teenagers were expecting their usual "traveling bag" when we flew east for Christmas the last year before my daughter planned to be married. They may never outgrow them!

### Farewell

When a goodbye must be said to a friend moving away, it can be a time of great difficulty. Finding something to remember each other by is saying that you value the friendship and you don't want to be forgotten. A picture collage of her friends, home, and hangouts make a nice gift. If you want her to keep in touch, stationery with a book of stamps leaves her no excuse. A group of friends could compile a list of their e-mail addresses. This is another way of saying, "Please stay in touch."

## Housewarming Gifts

Usually, housewarming gifts range from live plants to bathroom soap. Small gifts of permanent use are usually given at a housewarming. A set of cloth napkins with matching napkin rings, guest towels, a print for the wall, or a brush for the new fireplace are a few ideas.

## Thank You

Thank you gifts can be as versatile as birthday gifts. Although a simple card is sufficient, anything more would be an extra expression of gratitude. Finding something that is related to the situation makes the gift specialized. A few examples are, a set of napkin rings sent to a dinner party hostess, or a new baseball glove presented to a coach after a successful game. If you were thanking someone for his or her hospitality, a live plant with the card attached, placed in the guest bedroom would show your gratitude nicely.

## Handmade Gifts

Handmade gifts are appropriate for anyone! If you enjoy baking, this is a delicious gift to give someone. It's a great gift for a teacher; she can take it home and eat it. It's not another trinket to go with the two-hundred and fifty others she has received from students over the years. In cooking, take care to be clean and neat. Cookies presented in a baggie, smeared with cookie dough are not very appetizing. It may appear that you are careless in the kitchen if you don't take the time to make your finished product appear clean and appetizing.

Crafted items are special to give. Something crocheted, sewed or stitched can send a message of love and sacrifice. Keep in mind the person's colors, decorating style and special favorites when giving a hand-crafted gift. I cherish the quilt my husband's maternal grandmother gave us for our wedding. I have another beautifully hand crafted quilt. It is very special not only because our church family gave it to us, but also because it was handmade by a very special friend.

### ๑๛ Grace Notes: ๑๛

*Are you fresh out of ideas? Browse through a magazine before going to the department store. You may come up with some ideas while comfortably sitting in your easy chair rather than wearing your feet out wandering around a store.*

## Gifts are opportunities to share kindness.

# 29
## *Accepting Gifts*

As Christians, sometimes it is easier to give gifts than to receive them. It may feel uncomfortable at first, but the gracious woman will accept gifts with pleasure and make a mental note to show genuine gratitude, whether it is something she "loves" or not. The simple expression of giving is the true gift. The fact that someone thought of you, made the effort to go to a store and pick out a gift is enough to warrant gratefulness. Accepting a gift graciously is similar to accepting a compliment. A gracious thank you is better than false humility when someone compliments your successes. By the same token, a simple "Thank you," is better than "Oh, you shouldn't have," when in your heart you are very happy the one who shouldn't have, did! If you are glad someone gave you a gift, say so! It will mean more to the giver to say you are pleased than to respond with a statement that you don't really believe yourself. Someone who is ungrateful will say things like "This isn't what I wanted" or leave the impression without saying the words. Gifts are fun to receive as well as give, we just don't like to admit it. We don't want people to think we are greedy or in need of anything. *Gifts are opportunities to share kindness. Accepting them can also be an opportunity to share with a kind heart.*

A gift should be opened when it is received. This shows the giver you are grateful and anxious to receive such a kind gesture. A verbal *thank you* is appreciated, but a written note of thanks is proper and should be written within a few days of receiving the gift. (*Thank you notes are covered on pages 138 and 139.*)

# Part Six

# Weddings

# *30*

# *Wedding styles*

The four different types of weddings are: very formal, formal, semi-formal, and informal. The number of guests, size of the wedding party, and choice of a wedding gown can be elements that determine which kind of wedding is appropriate. Although most Pentecostal brides use more traditional ideas, there are times when styles will cross over. The most important thing for a bride to remember is that this is one of the most important days of her life, and she will want to make it full of memories she will always cherish leaving no regrets.

## The Very Formal Wedding

The very formal wedding is usually held in a church or hotel ballroom with two hundred or more guests in attendance. Although an evening setting is traditional, brides are now scheduling early evenings or late afternoons giving plenty of time for the elaborate festivities. Very formal weddings were more stringent in the past, with the bride's family paying close attention to proper protocol and etiquette. A less strict stance has been taken with modern weddings even among Christians.

The invitations are engraved with traditional wording. The bride's gown is a traditional style with long sleeves (short gloves are optional) and a cathedral or chapel train *(see illustrations beginning on page 236)*. If she wears shorter sleeves, she may wear gloves to cover her arms. A shorter train is acceptable if she sets the time for earlier in the evening. There will usually be four to twelve attendants wearing floor-length dresses escorted by men in cut-away coats or tuxedos. White tie and tails are reserved for weddings after 6:00 p.m. Following the ceremony, an elaborate reception is held which usually includes a seated meal.

### The Formal Wedding

The formal wedding can be held in a church, hotel, club, or private home with one hundred guests or less. This is probably one of the most popular wedding types for Pentecostal brides whether or not she can come up with one hundred guests. This wedding may be scheduled either in the afternoon or evening.

Engraved or printed invitations are sent with traditional or personalized wording on them. The bride wears basically the same attire as in a very formal wedding, a long gown with either a chapel sweep or detachable train. She can wear a hat or veil, keeping in mind a length that compliments her gown. Wearing gloves is optional. If she has the wedding earlier in the day, she may desire to wear a shorter dress. The formal bride will carry a full bouquet, a flower-trimmed Bible or a prayer book. There will be from two to six attendants wearing dresses that are long or short. The groom and attendants wear cut away or regular suits. For the formal wedding they rarely wear dinner jackets. The formal reception usually includes a seated meal.

## The Semi-Formal Wedding

The semi-formal wedding is more versatile and usually smaller, involving fewer than one hundred guests. It can be held at a church, hotel, home or other location. The engaged couple can chose either engraved or printed invitations. For this style of wedding the bride's dress has more options. It can be floor-length or shorter and white or pastel; the veil may be short or long, from floor-length to flyaway *(see illustration on page 239)*. The train is optional; many brides use the chapel sweep for the semi-formal wedding or a detachable train that can be removed for the reception. The bride will carry a simpler bouquet, a flower-trimmed Bible or prayer book. Usually, there will be one or two bridesmaids in suits or street length dresses. The groom and attendants may wear either suits or tuxedos. Dinner jackets are also acceptable for a daytime wedding. A semi-formal reception consists of light refreshments either around tables or audience style seating with chairs facing the bride and groom's table.

## The Informal Wedding

The informal wedding can be held in the daytime anywhere. The restrictions are less stringent, lending a more relaxed atmosphere at the city hall, restaurant, beach, park or any other place suitable to the number of guests. The informal wedding is a popular choice for a second marriage, or perhaps for an older couple that have lost their mates.

There are usually fifty or fewer guests at the informal wedding. Of course this may vary slightly according to the situation or location. The invitations may be handwritten invitations or extended personally. The bride wears a suit or dress; white is optional. She may choose a veil, hat or other decoration for her hair and carry a small bouquet. There is usually only an honor attendant wearing a short dress and the groom and best man wear suits or blazers with coordinating trousers. The reception is intimate, being held at a private home or restaurant.

# *31*

# *Wedding Coordinator or Bridal Consultant*

Many brides are well capable of planning and organizing every aspect of their weddings. Purchasing a wedding planner and following the organized suggestions is all the direction many brides need.[1] If you do not feel comfortable with this or just don't have the time, a wedding coordinator or bridal consultant can be very helpful. A bridal consultant is a professional you can hire to do everything from finding the best buys on flowers and photography to calming your mother down during the wedding. A wedding coordinator is either one of your choice or someone the church has appointed to help with wedding ceremonies conducted in that facility.

To locate a bridal consultant you may look in the yellow pages under "Wedding supplies and services," or ask various bridal salons. Brides who have used consultants in the past are usually very helpful if they have been pleased with their services. Florists, photographers, and caterers may also be able to help locate the perfect consultant for you. Be sure to ask for references before hiring and note how much experience the consultant has. The charges vary with the

---

[1] Several software programs are available to organize wedding plans. Internet web sites offer assistance in this area as well as trial versions of their software.

amount of services you expect from your consultant. You can hire a consultant to help plan the wedding from start to finish, or just a day-of-the-wedding service.

A full-service consultant will do things like find ceremony and reception sites that will compliment the style of wedding you desire. She/he will scout out the best photographers, florists, and caterers. After researching prices and services, she/he will present you with the names of those who will do the best jobs within your budget.

A consultant hired for the wedding day only will help with last-minute planning, such as telling the caterer when to start serving and where the reception musicians should set up. Whether they charge a percentage of the overall cost of the wedding, charge you by the hour, or have a flat fee, many times they will save you money, advising you on budget cuts and money saving tips.

Many times a bridal consultant is hired when a bride is planning an out-of-state wedding or when she works full-time and has no time to scout the places, getting the best value for the things she needs for her wedding.

A wedding coordinator is either someone of your choice, or someone the church provides. If the church has a wedding coordinator, she will help you with the pastor's schedule and coordinate your plans with his. She can clear up many questions regarding church regulations, give you suggestions on music, reception, decorations, and help you walk through the rehearsal and ceremony. The coordinator will work closely with the clergy or pastor during the rehearsal. The pastor often knows ceremony etiquette and will be the primary spokesman, but it is nice to have a liaison between you and well-meaning family or friends especially if things start to get out of hand. Having someone else there with knowledge about weddings, who will preserve your wishes is very helpful. She is the perfect person to remind relatives this is your wedding.

Even if the church has a wedding coordinator, you may want to use a personal coordinator, someone of your choice, for the rehearsal and ceremony. When looking for someone to be a personal wedding coordinator, you need to find one who is not afraid to take charge and with initiative to follow through. This person can help the pastor during the rehearsal by seeing that it starts on time, goes smoothly, and reflects your wishes. When it is time for the ceremony, she will help pin corsages, keep mom calm, tell bridesmaids when to enter the procession and help you with last minute touches before you hear *The Wedding March* and enter the sanctuary.

## Notes

_____
_____
_____
_____
_____
_____
_____
_____
_____
_____
_____
_____
_____
_____
_____
_____
_____
_____
_____
_____
_____
_____
_____
_____
_____
_____
_____
_____
_____

# *32*

# *The Wedding Party*

## Maid of Honor/Matron of Honor

The maid or matron of honor is usually a very close friend or sister. The maid of honor is usually single and the matron is married. It is proper to have one or the other or both, depending on the wishes of the bride. Traditionally, the maid/matron of honor was there to assist the bride and help her in any area she needed her. Should you choose to have one or both maid and matron, their responsibilities can be shared. Some of these responsibilities include:

1. To assist making arrangements with the bridesmaids for their final gown fittings.

2. To help plan and organize a shower or luncheon.

3. To help the bride get dressed, arrange her hair and see to other personal details just before the ceremony.

4. To hold the bride's bouquet during the ceremony.

5. To help with the bride's train and veil, keeping her looking "picture perfect."

6. To hold the groom's ring and hand it to the bride at the proper moment.

7. To sign the marriage license as a witness.

8. To help the bride change into going-away clothes.

There has been some discussion among contemporary etiquette authorities suggesting that it is proper to use a male in the position of honor attendant. However, because of the personal responsibilities of the maid/matron of honor, it would be difficult to have a man as the bride's honor attendant. Likewise it would be awkward to have a female serve as the groom's attendant (best man). According to Emily Post, the answer is obviously clear. Because of their responsibilities, crossover attendants are not used in traditional weddings.[2]

## Bridesmaids

The original purpose of the bridesmaid was also to assist the bride wherever possible. They can help in any area the bride designates. Some suggestions are distributing the attendant's gifts, helping with the child attendants, and tidying up the dressing room. Another suggestion is to have the bridesmaids help with the overall clean-up after the wedding and reception are over.

The bridesmaids can be any age, married, or unmarried. The number of bridesmaids will vary according to the availability of women and the size of the facility you are using. The female attendants traditionally will equal the number of male attendants. While it is not required, it is customary to use the groom's sisters in the wedding. If you do not want to use them as bridesmaids, another place in the wedding or reception is a thoughtful gesture that can help reinforce family ties in the beginning. They can be used as guest book attendants, gift coordinators, or honorary hostesses at the reception. In this capacity, your future sister-

---

[2] Elizabeth L. Post, *Emily Post on Weddings* (New York: Harper Collins Publishers, 1994), 43.

in-laws would see guests to their tables, take presents to the gift table, assist the wedding party, mingle among the guests and take candid pictures. They would be used in addition to the servers.

## Best Man

Traditionally, a brother, close friend, relative, or father of the groom serves as the best man. The responsibilities of the best man are as follows:

1. To make sure the groom and ushers are at the ceremony on time.

2. To assist the groom in dressing for the wedding; making sure his tie is straight, and his coat collar is down.

3. To keep the groom calm before he walks down the aisle.

4. To hold any envelopes containing fees or tips for the groom (i.e., for the minister, limousine service, etc.).

5. To be responsible for carrying the bride's ring and handing it to the groom at the proper moment during the ceremony.

6. To sign the marriage license as a witness.

7. To help with the ride to the airport for bride and groom.

8. To organize the return of all rented formal wear.

## Ushers

There is one usher required for every fifty guests. The ushers are usually the groom's brothers, cousins, future brothers-in-law, and friends. Although in smaller weddings the ushers can double as groomsmen, they can still carry out their responsibilities as follows:

1. Seat the guests.

2. Unroll the aisle runner.

3. Make sure all guests have rides and directions to reception.

4. Hold umbrellas while escorting guests to cars if it rains.

5. Decorate the getaway car.

6. Help with clean up. Carry the wedding decorations (ie. Arch, flowers, candelabras), the chairs and tables to respective storing areas after the reception.

## Child Attendants

The ages of child attendants may vary depending on the wishes of the bride. Some brides prefer older children between the ages of eight and twelve because they are more predictable, while others find the whimsical personalities of smaller children (as young as two-and-a-half) add zest and vitality to an otherwise formal occasion.

1. Flower Girl – strews rose pedals or flowers along the pathway the bride will be walking.

2. Miniature Bride and Groom – sets the stage for the "big kids" getting married.

3. Ring Bearer – carries wedding rings on a pillow for a ring ceremony. There are a few options if the wedding is performed without rings. I've seen a Bible bearer; a child carrying a small white Bible or prayer book on a white silk pillow. The Bible could be used by one of the ministers before the prayer, or at the unity candle. Another option is a bell ringer; one or two little boys carrying bells and ringing them down the aisle to announce such a grand occasion.

4. Pages or Train Bearers – follow the bride and carry her train.

5. Candle lighters – may be children or older participants. Their responsibility is to see that all the candles are lit and ready for the ceremony. This is usually done at the beginning of the ceremony with music playing or while a special song is being sung.

# Notes

# *33*
# *Planning Timetable*

The advantages of pre-planning a wedding are obvious. Although you may be ready to start, knowing when and how to begin can be overwhelming. The following is a helpful timetable to assist you in organizing the details of your wedding.

## 12 Months before

- ❑ Announce your engagement
- ❑ Arrange for your two sets of parents to get together if they haven't already met
- ❑ Select a date
- ❑ Choose the kind of wedding you want – evening wedding with sit down dinner, afternoon wedding with buffet, garden wedding, etc.
- ❑ Go over the budget (Include both sets of parents if they will be paying for any portion of the event.)
- ❑ Work on guest list to get a rough guest count
- ❑ Reserve the ceremony site and talk to the pastor
- ❑ Reserve a reception site

## 6-9 Months before:

- ❑ Purchase a wedding planner if using one
- ❑ Choose your wedding party
- ❑ Decide on a caterer
- ❑ Enroll in bridal gift registry
- ❑ Shop for a gown
- ❑ Shop for bridal attendants' dresses
- ❑ Choose a photographer and, if desired, a videographer
- ❑ Hire a florist
- ❑ Book musicians and/or DJ

## 4-6 Months before:

- ❑ Order wedding invitations, envelopes, thank-you cards and any other wedding stationery you might want
- ❑ Order wedding gown
- ❑ Order tuxedos for groom and groomsmen
- ❑ Shop for cake
- ❑ Scout accommodations so you can send guests a list of nearby hotels in various price ranges. (Most hotels offer lower rates when you tell them a group is coming.)
- ❑ Meet with caterer or banquet manager to discuss menus, service style, etc.
- ❑ Complete guest list (Assume 20% of the invitees probably can't come.)
- ❑ Arrange rehearsal dinner

## 2-4 Months before:

- ❑ Call county clerk's office to find out about requirements for marriage license
- ❑ Check state requirements for blood testing
- ❑ Make honeymoon reservations, and compile all necessary travel documents
- ❑ Pick ceremony and reception music (Check with ceremony site about any restrictions.)
- ❑ Order wedding cake
- ❑ Complete honeymoon plans
- ❑ Meet with party-rental companies if special supplies (candelabras, tables, chairs) are being used for the ceremony or reception

## 4-8 Weeks before:

- ❑ Mail invitations eight weeks ahead of the date
- ❑ Have final dress fitting and select headpiece
- ❑ Buy your fiancée's wedding gift and thank-you gifts for the attendants
- ❑ Look over insurance papers with your fiancée (car, life, medical, home) – You may need to make changes in the policy when you go from single to married

## 2-3 Weeks before:

- ❏ Arrange seating for the reception
- ❏ Confirm details with caterer, florist, etc.
- ❏ Give caterer final head count
- ❏ Send an engagement photograph with a wedding announcement to newspapers

## 1 Week before:

- ❏ Place fees in envelopes to be given to the organist, soloist, minister, etc., on the big day
- ❏ Appoint a punctual pal to bring a cake knife, toasting glasses or other heirlooms to the wedding site early (and to be responsible for getting them home again)
- ❏ Get a manicure, pedicure, facial, massage or other beauty treatments of your choice
- ❏ Pack for the honeymoon (Arrange for someone to bring your luggage and going-away clothes to the reception site if you are leaving from the reception.)

## The day before:

- ❏ Greet out-of-town guests
- ❏ Go to the gym, take a long walk, or do some other stress-reducing activity
- ❏ Schedule time for a bubble bath, facial or a hair-styling appointment – before the rehearsal dinner
- ❏ Attend wedding rehearsal and dinner

# Notes

# *34*

# *Pre-Planning*

## Determine a Budget

Before planning a wedding, you and your fiancée should sit down and decide what kind of wedding you want. From there you will have to decide what your budget is going to be. Part of this planning will include how many guests you plan to invite. The guest list is important because the reception is a large part of the cost. You will also need to decide who will pay for what.

The traditional views on dividing the expenses have changed over the years. More than ever, the bride and groom shoulder the costs of the wedding. The emphasis on career-finishing goals before marriage has changed the financial status of most couples. The groom's family many times offers to pay a portion. It is quite appropriate for the bride's parents to accept. In modern society, the bride's parents are no longer obligated to pay for the entire wedding. They are at liberty to set the budget they are willing to spend. The groom and his parents are free to offer to pay any expenses that exceed the bride's parents' budget. It is a good idea to meet with both sets of parents to discuss your budget. You may use the following list as a guide to what costs have been the traditional division and then make the necessary adjustments to fit your needs.

**The Bride and Her Family:**
- ➤ The engagement photograph and announcement
- ➤ Gifts from the bride to the groom, including his wedding band, her parents' gifts and the bridesmaids' gifts
- ➤ Flowers carried by the bridesmaids and flowers decorating the church and reception
- ➤ Musicians and singers at the church and reception
- ➤ Decorations for the ceremony and reception such as the candelabras, arch, aisle runner, and other accessories
- ➤ Wedding photographer
- ➤ Lodging for bridesmaids if necessary
- ➤ Transportation for the wedding party to and from the wedding reception
- ➤ All expenses connected with the reception, including food, beverages, and room rental
- ➤ Invitations, announcements, and personal stationery for the bride
- ➤ The bride's wedding clothes and her trousseau

The bride's family should make reservations for out-of-town guests, but they are not obligated to pay for their lodging. It is acceptable to find free accommodations with friends and relatives.

**The Groom and His Family:**
- ➤ The bride's engagement and wedding rings and her wedding gift, if there is one
- ➤ The marriage license
- ➤ Gifts for the best man, ushers, and the groom's parents, if he chooses to give them something
- ➤ The rehearsal dinner
- ➤ Matching ties and gloves for the ushers

- ➢ The bride's bouquet and corsage, flowers for the mothers and grandmothers, and boutonnieres for the men in the wedding party.
- ➢ The clergy's fee
- ➢ Overnight lodging for the groomsmen if they are from out of town
- ➢ The honeymoon trip

If you have a certain amount you are allowing for your wedding, it would be helpful to break down the different expenses into percentages. Use the following percentages as a guide.

| | |
|---|---|
| Bride's Attire | 10% |
| Flowers | 10% |
| Invitations | 4% |
| Miscellaneous | 6% |
| Music | 10% |
| Photography | 10% |
| Reception | 50%[3] |

**Invitations**

After receiving the guest lists from both parents, you may now order your invitations. The style of wedding you choose will determine the simplicity or formality of your invitations. Shop around for a stationer that is within your budget.

It is a good idea to order your invitations four to six months before the wedding date. This leaves you plenty of

---

[3] Cele Goldsmith Lalli, *Modern Bride, Guide to Etiquette* (New York: John Wiley & Sons, Inc., 1993), 13.

time to address and mail your invitations six to eight weeks before the wedding.

You may choose either a single sheet invitation or a large double sheet that is folded in half. Your stationer will assist you in your selections. At this time you will decide what print type you want and what wording you will use on the invitation.

Wedding invitations can be engraved, printed or handwritten depending on the style of wedding you are having. The very formal wedding uses only engraved invitations. The letters are actually "cut" into the paper resulting in a raised effect. The formal and semi-formal wedding may use engraved or printed invitations.

Printed invitations are gaining popularity because of the superior quality in modern printing. Many printed invitations have the appearance of being engraved. Handwritten invitations are used exclusively for the informal wedding.

The wedding invitation comes with two envelopes, an outer envelope and an inner one. The invitation and all the enclosures are placed inside the inner envelope facing the back. Insert the folded edge first of a folded invitation. The left edge is inserted first for a single sheet.

Tissues were originally used to prevent the ink from smudging. These may be included, but they are not necessary. If you use tissues, they are placed in front of the printing on the invitation.

If you are hosting a sit-down dinner at your reception, a response card is suggested. A response card is necessary for the purpose of determining how many guests will be in attendance. Insert the response card and self-addressed, stamped envelope into the inner envelope in front of the invitation *(see illustration on page 218)*.

The inner envelope will have the guest's formal title handwritten on the front. To address a pastor's family on the inner envelope, Rev. and Mrs. Smith, Jonathon and Amanda would be appropriate. A married couple would be addressed simply as Mr. and Mrs. Fox.

*Rev. and Mrs. Smith*          *Mr. and Mrs. Fox*
*Jonathon and Amanda*

The unsealed inner envelope is placed in the outer envelope. The guest's name should be visible when the outer envelope is opened.

It is preferable to address your invitations by hand. Calligraphy writing looks more formal but it is not necessary. If you have poor penmanship, you may want to ask a friend with exceptional handwriting to help you address your invitations. A computer program to address your envelopes is acceptable, but it is best to use a calligraphy or script font *(see page 147)*.

When addressing the outer envelopes, the recipient's full name should appear. Do not abbreviate anything except Mr., Mrs., Jr., Rev., etc. The address, city and state should be completely spelled out, including "street," "drive," and "circle." Children are omitted from the outer envelope.

*Rev. and Mrs. John Smith*          *Mr. and Mrs. Travis Fox*
*22 West Monroe Street*          *25 Royal Drive*
*Anytown, California 99999*          *Anytown, California 99999*

## Marriage License/Blood Tests

State Requirements will vary from state to state. It is a good idea to see what is required in the state where you will be married. Some states require the minister to be registered, others do not. Before deciding who will sign the marriage license, make sure that person is qualified to do so. Your city or county clerk's office will know what the requirements are for a marriage license. A telephone call will help narrow down your options for which office to go to. You will need to take with you:

➤ Proof of age
➤ Proof of divorce, in the case of a prior marriage
➤ Proof of citizenship (if necessary)
➤ Documentation of required blood and medical tests
➤ Necessary fees

The amount of time it takes for the marriage license to become valid varies. Check on these regulations and time limits to avoid problems.

In some states blood tests are necessary. You can find out what is required by calling your local Health Department. These tests only take a few moments, but it may take several days to receive the results. Schedule your tests in plenty of time to avoid delay in procuring your marriage license. You may want to ask what your blood type is at the time so you will have that necessary information in the case of an emergency.

## Choosing your Officiant or Minister

While doing research on preparing a wedding you will see the term "Officiant" used. This is the person officiating your wedding ceremony. Although we usually use the bride's current pastor or other minister to conduct the wedding ceremony, there are others qualified to do the job. The Officiant can also be a Judge, Justice of the Peace, or Mayor. You need to find out what fees there are regardless of which person is doing the ceremony. It is always in order to offer the officiant a monetary gift if they say the fees are waived. If the minister has no set fee, it would depend upon the extent of obligation he is involved in, or the amount of time he has invested as to how much the payment should be.

Paying a minister can be a delicate subject. If you were to go to a medical office, there is a base fee just to see the doctor. Any treatment would be extra. What you are paying for is his knowledge.

The same principle applies to a minister. Many ministers spend several years going to college or seminary, spending thousands of dollars on their education and then pay dues to belong to an organization that allows them to perform services such as wedding ceremonies. Ministers do many things that they wouldn't consider charging for, but it would be a gracious act to compensate them for something they have been trained to do. It is also a nice way to say "thank you" for participating in one of the most important days of your life.

One time, many years ago, my father, who was a pastor, married a young couple. When the young man asked my father how much he owed him, my father replied, "Well, whatever you think it's worth." The young man's face lit up with a huge grin. He shook my father's hand vigorously and said, "Gee, thanks!" and walked out the door. What a bargain! Well, I guess you know what he thought it was worth!

Some churches have a basic fee for the services they provide their members. This amount many times includes the minister's fees. Make a point to find out if this is the case, and if so, it would be included in the amount you paid for the package. I wish all churches would organize their wedding services in this way. It sure clarifies the costs for a bride and groom.

A minister does more than just tell you to say, "I do." He will help you with ceremony protocol, answer questions, offer pre-marital counseling and many times help you with other etiquette during the wedding. Be sure to ask what the protocol is for the particular church you are using. Some churches have certain criteria for areas of dress, limits on number of attendants, ceremony length, songs, etc. Usually these regulations have good reasons and should be accepted with due respect for the privilege of having your wedding in their facility.

### Pre-marital Counseling

Often times the minister of the church you are presently attending will give you and your groom pre-marital counseling. These counseling session are to be scheduled not more than six months before the wedding date. Sometimes they will require you to read a good book on relationships between husband and wife. This may take a few weeks, so that needs to be scheduled in plenty of time for you to complete it. If the minister is not comfortable with pre-marital counseling, he may refer you to a good Christian counselor. If your minister does not feel this is necessary for you, there are many wonderful books written on the subject. Here are a few:

> *Battle of the Sexes,* James D. Mallory, M.D.*
> *Before the Ring,* William Coleman*
> *Before You Say "I Do,"* Dr. H. Norman Wright and
> Wes Roberts

*Communication: Key To Your Marriage,* H. Norman
      Wright*
*Hidden Keys of a Loving, Lasting Marriage,* Gary
      Smalley*
*Preparing for Marriage,* Dennis Rainey*
*Secrets to Lasting Love,* Gary Smalley*
*So, You're Getting Married,* H. Norman Wright*
*Starting Your Marriage Right,* Dennis & Barbara
      Rainey*
*The Act of Marriage,* Tim LaHaye
      (*Available through Pentecostal Publishing House)


## Hospitality Committee

   A rather novel idea to help relieve uncomfortable
lulls in your guests' time between the ceremony and the
reception is to appoint a hospitality committee. Ask some
friends or several couples to mingle with the guests while
they wait to go through the receiving line and arrive at the
reception. You need gregarious couples that are not afraid to
talk to strangers and who have delightful, drawing
personalities. Sometimes a single person does better when
coupled with another person. It is important to choose those
outside the wedding party so they will be free to visit among
the guests.


## Flowers

   While you consider what kind of flowers you want
for your wedding, the availability and cost may influence
your decision between the use of silk (artificial) or fresh
ones. If using fresh flowers, keep in mind which ones are in
season at the time of your ceremony. A florist or nursery can
help you with a list. You may consult the resources in the

back of this book or keep an eye out for articles in local newspapers or magazines with some helpful ideas along these lines. Although you can get artificial flowers all year long, it is good etiquette to use the ones that are seasonal to your area even though they are not real Roses, statice, gladiolus, and several lilies are easy to find year-round in most regions of the United States.[4] Other flowers are available, but may be more expensive. The best way to know is to shop around. You may want to mix fresh and artificial flowers. If your bouquet and your bridesmaids' bouquets are fresh flowers, the arrangements at the end of the pews, on the guest book table, and reception area may be artificial without clashing because of the distance from the wedding party.

### Photographs and/or Video

Much discussion will take place on how to cut the costs of an otherwise expensive wedding. There are many areas you can cut costs, but I would not suggest you do it with your photographer or videographer. Your wedding album will be the most precious memory after the wonderful occasion is in the past. To settle for someone who is not a professional may prove to be more disappointing than trying to work your budget around a more expensive, professional one. I am reminded of a couple that recently got married and had a well-meaning friend offer to take the pictures in order to save a little money. To their utter dismay, the pictures looked like the snap shots they took while on their honeymoon. The bride confided to me that if she had any regrets, it was opting to use a novice photographer.

---

[4] Bride's Magazine, *Bride's Book of Etiquette,* 6th ed. (New York: Putnam Publishing Group, 1989), 180.

Plan ahead. Look at other brides' wedding albums and when you see pictures you like, make a note. When you meet with your photographer, if you know what you want, your picture planning will go much more smoothly.

## Posed Pictures

The following may be used as a checklist for the posed pictures you may want to include:

- ❏ A full length of the bride alone
- ❏ Bride and groom
- ❏ Bride alone with mother (before the ceremony)
- ❏ Bride alone with father (before the ceremony)
- ❏ Bride with mother and father
- ❏ Bride with groom's parents
- ❏ Bride with attendants (either in a group/groups or individually)
- ❏ Groom with groomsmen
- ❏ Wedding party (after the ceremony usually at the altar)
- ❏ Bride and groom with pastor and his wife
- ❏ Bride and groom with the musicians and singers
- ❏ Bride and groom with other relatives and close friends

## During the Ceremony

Pictures taken during the ceremony usually are:

- ❏ Each attendant walking down the aisle
- ❏ Bride's mother walking down the aisle with an usher
- ❏ Groom's parents walking down the aisle with an usher
- ❏ Wedding party assembled at the altar
- ❏ Singers and musicians
- ❏ Exchanging of vows, rings, unity candle, and kissing

## Candid pictures may include:

- ❑ Bride putting on veil (perhaps with mom or an attendant helping)
- ❑ Informal shots of bride with attendants just before the ceremony
- ❑ Informal shots of groom and attendants
- ❑ Bride and father leaving for the church
- ❑ Guests sitting at tables during the reception
- ❑ Cutting the cake and feeding it to each other
- ❑ Toasting (punch or sparkling cider of course!)
- ❑ Tossing the bouquet
- ❑ Tossing the garter
- ❑ Kissing the parents good-by
- ❑ Bride and groom leaving in the car or limousine

### The Bridal Portrait

You may choose to schedule professional photographs in your gown ahead of time. This is optional and by no means expected. Many photographers will come to the bridal shop during your last fitting, or if you prefer they will come to your home for a special portrait. Others prefer to do it in the studio. Some brides feel more relaxed and take better pictures in the serene atmosphere of a professional studio rather than the whirlwind on the day of their wedding. Of course, these pictures would not take the place of the ones you have scheduled for your wedding day.

If there is a receiving line, pictures should be taken afterward so your guests can proceed to the reception *(see Chapter 39).*

Videography is becoming more popular as a preservation of the special moment. You can hire a professional, or have a friend film your wedding for you. Ask to see a sample of their work, keeping details that are important to you in mind. Their prices can range from

$100.00 to $2000.00 or more, depending on how many cameras you want and the extent of editing. To avoid long, boring films with eternal lulls, make a list of the special moments you want to include in your video. Your list of still photography will help in this area. Then ask the videographer to edit the long edition to a shorter, faster-paced version that you and your family can enjoy for years to come.

It is my feeling that video should not take the place of traditional photography. Let me remind you that the difference in quality will be as vast as it is between a professional photographer and someone untrained to take pictures. If your budget won't allow the expense of a professional cameraman, however, a friend's edited version can be quite satisfactory.

## Music

It is a good idea to plan ahead when picking out the songs you want performed at your wedding. Now is the time to decide whether you want to use CD's, soundtracks, a piano, organ, or other instruments. If you use live musicians, who will they be? Do you want the traditional processional or something else?

After choosing the songs you want, you must decide who will perform them. Try to ask ahead of time, providing the singer(s) with a tape, and/or sheet music. Give them plenty of time to practice the songs and feel comfortable. Let them know who the musician(s) will be or if they will be singing with a soundtrack. If using a soundtrack, give them a copy of the track so they can practice with it. If they are singing with a musician, schedule a practice session closer to the date of the wedding. Live music is nice, but keep your budget in mind; most musicians have fees.

# Notes

# 35

# *Wedding Attire*

*Something old,*
*Something new,*
*Something borrowed,*
*Something blue,*
*And a lucky sixpence*
*in your shoe!*

It has been an old custom for the bride to wear something for each line of this Old English rhyme. "Something old, something new" signifies continuity, a lifetime of happiness, moving from the old unmarried state into the new married life. A treasured handkerchief from your mother or grandmother, or heirloom Bible serves as "something old." "Something new" could be your gown, other accessories you are wearing as part of your wedding outfit, or perhaps your bouquet. "Something borrowed" is many times a handkerchief, gloves, or other accessory lent by a bridesmaid or close friend signifying borrowed happiness. It is suggested that "something blue" may be a carry over from an ancient Hebrew custom where Israelite brides were said to have bordered their wedding gowns in blue as a symbol of fidelity, purity, and love.[5] Whether this

---

[5] Tad Tuleja, *Curious Customs* (New York: Harmony Books, 1987), 58.

is true or not, it is a worthy tradition that many have enjoyed implementing. Some suggestions for wearing blue would be to carry a soft pastel blue purse, to use a blue garter, or attach a small ribbon bow to the underside of your gown. A dime, tucked safely inside your shoe would serve as the "lucky sixpence" signifying good fortune.[6]

## The Trousseau

The word "trousseau" comes from a French word meaning "little *trusse*" or "bundle" of clothing that the bride carried with her into the house of her husband.[7] You do not need a whole new wardrobe, but a few new items carried into the marriage are needful. Many times the lingerie shower will help meet the need for some new personal items such as slips, panties, bras, robes and gowns. Other items may include slippers, hair accessories, nylons and toiletries. You should, at the very least, indulge in the purchase of a new set of underclothing to wear beneath your wedding dress. After all, this is a special day and you will feel your best if you are dressed in brand new clothes from the inside out! Following are the basic items for the trousseau:

### The Wedding Gown
*The Wedding Gown* is traditionally white, symbolizing purity and innocence. I have noticed that in many bridal magazines and resource books, white also signifies joy and celebration, presenting the option for a second-marriage bride to wear white also. Some brides prefer to borrow or rent a gown. Wearing an heirloom gown,

---

[6] Marjabelle Young Stewart, *Your Complete Wedding Planner* (New York: St. Martin's Griffin, 1989), 15.

[7] Peggy Post, *Emily Post's Etiquette*, 16th ed. (New York: Harper Collins, 1997), 673.

perhaps the one your mother or grandmother wore, may be what you have always dreamed of. Whatever your choice, it is still considered part of your trousseau.

There are several types of wedding dresses and lengths. It is good to keep in mind what style looks best on you.

A sheath is a straight gown with no vertical seams. It is shaped in at the waist with a narrow skirt. A sheath can be accompanied with a detachable train to fit the formal bride, or left without one for the semi-formal.

*Sheath with detachable train*

You may prefer something with a full skirt such as a ball gown with a *basque* waist. This gown usually has a tight bodice with a sewn-in waist, and a full romantic skirt. A ball gown usually looks good on all shapes and sizes of bodies.

*Ball gown with Basque waist*

A princess style A-line dress is designed for slimming the body, with vertical seams flowing from the arms to the hem of the flared skirt and having no definite waist. This style is very versatile, being appropriate for very formal to semi-formal weddings.

*Princess line gown*

An empire waist has a small bodice featuring a high waist that falls just under the bust line and styled with either a slender or an A-lined skirt cascading to the floor. This style looks great on petite girls.

*Empire waist, A-line gown*

*The Train* – The style of dress you wear, should be in agreement with the type of wedding you have chosen. It has been the tradition that the longer the train the more formal the wedding. The lengths vary almost as much as the styles of dresses.

> - The **Sweep train or Chapel sweep** is the shortest train, which barely sweeps the floor.
> - A **Chapel train** is the most popular and is about 3 ½ to 4 ½ feet long.
> - The **Semi-Cathedral train** is just a little longer than the Chapel train, usually flowing about 4 ½ to 5 ½ feet from the waist.
> - The **Cathedral train** will extend 6 ½ to 7 ½ feet from the waist.
> - The **Monarch train or extended cathedral train** is the longest and flows twelve feet from the waist. If you can walk up several steps, stand at the top with a train that covers the steps, you are wearing a Monarch train.
> - A **Detachable train** can be any length. It is very popular because it attaches with hooks and loops and can be removed.

Look through magazines and books to help you narrow down the style of dress that will look best on you. If you are on a tight budget, keep in mind that there are other brands which make beautiful dresses similar to the "name brand" ones in the magazines. You may want to visit several bridal salons to compare prices and products available. With the help of the gown consultant, you may feel free to try on different styles to find what is best for you. Try not to limit yourself to gowns you think will look best. It never hurts to venture out into a different style. Who knows, maybe you will find the perfect dress hidden among the styles you never would have dreamed of trying on.

Once you have chosen the dress you want, the salon will order it for you. Depending on their policy, the establishment may require a deposit at this time. This amount could vary from ten percent to half of the total cost. Ask questions freely. Anything you are not clear about, whether it is the price of the dress, the contract you have to sign, or what the price includes, could be answered by simply asking questions. By taking your measurements, the manufacturer will tailor the dress to fit you. It takes anywhere from four to eight weeks for a dress to arrive after it has been ordered. You will return at that time for a "fitting." Wear shoes the same height as the ones you will wear in your wedding so that if the hem needs adjusting,

they can do that for you. Some shops include the hem adjustment in the price of the dress, others don't. You may want to find out their policy before you order the dress so alteration charges won't take you by surprise. Also, wear your hair as it will be arranged for your wedding, so you can try on veils to see which style will compliment your dress. Whether you buy your veil at the same shop or not, it is still good to try a few on so you can see how they look with your gown.

*Chapel Sweep*

*Chapel Train*

*Cathedral Train*

**The Veil**

*The Veil* was originally a symbol of the bride's youth and virginity. Early Christian brides wore white veils to signify purity.[8] The veil used to be worn the same length as the train, but recently many brides have paired a short veil with a long train and visa-versa. The veil should compliment the length and proportion of the dress. Try your headpiece on at the same time as your dress, so you can see them together. Your headpiece should be the same color as your gown. If you have beautiful detail down the back of your dress, you may either choose a shorter veil, or a detachable one that can be removed during your reception. When trying on a veil, make sure it is comfortable and that you are able to turn your head from side to side with ease. Wear your hair similar to the way you will on your wedding day. There is some varying opinions of the names of the different lengths of veils, but to help identify which one you would like to use, here are some general descriptions.

1.  The **Blusher** can be added to any length veil and falls down over the bride's face at the beginning of the wedding ceremony. The groom usually lifts it when he kisses his bride for the first time as they become husband and wife.

2.  The **Birdcage or Madonna** veil is short, falling just below the chin. It is usually worn at informal weddings and often attached to a hat.

3.  The **Flyaway** veil has multiple layers that touch the shoulder. It is best worn with informal ankle-length dresses.

---

[8] Bride's Magazine, *Bride's All New Book of Etiquette,* (New York: Putnam, 1993), 12.

4. Petite brides prefer the **Elbow-length** veil. It is usually worn in informal or semi-formal weddings.

5. The **Fingertip-length** veil is probably the most popular style. It looks good on all heights and is appropriate to wear with almost any length gown except one with the Monarch or Extended Cathedral Train.

6. The **Ballet or Waltz length** veil falls to the ankles.

7. The **Chapel** veil is about seven feet long and is worn with a floor-length dress or a chapel sweep.

8. The **Cathedral** veil (not shown) is about ten feet long and is worn in formal and very formal weddings.

## Underclothing

Wearing the proper underclothes beneath your wedding gown is more important than it first may seem. If you have on the wrong size and you see folds through your wedding gown, it could mar an otherwise beautiful effect. It is important to find your proper size. If you have never had professional advice on purchasing a bra, now is the time to get it. *Pamper yourself.* Go to a nice department store with a full line of lingerie, and ask the clerk to help you determine your true size. If you cannot find anything there to please you, at least you know how to fit yourself from then on. Your slip, panties, bra, and hosiery should blend with your gown. If it is white, wear either white or light flesh tones. Wedding dresses often have the bodice lined so the fear of a white bra showing through should be minimal.

White or natural colored hosiery is the best accent from underneath a white wedding gown. There is some beautiful hosiery on the market today. Shimmering silver undertones and glistening highlights are just a couple of the many choices available. Have fun wearing something different for a change. You only get married once in a lifetime!

## Handbag

You may want to carry a small handbag down the isle. If so, it needs to coordinate with your gown and may be in addition to your bouquet. You may choose to carry a smaller bouquet if you have a purse also. There are some beautiful evening bags available in either soft material or more constructed shapes of satin or silk.

**Shoes**

When shopping for your shoes go in the afternoon. Your feet tend to swell during the day and in the afternoon they will be the largest. This way your feet won't tire at the reception because they are a tad bit too tight. Be sure to have the correct height heel when having your gown fitted, so the hem will be appropriate for the shoes you will wear.

**Bible or Prayer Book**

Some brides carry a family Bible or small white prayer book decorated with lace and flowers in the place of a bouquet. When I refer to "family Bible," I am not alluding to the fifteen pound, eleven and a half-inch hardbound book passed down from your father and mother. Can you image yourself struggling up an aisle with one of these under your arm, trying to keep your balance? You would definitely need your Dad with you, helping you carry a binding of that magnitude! In actuality, the book the bride carries is rather small, and when decorated with flowers is no larger than a full bouquet would be.

**Garter**

Wearing a garter is optional for the Christian Bride. It evolved as a form of self-preservation rather than a virtuous symbol. It is my understanding that in ancient times, guests would rush the bride at the altar, ripping pieces of her dress to keep as good-luck tokens. In pure self-defense, the bride began removing the garter herself and throwing it to the crowd. If you want to keep this tradition as part of the reception festivities, you may want to wear the garter below the knee so that your modesty is preserved. Tradition says your new husband removes it to throw to the bachelors, with each one hoping to be the next "married man."

**Going Away Outfit**

These are the clothes you wear if you choose to change before leaving the reception site. When shopping for your going-away outfit, you may want to coordinate the new underclothes to match what you plan to wear under your gown. Of course, there is nothing wrong with another set of underclothes to match your going-away outfit. This would just be another nice addition to your Trousseau.

## Attendants

The bridesmaids' dresses should compliment your wedding gown in style and formality. It is nice to consider the figure of each attendant and try to find a style that will compliment them all. They may be ordered from a bridal salon, department store, or be hand-sewn. Customarily, each attendant is responsible for purchasing her own dress. There is the option as the bride, to buy the outfit, as a gift for some or one of the attendants should there be someone who could not participate because of financial challenges. No other gift is required if the bridesmaids' dresses are a gift from you.

### ෨ *Grace Notes* ෨

*If you want to do something special for the bridesmaids and you cannot afford to buy their gowns, you may find a pretty hair accessory that would comfortably fit your budget for a gift. Or you may want to do something like that in addition to a special gift you have purchased for their participation in your wedding.*

## The Groom and Groomsmen

Depending on the formality of the wedding, the groom and his attendants are more limited than the bridesmaids in their formal wear options. From the very formal tuxedo to the formal/semi-formal cutaway jacket or suit, the options may be only in the vest or what type of tie should be worn. As earlier stated, the dinner jackets or sport coats should be reserved for less formal weddings. The groomsmen are responsible for renting or buying their wedding attire.

> *The tradition of wearing something blue is believed to originate with ancient Israelites, who bordered their wedding gowns in blue as a symbol of fidelity, purity, and love.*[9]

---

[9] Deborah Chase, *Every Bride is Beautiful,* (New York: William Morrow and Company, 1999), 86.

# *Notes*

# 36

# *Pre-Wedding Parties*

Life moves into the fast lane after the announcement of the bride's engagement. Several people will want to have parties and showers in your honor. The exact number of these festivities will depend on your friends and family.

*Engagement parties* are usually the first ones to be attended. This party is thrown after the bride's announcement but before it is put in the newspapers. The bride's parents usually give this party, but it is becoming more common for both parents to participate and split the cost. This type of celebration can be a casual get together but it is usually a dinner party.

Showers are parties hosted by friends and family to help the couple acquire needed essentials to set up a household. This time of fun can also prove to be essential as friends and family meet each other. There are several different types of showers and themes. Some are appropriate for the couple to attend, and others are reserved for girls only. For more information on wedding showers, please see chapter 21.

The Bride's Luncheon is a time to get together with the bridesmaids as a thank you for being in the wedding. This is a good time to present the bridesmaids with a thank you gift rather than at the reception. If you wait until the day of the wedding, the hype and excitement may cause you to miss the intimate moment of their receiving your gifts and opening them in front of you. Traditionally, a luncheon was served, but it can be held at any time of the day and suit the style of the bride. If she wants to have pizza, then do so and have fun! The bride pays for the lunch and makes all the arrangements. She can either have the luncheon in the privacy of her home, at a restaurant, or as a small, catered, garden party. It is usually given closer to the wedding when all the bridesmaids can be in attendance.

The Bachelor Party is just that—a party given in honor of the groom-to-be; no girls allowed! Bachelor parties given in the world often end up as beer bashes, but they don't have to. The groomsmen, best man, family, or friends give the bachelor party. In fact, the groom can host a bachelor party himself. Both fathers may be invited, but they usually don't stay as long as the younger friends. It would be so nice if the guys went together and "showered" the groom-to-be with a chest of tools or other items he would use in his own garage. You know, he doesn't get to register for such necessary items. Sorry pretty bride, you are not to come to this party under any circumstance!

The Rehearsal Dinner is hosted by the groom's family either before or after the rehearsal. This gives the wedding party time to be exclusively with the bride and groom and their families for a few hours. The dinner can be held at a restaurant with an extravagant five-course meal or in a private home with a simple menu. The formality and size depends on the type of wedding and the budget. Those invited should include the complete wedding party, their spouses, the parents of the children in the wedding, and the pastor and his wife.

# 37

# *The Rehearsal*

The wedding rehearsal is one of the last things on the agenda during the countdown to the wedding. It is held one or two days before the ceremony. A walk-through of the processional and recessional is necessary for each member of your wedding party to know what to do and to feel comfortable doing it. If you are assured of their confidence, it will help alleviate your last minute stress.

After arriving at the church or other ceremony site, the first thing to decide is which aisle you are going to use. The bride usually walks down the center aisle if there is one. If not, choose the one most convenient for you, or use one for the processional and the other for the recessional. This would not work if you were using an aisle runner.

Take a few moments with the pastor and coordinator to review your plans for the ceremony. The order and other special wishes should have been discussed with your minister at prior meetings, so this should be a review of your plans. If you are doing anything special or made any changes that he is not aware of, mention them before the rehearsal begins. It is good to have an "Order of Ceremony" written down and copies given to the pastor, the coordinator, musicians, and singers. The following is an outline of the ceremony with the songs included to help clarify any questions during the rehearsal.

## ORDER OF CEREMONY

1. Music plays
2. Mother of groom ushered in
3. Mother of bride ushered in
4. Guest book attendant ushered in
5. Candle-lighters light candles
6. Minister, groom and attendants enter from side
7. Song:
8. Bridesmaids
9. Maid/Matron of honor
10. Flower girl and ring bearer
11. Song: Wedding March played
12. Bride and her father walk down center aisle
13. Minister seats audience
14. Father gives the bride away
15. Groom takes bride and escorts her to the minister
16. Minister's opening speech
17. Bride and groom recite vows
18. Bride and groom exchange rings (optional)
19. Prayer over bride and groom
20. Unity candle with song
21. Minister pronounces "Man and Wife"
22. Husband kisses wife
23. Recessional with song

## Walking Through the Ceremony

The pastor will officially begin the rehearsal with prayer. Then the wedding party is asked to line up on the platform in the positions where they will be standing just before the recessional.

## Ceremony Standing Positions

The wedding party practices the **recessional** first. When they have exited the sanctuary, the groom and best man may practice entering from the side where they will be waiting with the minister(s) for their cue to enter. While they are practicing this, the attendants assemble in the order they will enter the sanctuary to practice the **processional**. While this may seem backward, it is the best way to assemble everyone in order.

➢ Candle-lighters begin the ceremony so they should practice entering first.
➢ The ushers enter singly or in pairs.
➢ The bridesmaids also enter singly or in pairs.

> The maid and/or matron of honor appear either together or separately.
> The ring bearer and the flower girl usually walk together.
> And finally, the bride and her father enter with the bride on her father's left arm (which is the side his heart is on).

## The Processional

## The Recessional

The attendants usually pace themselves at least ten feet apart and walk in a slow, graceful manner. Nowadays, "*Pomp and Circumstance*," the step-stop-step-stop procession is reserved mostly for graduations.

In the past, it was traditional that the bride refrain from participating in the rehearsal. That custom has changed, helping many brides feel more comfortable on their wedding day with a little practice at the rehearsal. With that in mind, as the bride, you may enter with your father when the last attendant is halfway down the aisle. If you prefer, you may wait until all the attendants are assembled at the altar.

When you reach the steps, remove your hand from your father's arm and move your bouquet to your left hand. Wait for the minister to ask, "Who gives this woman to be married to this man?" When your father replies, "I do," or "her mother and I," he steps to your mother's side and remains there during the ceremony, unless he is a minister involved in the rest of the ceremony.

The groom takes his place on your right and together you ascend the steps to stand before the minister. The minister will help you walk through the procedures from there, guiding you through the protocol of vows and prayers. Many ministers prefer to save the vows for the actual ceremony and will not practice them during the rehearsal.

It is good to practice the processional and recessional once again with music to help coordinate timing. Afterward everyone should meet up in the front of the church to discuss any questions. At this time the ushers can be briefed on the proper way to seat guests.

# *Notes*

# *38*

# *The Ceremony*

## The Guest Book

On an elegantly decorated table just inside the entrance of the church or reception hall, a small book lies open with a feather pen nestled neatly in a pearl and gold holder. A young woman smiles as she encourages guests to sign the guest book. You will treasure the small book forever, for it will hold the signatures and well wishes of some of your closest friends. This little treasure will forever be a reminder of those who took the time to celebrate the beginning of your lives together. A guest book can be purchased at most stationery stores or gift shops. It will be well worth your investment.

## Seating the Guests

Once they have signed the guest book, it is the ushers' responsibility to politely escort your friends and family to a comfortable pew where they can enjoy the ceremony. The groom usually designates a head usher who in turn, coordinates the others, keeping order and answering questions. Before the wedding, the ushers should make themselves aware of the amenities of the facilities in case someone needs a drink, restroom, phone or some other necessity.

The ushers will proceed following the instructions given to them at the rehearsal. They should escort guests of the bride and her family to the left side of the church as you face the altar. This is the same side the bride will be standing on as she faces the altar.

The guests of the groom and his family are traditionally seated on the right side of the church. If the church has no center aisle, the bride's family and friends are seated on either side of the left aisle and the groom's family and friends on either side of the right. If one family is from out of town, rather than the congregation being obviously lopped-sided, they may all sit together.

As the usher approaches the newly arrived guest(s), he asks discreetly if there is a seating preference; bride or groom. If not, he seats the guest on the side least filled. If the usher is seating a couple, he extends his arm to the lady and walking ahead of the gentleman escorts them to their pew. If a group of ladies arrive together, the usher offers his arm to the oldest, or following a more modern custom, he walks in front of the group.

Certain pews may be reserved for family members and special guests. The parents of both the bride and groom will be seated on the first pew of their respective sides. Grandparents are seated in the second pew close to the aisle. Next to them, on the same pew, are the siblings of the bride and groom if they are not in the wedding party.

Other pews may be reserved for honored guests such as the parents of the flower girl and ring-bearer (just in case the children need their mommy and daddy). Blended families with stepbrothers and stepsisters would be included in these special reservations. You can mark the reserved pews by decorating them with ribbon or special bouquets and instructing the ushers to seat others there if the pews are not needed.

## Divorced Parents

The family situation determines the seating if your parents are divorced. For example, if you are living with your re-married mother and she has contributed to your wedding and upbringing the most, then she is seated on the first row with her husband. Your father takes the third pew with his wife if he is remarried. If the custodial parent is your father, the case is reversed. If neither are remarried and they are on friendly terms, they may sit in the front row together.

## Last But Not Least

The ushers should seat the guests from the front to back as they fill the pews. During the last few moments before the ceremony begins, the grandparents are ushered in and seated in the second pew. Five minutes before the ceremony begins an usher escorts the groom's mother down the aisle with his father following behind. They are seated on the front pew on the right side, the mother closest to the aisle. Lastly, the bride's mother enters. Elegantly escorted by the groom (a wonderful suggestion) or the head usher, she gracefully takes her place on the first pew. Some larger churches leave the first pew vacant and place the mothers on the second pew. Whatever the choice, no one is seated in front of the mothers. This is the signal that the ceremony has begun.

The ushers should seat no one after the mothers have been seated. Anyone coming to the wedding after the ceremony has begun should quietly slip in and find a place to sit.

Bride's Side                    Groom's Side

1) Mother of the Bride        5) Grandparents
2) Father of the Bride        6) Brothers and Sisters
3) Mother of the Groom        7) Other relatives
4) Father of the Groom

### Escorting the Bride

Usually the father of the bride has the honor of escorting her down the aisle. If your father is deceased, it is perfectly proper for someone else to do the honor. Your mother, a sibling, relative, or close friend are optional choices for an escort. If you have a stepfather and wish him to escort you, it is fine to do so. If your parents are divorced, your father still has the honor. There is some controversy as to both father and stepfather escorting the bride if they are on friendly terms. Emily Post holds the view that the father should not give up his prerogative or be asked to share the honor, no matter how cordial the daughter and stepfather are.[10] Several modern references have a more liberal view on this matter even suggesting the mother as an escort or choosing none at all.

----

[10] Elizabeth Post, 105.

If your situation is special, you will have to be the one to make the call. How will your father feel if he is sharing or giving his place of honor to another man? How will your mother feel if you ask her to walk you down the aisle? Who will be the most adversely affected by your decision? Will the long-term repercussions be good or bad? You must weigh it all out and make the decision that will cause the least amount of friction.

### Giving the Bride Away

Traditionally, the father of the bride gives her away. The father may respond to the question, "Who gives this woman to be married to this man?" with, "Her mother and I" or "I do." The stepfather may give her away if the bride has been living with her mother and feels closer to her stepfather. If she has no father she has the option to delete it from her program.

### The Vows

There is nothing wrong with the traditional vows your minister has in his little black book. Some couples wish to have something that says the same thing in more modern language. There is nothing wrong with that either. The problem comes when you want to leave out vital promises that do not agree with the Bible. Here are some suggestions if you are planning to write your own vows.

1. Talk to your minister. He can help you personalize your vows without compromising your biblical commitments.

2. Work on your vows as a couple. Don't try to write both sides from your own perspective.

3. Look at traditional vows as a guideline and decide which ones are particularly meaningful to you.

4. Think about what makes you a unique couple and include that in your vows.

5. Include what marriage means to you. What do the words commitment, forgiveness, and trust mean to you when applied to marriage?

6. The vows should only take from one to three minutes. Keep it short.

7. Put them on paper and give them to your minister. He needs to see them before the ceremony. It is a good idea for him to have a copy well in advance of the wedding to approve them.

## The Program

In more recent times, couples may choose to print a wedding program. The wedding program will help your guests follow the sequence of the wedding and identify who the key participants are. Below are some suggestions for information that may be included in the program:

➢ The names and relationship of your family, attendants, and musicians.

➢ A list of songs and lyrics to one that is especially meaningful.

➢ *Thank you* to the guests for sharing your special day.

## Unity Candle

It is not required to have a unity candle if you are having a Christian wedding, but it is a meaningful and popular item to consider. A unity candle can be expensive or plain. The general idea is that the two of you have become one; two families have united as one.

I have seen the unity candle incorporated in various ways. Usually, before the procession begins, the mothers of the bride and groom step up to a table pre-arranged with three candles; two taper candles on each side of a large pillar candle. They light the taper candles and return to their places. When it is time for the unity candle in the ceremony (after the vows), the bride and groom step to the table, each taking the candle their mother lit and simultaneously lighting the large candle.

Unity candles do not do well in outdoor weddings unless you provide a wind shield. Give some thought to the idea ahead of time so you won't be disappointed with an unexpected windy day. If plan "A" does not work, have a back-up plan. You will feel more comfortable if you have another option in mind, "just in case...."

## Personalize Your Wedding

You can personalize your wedding by implementing special effects that you may or may not have seen others do at their weddings. If you have a favorite poem or song that is special to you as a couple, you may want to include it in your wedding just for the two of you to enjoy. Have it recited or sung in the ceremony or include it in your program.

My groom composed a beautiful poem for me that I will cherish forever. We printed it on our wedding programs as a declaration of love to each other. As time goes by, I steal a few moments alone, remove the piece of paper from its special hiding place and relive the treasured memories of the day my one true love expressed his heart to me on paper.

Many unique ideas are acceptable for a wedding even if you have never seen them before. It is not so much from following etiquette that we see common trends among weddings as it is a lack of adventure and individuality. Some of the unusual but impressive things we have seen are:

> ➤ The groom escorting the mothers to their places.
> ➤ Little boy bell ringers announcing this grand celebration.
> ➤ A bride sitting at the beautiful grand piano and singing a song composed just for her groom.
> ➤ A miniature park bench positioned on the platform for the children to sit on during the long ceremony.
> ➤ The bride's parents greeting the guests at the front of the church before the ceremony begins.
> ➤ A horse-drawn carriage carrying the bride and groom to an outdoor reception site.

# 39

## *The Reception*

### The Receiving Line

The receiving line can be assembled in two different places, depending on when you have the pictures scheduled and where you will have your reception. In the past, the receiving line was immediately following the recessional. The wedding party lined up in the foyer or lobby as the guests were leaving for the reception. This caused some of the guests to wait twice, once for their turn in the receiving line and a second time while the pictures were being made. It was a constant dilemma to know what to do for the waiting guests until the bride and groom appeared at the reception. To value the precious time of the guests, most brides who schedule pictures between the ceremony and reception assemble the receiving line later or omit it from the program altogether. These brides prefer to mingle among their guests at the reception. Allowing your guests to make their way to the reception can save time for both the guests and your wedding party. The question is what do they do while your wedding party is having pictures made? Here are a few helpful hints:

➤ Select a hospitality committee to help greet guests by visiting and offering drinks when they arrive at the reception site *(see page 223).*

> ➤ Select someone not in the wedding party to do some stand-up comedy to entertain the guests before the wedding party arrives.
> ➤ Begin serving your guests before the wedding party arrives.
> ➤ Allow the guests to remain seated and observe the pictures being taken.

Once your pictures have been made, you will make your way to the reception. The reception officially begins with the receiving line. It is usually formed just inside the reception entrance to greet your guests, but if the majority are already there you may have it assembled in the most convenient location for the crowd. You may prefer the fathers and attendants to mingle among guests rather than stand in the receiving line. From the door or from the left, the order is as follows:

1) Mother of the bride; 2) Father of the bride (optional); 3) Mother of the groom; 4) Father of the groom (optional); 5) Bride; 6) Groom; 7) Bride's honor attendant (optional); 8) Best Man (optional) 9) Bridesmaids (optional) 10) Ushers (optional) Bridesmaids (optional).

## Location

If your church has a fellowship hall and it is large enough to accommodate your wedding guests, it would be the choice location. If your church does not have a fellowship hall, you will have to find a place to have your reception. The best way to find out what is best is to ask friends and others that have used similar facilities. You may want to inquire as to where the church holds banquets or large parties. Sometimes community centers are available at little or no cost to citizens. A local bridal salon may be helpful.

Your reception can be a five course meal, a buffet line, or cake and *hors-d'oeuvres*. Whether you choose to go extravagant or simple, the important thing is to reserve a time when your friends and family can come together to wish you and your groom happiness.

Look for a place with enough space for your planned activities. There should be enough room for those attending your wedding to have some refreshments and cake, and spend some time with you.

## Food For Thought

If you use a caterer, you will need to make arrangements ahead of time, letting them know the number of guests you expect, what style of service you plan and the length of time you will be engaging them. Asking each guest to return a response card provided in your wedding announcement is an excellent way to determine the number of guests planning to attend your reception.

Your caterer will need to know how you plan to serve your guests, either seated at tables or in a buffet line. If you have a buffet line, the service of your caterer would not include table servers, unless you want to serve drinks at the tables. You may prefer to ask a few friends to be servers if the caterer agrees.

Whatever you choose to serve, the wedding cake is usually the dessert. If you want to save a little money, you may have a smaller wedding cake with sheet cakes to serve the bulk of your crowd. It is still exciting to watch the bride and groom cut the cake and serve it to each other.

### Master of Ceremonies

Ask someone comfortable with crowds to be your Master of Ceremonies (emcee). This person is usually a male, but not necessarily required to be. He can fill in time before the wedding party arrives, provide entertaining stories and interesting tid-bits about the couple, and announce the arrival of each member of the wedding party.

After the bride and groom join the guests at the reception, the emcee will announce each scheduled event such as cutting the cake and tossing the bouquet and garter.

## The Head Table

If you are planning a sit down dinner with a head table, the seating arrangement should be as follows: 1) Bride; 2) Groom; 3) Bride's honor attendant; 4) Best man; 5) Bridesmaids; 6) Ushers

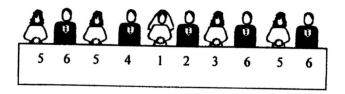

| 5 | 6 | 5 | 4 | 1 | 2 | 3 | 6 | 5 | 6 |

## The Gift Table

It is customary in some parts of the country for guests to bring a gift to the reception. To one side of the reception hall, a long, tastefully decorated table is placed with a young girl attending to the gifts, making sure the cards stay with each gift. It is appropriate for guests to bring gifts to the reception, but they may not receive the joy of watching you open them. Whether you have had a wedding shower or not, you are not obligated to open the gifts received at the reception because there just isn't enough time. Of course, the ultimate decision is yours, which may vary depending on the size of the reception and the number of gifts. If a wedding shower was given, there will be fewer gifts at the reception so it may be feasible to unwrap them while the guests are there. On the other hand, it is easier to transport the gifts if they remain wrapped, keeping the cards with the correct gifts. Whether you open them or not, you will need to have your maid of honor or another dependable friend transport them to your new home while you are on your honeymoon. When you and your husband return from the honeymoon, the joy of opening your wedding gifts together and spending time remembering each giver can be a very special time. Remember to send a thank you for each gift with a small note about how you will use the item in your home (*see Thank you Notes in chapter 19, pages 138-140).*

With the growing popularity of showers, and the potential loss due to theft and damage, several wedding planning guides have not even included gifts as part of the reception.

Receiving *monetary gifts* at your reception is very common. If you prefer monetary gifts, let a close friend or family member spread the word discreetly. Never put your gift preference on your wedding invitations. A trustworthy friend may be appointed to hold checks and cash you receive at the wedding and/or reception. A decorated basket sitting on the gift table is nice for keeping the cards with money in them from being lost among the gifts. They should be safe with a gift attendant close by.

*Damaged* gifts are rare, but you may receive one by mail that has had a nasty trip. Try to determine where it was purchased and call the company's customer service. If it is from a store where you were registered, the registry department may be able to help you. Explain the problem and most stores will replace it. There is no need to contact the person who sent it to you if you are able to replace it. If not, check the package to see if it was insured. If so, you may need to contact the giver so they can be reimbursed by the post office. They will probably send you a replacement gift. Call the giver and explain what happened.

If you want to exchange a gift, first think about it carefully. If the person who gave it to you is a frequent guest in your home, he or she may miss seeing their gift on display. It may be better to keep it, making room for it in a less prominent place rather than risk hurt feelings.

On the other hand, if the gift is from someone who will never know you have exchanged it, feel free to do so. It is not proper however, to ask the person where the gift was purchased or how much it cost. If you cannot determine the origin of the gift by looking at the packaging or tags, you may just have to keep it.

### Gifts for Attendants

If you have not already presented your attendants with thank you gifts, it is good to do so before you leave the reception for your honeymoon. Beautifully wrapped packages may be waiting at their places at the head table. If you don't mind spending the extra time, you may want to present them yourself. If you have given them their gown for the wedding as a gift, a small card of thanks is nice at this time. If you can afford it, a small token gift is appropriate in addition to their gown, but not necessary.

### Leaving the Reception

It is time to take your leave from the reception. You may want to change clothes before leaving for the honeymoon. It is good to let the master of ceremonies know when you are going so he can announce that the bride and groom are preparing to leave.

After changing clothes, you and your new husband may want to invite your parents to your changing chambers or seek them out to tell them goodbye. You are not obligated to wish anyone else farewell, but your parents are now the second most important people in the world. This is an excellent way to get the relationship off to a good start with the new mother and father-in-law.

When you are making your way to the car or limousine, well wishers may want to shower you with birdseed, or bubbles. These items are often provided for the bridal party and interested guests.

# Part Seven

# Christian Hospitality

# *40*

# *Christian Hospitality*

The art of entertaining guests has been around as long as man has existed. God entertained Adam as they walked together in the cool of the day. I'm sure when Eve came on the scene a re-decorating project was born in the Garden of Eden. With her choice of fruit, berries, beautiful flowers and foliage, any woman would have a heyday!

Hospitality defined by the *Encyclopedia Britannica Dictionary* is, "to be disposed to behave in a warm way and manner, and to entertain with generous kindness." In other words, demonstrating hospitality is to conduct yourself with a gracious and friendly attitude, entertaining with great kindness.[1]

> *Do not forget to entertain strangers, for by so doing some people have entertained angels without knowing it (Hebrews 13:2 NIV).*

### Hospitality Is a Gift

Just as God makes each one of us unique physically, He gifted us differently for various uses in His Kingdom.

---

[1] Doris W. Greig, *We Didn't Know They Were Angels, Discovering the gift of Christian Hospitality,* (Ventura, CA: Regal Books, 1987), 22-23.

Hospitality comes in many forms regardless of how you respond to guests. Sometimes it means weeping with a friend or a neighbor or staying up late just to listen. It may be babysitting when a mother is sick or taking food to the home of someone new in the neighborhood. Asking God to help you see and grasp the opportunities of hospitality that come your way is a great start to discovering the gift of *Christian Hospitality.*

Mary and Martha had the gift of hospitality. Mary had the gift of listening and Martha had the gift of serving. What a wonderful combination! Martha may have been a little frustrated with Mary for not doing the things she felt she needed to do, but Mary was intent on building a closer relationship with the Lord. Mary's desire was not a bad one, neither was Martha's. Both women needed to learn something from each other. A balance of each other's gifts was needed to be complete. Martha needed to learn how to relax and enjoy her company, complimenting Mary's gift, rather than expecting Mary to have the same passion for entertaining as her own. Mary needed to learn sensitivity to her sister's needs, helping Martha with the load so they both could enjoy themselves at the feet of Jesus. Martha probably secretly wanted to be where Mary was—with her friend. Unlike Martha, to Mary, everything else was secondary. Jesus commented on the desire in Mary's heart to practice hospitality beyond the mere entertaining of company.

Whatever your personality, God can use your gift in the area of hospitality. You are learning, like Mary and Martha, to be a perfect hostess. Don't be too hard on yourself if you have a ways to go before you have mastered the gift of hospitality. It takes time, patience, and lots of practice! Keep trying and don't give up.

## Hospitality is Sensitivity

Missed opportunities! We all have them, but we need to learn to grab them! Every day opportunities come to share your home, friendship, money, time, and your love with family, friends and a hurting world. The old Chinese proverb: "Time is a river in which no man steps twice" is true in today's fast-paced world. As our opportunities rush past us, we must reach out and touch them, using each one to glorify God. Once an opportunity is gone, that particular situation will never come back again. We must be sensitive to opportunities to take advantage of them.

As you become more sensitive to opportunities, you will experience a depth of awareness in other areas as well. Your sensitivity to the natural needs of others will make you aware of other less obvious needs. As you minister to the natural needs of others, their spiritual needs will also begin to be fulfilled.

## Hospitality is Availability

For the Christian, hospitality involves availability as well as sensitivity. Sensitivity and availability are like *Siamese twins*; with one comes the other. As you become more sensitive to opportunities and needs, your willingness to be available grows.

*To behave in a warm way* can mean different things to different people. It can be listening when someone wants to talk. This can be the best therapy for someone with a need. When you don't have the answers, it's okay. Sometimes others don't want answers, they want understanding and reassurance that they are not alone.

Being available is one of the greatest gifts you can give. It may mean altering plans to accommodate someone else's need. Doris Greig shares her thoughts on availability in her book, *We Didn't Know They Were Angels*. "Being available is not only listening to what your friend is saying, but listening to what she is not saying also. Or to hear what she is trying to say and cannot."[2]

The fact that you sense a need in a friend is proof that you have listened past her vocal plea and plugged into her heart, the place she stores the greatest hurts and fears. To be sensitive to other people's needs without them saying so is a true demonstration of Christian hospitality.

I like the way the New International Version of the Bible describes Jesus' thoughts on hospitality:

> *When you give a luncheon or dinner, do not invite your friends, your brothers or relatives, or your rich neighbors; if you do, they may invite you back and so you will be repaid But when you give a banquet, invite the poor, the crippled, the lame, the blind and you will be blessed. Although they cannot repay you, you will be repaid at the resurrection of the righteous (Luke 14:12-14 NIV).*

Jesus admonishes us to extend hospitality without any thought of return or reward. Give unconditionally. The rewards are far beyond natural payment.

---

[2] Greig, 110.

## Hospitality is Generous

Hospitality is more than giving parties and having guests. Jesus describes it as feeding the hungry, quenching the thirst of the thirsty, inviting the stranger in, clothing the needy, looking after the sick, and visiting the prisoners.

*Then the King will say to those on his right, 'Come, you who are blessed by my Father; take your inheritance, the kingdom prepared for you since the creation of the world For I was hungry and you gave me something to eat, I was thirsty and you gave me something to drink, I was a stranger and you invited me in, I needed clothes and you clothed me, I was sick and you looked after me, I was in prison and you came to visit me.' "Then the righteous will answer him, 'Lord, when did we see you hungry and feed you, or thirsty and give you something to drink? When did we see you a stranger and invite you in, or needing clothes and clothe you? When did we see you sick or in prison and go to visit you?' "The King will reply, 'I tell you the truth, whatever you did for one of the least of these brothers of mine, you did for me' (Matthew 25:34-40 NIV).*

When you care for someone who is sick, you are caring for Jesus. When you open your home, sharing your food and accommodations with someone, you are doing it unto the Lord. Whatever hospitality you extend to others, you are including Jesus. *The rewards of a Spirit of Hospitality are far reaching.* They go beyond the satisfaction of meeting the present needs of others—they accumulate dividends in Heaven!

When you genuinely enjoy people, they can tell. When you open your home to friends, you don't need expensive china or a formal living room with ample furniture. If you are gracious and warm, unselfishly entertaining with kindness, friends will flock to your door. It doesn't matter if they are stacked on top of each other, if you love having them there, they will come back.

My husband's grandmother, Zealous Baughman, is the perfect example of exhibiting hospitality *with great kindness*. She loves to have company come into her humble home, a mobile home/house combination with a wall-to-wall table in her small kitchen. It doesn't matter what time of day or night we drop in on her and her husband, Mark, she has something she has "just whipped up" or "something she wants you to try." I've watched her cut a small pie into enough pieces for everyone to eat, graciously choosing a cookie for herself so there will be enough to go around. She is never happier than when her wall-to-wall table is full and she is the queen of the kitchen. One of the side benefits of hospitality is gaining many friends. Who can resist a warm personality with *generous kindness*?

ھ~৶ *Grace Notes* ৶~৶

ھ *Special little thoughtful things are what make people like coming to your home. Here are a few suggestions to help make them feel at home.*

ھ *If guests are staying over Sunday afternoon let them know they are welcome to take a nap. You may want to assure them that it is your custom to do the same.*

❧ *Leave a basket of fruit in their room for a midnight snack.*

❧ *Slip into a modest robe after church and suggest that your guests do the same.*

❧ *Keep extra "footies" or slippers handy for guests to remove their shoes and relax.*

❧ *Walk your guests to the door when they are leaving. This lets them know you want to spend every single moment left with them.*

❧ *Keep a basket of toys and books just for your guests' small children even when your own are grown. A doll tucked in a blanket and a tin can full of small metal cars can occupy a young guest for hours.*

## HOSPITALITY

You want me to be hospitable?
Well, Lord you'll have to make a way;
There's not much cash left in the bank
When the bills have all been paid.

Are you sure you don't mean the neighbor, Lord?
They have much more space,
We're sure cramped with all these kids
Living in a real small place.

What's that You say, You're hungry?
You're in need of some warm clothes?
How can this be? You own it all,
The cattle on a thousand hills.

Yes Lord, I think I would be willing
To give a little of my time,
Thank goodness that it is real cheap,
And will cost me not a dime.

What's that Lord, You are saying?
You're talking straight at me?
When I've done it to the least of these
I've done it unto Thee?

Forgive my selfishness, Dear Lord,
And help me now begin to see
That any way I help my neighbor
Is Hospitality!

By Gayla M. Baughman

# *41*

# *Manners at Mealtime*

During our travels we have eaten in many restaurants and I have noticed a general decline in the practice of simple table manners. I'm not sure how people act at home, but it is my guess that things are much more casual. Shudder! If you have looked across the table and to your horror, noticed your husband or child doing something embarrassing, perhaps it is time to tighten up the "manners" belt at home. Practicing table manners in private assures that they will be used in public.

Thankfully, not everyone is ignorant of basic table manners. You may feel the same way I do about manners being exploited in public. We may not be able to go on a crusade to revive manners and change the world, but we can start by practicing manners in our closest communities, our homes. Here is a review of the basics.

### Posture

Sit up straight and avoid slouching or slumping while dining. When you are not eating, keep your hands on your lap or resting with your forearms on the edge of the table. Mom always said "No elbows on the table," probably because it was easier than trying to explain when they are acceptable. For all we've heard against it, elbows on the table are acceptable at times. For instance, when you are in a

279

restaurant you may need to use your elbows to lean forward enough to be heard over the noise or loud music. You may need to use your elbows at a formal dinner with a large table, so you can gracefully lean over enough to hear or talk to someone else. Peggy Post states, " A woman is far more graceful leaning forward supported by her elbows than doubled forward over her hands in her lap as though she were in pain!"[3]    At home, there is no reason for leaning across the table, and even in the above situations, elbows are *never* on the table while you are eating.

Both hands should be used when passing a heavy dish or when a child is trying to drink from a large glass. This helps avoid spillage and possible injury.

### Stay Seated

It is extremely important to teach your children to stay seated during the meal. If you practice this at home, when you take them to a restaurant they will do the same. For safety reasons children should never be allowed to play on the floor in restaurants. I was in a restaurant with a friend of mine and a waitress shared this story:

> *While she was working at another restaurant, a little boy of about five years old was playing on the floor. He was not misbehaving in any way, just quietly playing. The waitress, a friend of hers, carrying a pot of freshly brewed hot coffee to a table nearby, could not see him over the tray. As she tripped over this little boy, hot boiling coffee caused second and third degree burns over most of his body.*

---

[3] Peggy Post, *Emily Post's Etiquette*, 16th ed. (New York: Harper Collins, 1997), 232.

*A nightmare for that family and the waitress
began that day. Money could not ease the
pain or buy back the baby skin of their little
boy, nor could it erase the guilt and anguish
of a very remorseful waitress.*

This may not seem as important for adults, but I have
been in a crowded restaurant after a church convention and
wished a preacher with a booming voice would stand up and
say "You may be seated," like they do in church! But alas,
that has yet to happen. I have wormed my way through a
maze of people, flattened myself against walls to let a
waitress pass with hot food and finally, after the hostess
kindly excused a gentleman with his hinder parts leaning on
our table, was safely seated with great relief. I can't say that
I have not been guilty of this spasm of visitation, but staying
put when the establishment is busy and waitresses are trying
to serve other tables is a courtesy not to be overlooked. If
you want to visit with someone, ask to be seated at a larger
table so you may visit sitting down—or move outside where
there is more room.

Several of our friends have discontinued the
restaurant scene after church at special conferences and camp
meetings. They stock their motel room with finger foods and
cold drinks and invite a few friends over. It is important if
you do this to be mindful of neighboring patrons who are
trying to rest. As a courtesy, if your party gets too loud, you
may always move to the lobby.

### The Prayer

We Pentecostals have the custom of praying before
we eat. A thanksgiving prayer for the blessings the Lord has
provided is offered either by one person or at the direction

from the host for all those present to join in prayer. If the pastor or a minister is present, he is always asked to give the blessing. If a group of ministers are present, the host or hostess usually asks the eldest of the group or another honored guest to pray.

## The Napkin

The napkin should be placed in your lap before picking up a utensil to begin eating. At a formal dinner, you as the hostess, should place the napkin in your lap first and then the guests should follow. If it is a large dinner napkin, fold it in half or diagonally. If it is a luncheon or paper napkin, it should be completely unfolded and then placed on your lap. Your napkin should never be tucked in your collar between the buttons of your shirt, or under your belt. Blot or pat your lips rather than wiping your mouth as you would with a washcloth. If you need to leave the table during the meal, refold your napkin with the soiled part turned in and either place it to the left of the plate or on the chair. When you are finished, the napkin should be placed either to the left of your plate, or if the plate has been removed, in the center. The napkin should not be refolded or crumpled. It should lie in folds close together, hiding the soiled parts. Unused napkins are only reinserted into napkin rings when they are being used in the home, never in a restaurant.

## Serving the Food

The most common way of serving is the "family style." The hostess serves the meat and the other dishes are passed counterclockwise (to your right) to each guest as they serve themselves. If a gentleman sits next to a lady, he does not offer her the dish first but serves himself, and then he may offer to hold the serving dish while she serves her plate. For a second helping, if someone at the end of the table asks for an item, another may intercept it after asking the first person's permission. He may say, "May I help myself first so it doesn't need to come all the way back?" Of course, you wouldn't do this if it is the last piece or portion left![4]

The formal style of serving is when the hostess serves the plates at the head of the table passing them to each guest. This should be started counterclockwise working toward the opposite end of the table. The last lady on the hostess' right keeps her plate first. The gentlemen continue to pass plates until each lady to their right has one, and then they keep one for themselves. After the hostess' has served each guest on her right, then the guests on her left are served in the same manner. The hostess is served last.

### When to Begin

The meal begins when you, the hostess, pick up your utensil to start eating. In a larger setting, it is not necessary to wait until everyone has been served to start eating. Since you will be the last served, you could say, "Please start so your dinner won't get cold." The guests may then proceed. If you forget to instruct them, a guest may pick up his/her fork or spoon after several people have been served. The others will probably follow. No apologies are necessary.

### During The Meal

When you begin your meal, there are some basic rules to remember. If you have been served salad at a formal meal, and the main entrée is served before you are finished

---

[4] Peggy Post, 234.

with your salad, you may place your salad plate to the left of your forks. This is where the salad plate is placed for informal settings, rather than on the dinner plate as in a formal dinner. If you are eating soup, spoon the liquid away from you. Sip your soup rather than slurping it from the side of the spoon. If your soup is too hot to eat let it sit until it cools. Do not blow on it.

When your food arrives, refrain from seasoning it before you taste it. Some cooks use more seasoning than others, so you may not need any extra salt or pepper.

Chew your food with your mouth closed. When I was young, we used to play a game called "chew and show." I can't believe I managed it without my mother knowing! I probably don't have to go into the disgusting details of the game. The fact of the matter is, no one else is interested in how your food looks once it has passed between your lips. If you cannot keep your mouth closed while chewing, the bite was too large. Smaller bites will accommodate the size of your mouth. This will also help keep the sound of smacking lips and other loud noises to a minimal.

With the exception of bread, you should not touch the food with your fingers. Use either a knife or a piece of bread for a "pusher" to help guide the food onto the fork. If food spills off your plate, pick it up with a piece of your silverware and place it on the edge of your plate. Finger foods should be served only during casual dining. It is proper to handle foods such as pizza, sandwiches, and fried chicken during informal meals.

Although it is possible to converse with a small piece of food in your mouth, do not talk with your mouth full. Lay the utensil you are using down between each bite. This slows you down and helps in the digestion of food. It also discourages the temptation to wave the fork while you talk.

The usual entertainment around a table is conversation. This cannot be accomplished if someone is performing a solo on the south side of the green beans. Humming, singing, or whistling should be reserved for audiences away from the dinner table. Besides, one can't whistle with food in his mouth.

If you need something you cannot easily reach, politely ask the person closest to the item to pass it to you. Do not reach in front of someone or over his or her plate to get what you need.

Generally, you should not leave the table during the meal except in an emergency. If food gets caught between your teeth, however, and you can't remove it with your tongue, you may leave the table to find a place you can remove it in private. If you must go to the bathroom or if you suddenly become ill, simply excuse yourself.

If you get a piece of bad food or tough gristle in your mouth, do not spit it into your napkin. Remove the food from your mouth as discreetly as possible, using the same utensil it went in with or your fingers. Place the gristle on the edge of your plate and cover it with some other food from your plate.

**In a nutshell—Don't:**

- ➤ Chew with your mouth open
- ➤ Talk with your mouth full
- ➤ Wave the fork
- ➤ Sing at the table
- ➤ Slurp your soup
- ➤ Leave the table without being excused
- ➤ Season your food before tasting it
- ➤ Pick your teeth
- ➤ Use your fingers

## Use of Silverware

Many people are intimidated by the number of utensils in a formal place setting and become nervous choosing the right piece with which to eat. This decision is not as difficult as it may first appear. Starting with the utensil that is farthest from your plate, work your way in, using one for each course. If the table has been set correctly, you will have no problems.

The rules that specify how the knife, fork, and spoon must be used have evolved over the years. The delicate manner in which utensils are held originated from the effort to prevent the utensils from having a threatening appearance. Thus, to hold any utensil in a fist, or in such a way that it points or waves at anyone would hint at potential danger and is to this day inappropriate.[5]

In general, all the silverware with the exception of the knife are held horizontally by balancing them between the first knuckle of the middle finger and the tip of the index finger allowing the thumb to steady the handle. This is much the same manner in which you hold a pencil. The knife is used with the index finger firmly pressing down on the handle as you cut.

---

[5] Diner's Digest, How to Use a Knife, Fork and Spoon, 10 March, 2001, on-line, (Copyright 1997 CyberPalate LLC); available from *http://www.cuisinenet.com/glossary/use.html*.

*American and European* styles are two ways to use a knife and fork when cutting and eating your food. Both styles are considered appropriate. The American style allows you to cut the food by holding the knife in the right hand and the fork in the left hand. The fork tines should face down, holding the food to the plate. Change the fork from the left to the right hand to eat, rolling the fork so the tines are facing up. Emily Post calls the unnecessary complicated act of changing your fork from one hand to the other the "*zigzag*" method.[6]

The *European or Continental* style seems to be much more convenient and still considered acceptable. This style allows you to retain the utensil in the same hand the meat is cut with. The fork remains in the left hand, tines facing down and the knife in the right hand. Simply eat the cut pieces of food by picking them up with your fork still in your left hand.

To push food onto a fork you may use a piece of bread or your knife. The correct way to hold the knife as a pusher is in the left hand, holding it in the same way as when cutting meat with your right. The natural motion of guiding your food onto a fork with the tip is correct. A left-handed person would switch the positions to accommodate his or her prominent hand.

### When You Are Finished

Never push your plate away when you are finished. Leave it for the hostess or server to remove. Place your utensils side by side, diagonally from upper left to lower right in the ten-four position (as if they are pointing to the numbers 10 and 4 on a clock face), across your plate with the handles slightly over the edge.

---

[6] Peggy Post, 238.

If you have used a knife, place it with the blade facing inward and a fork, tines down, to the left of the knife. Once you have used a piece of silverware, never place it back on the table. It is best to position it diagonally across the edge of your plate. Do not leave a used spoon in a cup, place it on the saucer. A soupspoon may be left in a large, shallow soup bowl, but not in a small cereal bowl. If a utensil is precariously balancing in a cup or bowl, this is a good indication it is not to be there. Any unused silverware is simply left on the table.

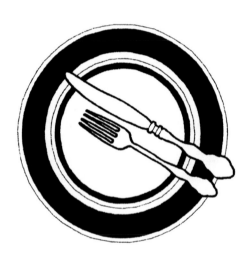

# 42

# *Setting A Table*

For either formal or informal dining put a linen or damask tablecloth on the table. This makes each meal special. Even if you are not entertaining guests, a cloth on the table is nice. This special touch is a good reminder to the members of your family that they are the most important people in your life. Be careful to make sure the folded seam or design is centered. Choose a centerpiece that can be left on the table as you eat with the guests still able to see each other over it.

## The Formal Place Setting

It is important to note that for the formal dinner, everything should be set symmetrically. The centerpiece should be in the exact center and each place setting evenly spaced apart leaving plenty of elbowroom. The dinner plate is placed in the center of the place setting with the design facing the diner. The salad plate may be placed on top of the dinner plate or brought to the table when the salad is served.

When setting a table, it is important to learn where each piece is placed in reference to what course is being served and when. The meat fork is placed directly on the left, next to the plate. Next to it the salad fork is placed unless the salad is served after the meat. In that case, the salad fork would be closest to the plate. The fish fork is placed on the far left. Directly to the right of the plate is the dinner knife, next the steak knife, and/or the fish knife (if needed) with the sharp edges facing the plate. The teaspoon and/or soupspoon, is placed to the right of the knives, and finally the appetizer fork to the right of the spoon. Note that the appetizer fork is the only fork on the right side. This convenient format allows the silverware to be used in order, from the outside in.

*Formal Place Setting*

Usually, no more than three of any type utensil are ever placed on the table at one time. The exceptions would be the addition of an appetizer or oyster fork, the butter knife (placed on the butter plate) and the beverage spoon. The long-handled beverage spoon, popular among iced tea drinkers, would be placed to the right of the soupspoon or provided at the time the beverage is served. For the formal dinner, the dessert spoon or fork is brought out on the dessert plate at the time it is served.

The use of a butter plate is relatively new to formal settings, but because of popular demand it appears above the forks slightly to the left of the plate. The butter knife is placed across the butter plate at a diagonal in the ten-four position with the sharp edge facing the edge of the table. The goblets and glasses are placed in arrangement according to size so the large ones will not hide the smaller ones. The water goblet, which is usually the largest beverage, should be placed directly above the knives to the right of the plate (directly across from the butter plate). Next to it and slightly to the right will be another cold beverage. It is not necessary to use wineglasses, since we do not serve wine unless it is used for a sparkling cider or grape juice. In that case the wineglass would be placed to the right of the water or tea goblet. The napkin is placed in the center of the dinner plate with the design or monogram facing the diner.

## The Informal Place Setting

The basic difference between the formal and the informal place setting is the latter uses fewer pieces of service because fewer courses are served. A damask tablecloth is nice, but for the casual setting you may use place mats or a brightly-colored tablecloth for a more festive atmosphere. The dinner plate is not usually placed on the table if you plan to serve the plates in the kitchen and bring them to the table hot. If you plan to serve "family style," the plate may be included in the place setting.

You will place the number of implements according to the number of planned courses. For a basic design, serving salad as the first course, start with the same pieces you do for a formal setting. The dinner fork is to the left of the plate, the salad fork next. The meat knife is to the right of the plate, with the serrated edge turned toward the plate, the teaspoon next to it. If you are serving soup, the soupspoon goes to the right of the teaspoon. You may add a beverage spoon to the right of the teaspoon if you are serving unsweetened iced tea. You may put the salad plate to the left of the forks. The butter dish, with the butter knife resting in it, is placed above the forks.

*Informal Place Setting*

If you serve coffee, the cup and saucer go to the right of the setting with the coffee spoon on the right side of the saucer. If the menu calls for a dessert fork and spoon, they may be placed above the dinner plate with the fork closest to the plate. The fork head should be facing the glasses and the spoon head the opposite. The napkin may be placed in the center if there is no dinner plate or to the left of the forks. It is never placed under the forks. (Unless you are dining outside and the wind is blowing!) Sometimes the napkin is placed in the tea glass with an artistic fold for either casual or formal. I'll share some of those folds with you later!

## The Family Setting

Daily servings such as breakfast and lunch seldom require several courses. You would not need to put as much silverware on the table at these times, but when it is just the family, the table still needs to be set in an orderly fashion. This is a great time to teach younger children how to set the table. The bare essentials from left to right are, a napkin, fork, dinner plate, knife, and spoon. The glass is placed at the upper                                                    right.

*Family Place Setting*

### ৵৵   Grace Notes   ৵৵

*Can't remember where the silverware goes? Try this, the utensils that have the same number of letters as "left," are the ones placed in that position. "Fork" has only four letters, while "spoon," and "knife" have five letters as does the word "right." Remember, the appetizer fork is the only exception. ☺*

# Notes

# *43*

# *Buffet Dinners*

There are many different ways to set up a buffet. It is best to arrange the items in the order of what is needed first to keep the line moving in a smooth organized fashion. If you set a buffet the same way every time, your guests will know what to expect.

### A Perfect Buffet

Starting with the **dinner plates** either move the line to the left or the right, or both sides if you are serving a large group. Place the **salads and dressings** next, then the **breads, vegetables, and main entree**. Finally, the **utensils** are at the opposite end of the plates if they are not placed on the tables. Keep the cold foods together and the hot foods together.

If hot plates are needed, line them up in a fashion to avoid any accidental burn hazard to the guests. You may want to fold your utensils in napkins to make them easier for the guests to carry. If not, place them close to the utensils or on the tables. For convenience, have the **drinks and desserts** at a separate table, moving the line in the same direction as the buffet table. Guests can then place their plates on the table where they will be eating. They can return for drinks without the fear of spilling a full plate of food while doing a balancing act with another plate, utensils, napkins and glasses. Usually smaller plates are offered for desserts. A separate table is ideal for serving foods such as pies, cakes, cookies, and other confections.

It is important when serving a buffet, to make the service convenient and keep the line running smoothly. Each year the *United Pentecostal Church International* sponsors the *Summer Institute* in various areas of the country for the faculty and staff of the colleges endorsed by the organization. For several years we have had the privilege of traveling to Toronto, Ontario, Canada, for the *Summer Institute*. We have been there about four different times since I have been a part of Christian Life College.

After multiple visits to Canada, I finally realized how several of the restaurants set up their buffets. I don't know if this escaped me because it is a northern practice, or if I have avoided buffets successfully enough to miss it. Unfortunately, I wasn't the only one confused at several of these buffets. To my utter amazement they started at both ends and worked toward the middle! It took me four years to figure this out! You can imagine the confusion with all these college professor-types trying to figure out what to do! The problem was the food on our end of the buffet was **not** exactly like the other end, and we wanted a little of everything! What a fiasco!

As we made our way from left to right, innocently filling our plates and graciously forcing a smile at the "rude" people coming toward us filling their plates, we bumped, said, "excuse me," and did all the other proper things we should do. Exasperated, I sat down facing the buffet to study what the format was. How embarrassing when I realized we were the ones being rude! We will know better next time, at least I will. Perhaps everyone else knew what they were doing, but in my confusion I thought we were all crazy. I promise to be patient and get in line again at the other end if I want that wonderful crab salad they make in Toronto!

# *Notes*

# *44*

# *An Afternoon Tea*

While my husband and I were pastoring in Arizona, I had the privilege of hosting several teas. I really didn't have any idea how to host a tea but I had a zeal and desire to put something together other women would enjoy.

My first experience was a learning springboard. I began my plans with the thought, "How would they do this in England?" Since I have never been there, my imagination was all I had to go on, besides a few favorite Victorian era magazines and pictures.

I started with lace. I put lace everywhere! On the tables, draped over the furniture and anywhere else I could arrange it. Then, I thought, we need flowers. Dried flowers were my favorite, but I had to settle for a few silk ones in case someone had allergies. Let's see, we need china teapots and cups and saucers. How about letting them bring their own cup and saucer and we'll have a crowd breaker with each lady telling a story about her special cup? Great idea! So that's what we did. I unpacked my silver serving set and polished it to a beautiful luster, asked friends to lend me their china tea pots and more lace tablecloths, sent some nice frilly invitations, and waited for the appointed day to arrive.

When the day finally came, I plugged in my coffee maker and started the hot water. I bought some herbal and spiced teas, made a pot of cinnamon coffee for those who weren't tea drinkers, arranged some crumpets and cookies on a silver platter, and TA DA! We had a tea! I must admit that first tea was probably a far cry from proper, but we had a wonderful time pretending!

Since then, I have learned a great deal about teas. You can have a tea in honor of a visiting celebrity, to welcome a new neighbor, or simply to entertain guests. The invitations are usually telephoned unless you plan a more formal tea where invitations on fill-in commercial cards or personal notes are sent. If you are giving a tea in your home,

the dining room table is the most convenient place to set up for serving. However, any room in the house will do with a smaller table set as a tea table. As long as your guests can move around the table freely, it may be anywhere. A cloth is always used on the tea table. I prefer the conventional lace cloth on the table, but white linen with needlework or one with appliquéd designs would be pretty also.

Two serving trays are set at each end of the table, one for tea and one for coffee. The tea tray should have a full pot of tea, tea bags (if the tea has not been made ahead of time), a sugar bowl, cream pitcher, and a small saucer with lemon wedges on it. Hot water should be nearby to replenish the teapot frequently. The coffee server should have a large urn or pot, a pitcher of cream, and a bowl of sugar. You may serve hot chocolate in the place of the coffee if you want to, in which case the sugar and cream would not be needed. Cups and saucers are placed within easy reach, the spoons, and small tea plates with luncheon napkins are stacked neatly in the middle.

The food served at a tea is usually sweet items such as cookies, cupcakes, crumpets, sweet breads or thin slices of iced cake. Use forks if iced cake is served. Sandwiches cut in wedges are nice for those who cannot consume sugar. A sugar-free tray is a thoughtful gesture if there are those who prefer it or who are required to avoid sugar for health concerns. Guests serve themselves, so a designated tea pourer is entirely optional.

## Notes

# *45*

# *Centerpieces*

A centerpiece should be placed directly in the middle of the table. The centerpiece used during a meal should be a height that each diner can see over. It is very frustrating to hear a voice coming from somewhere among the hydrangeas with no face that can be seen. The length and width of the centerpiece is much more versatile, depending on the length of the table and the number of place settings.

### Fresh Flowers

There are many different types of centerpieces. Fresh flowers are the most common and surely among the prettiest. A crystal vase with fresh flowers can brighten up an  otherwise dull table. Not only are fresh flowers beautiful, but they give guests the feeling that the hostess took time to make a trip to her garden to cut fresh flowers just for their benefit. Perhaps you did not cut the flowers and do not have a garden. You can still grace your table with beautiful fresh-cut flowers. Your local grocery store carries bouquets at a very modest price, making a lovely centerpiece surprisingly convenient to purchase along with your groceries. You can actually have fresh flowers on your table every day!

Artificial flowers should be used with caution. Some better quality silk flowers make beautiful arrangements to use for centerpieces, but flowers that look fake and unnatural will take away from the relaxed, friendly atmosphere you are trying to achieve at the dinner table. Avoid using plastic flowers. I tend to agree with Peggy Post that "plastic artificial flowers are out of place."[7]

## Crystal Bowls

Crystal bowls are a valuable investment for arranging centerpieces that are the right size to use during a dinner. You may fill a small one with colored marbles or perhaps water for a floating single rose. Fill a large bowl with water and place three floating candles in it for a lighted centerpiece. If you are in a hurry and need something with little preparation, a crystal bowl with potpourri can serve quite well as a centerpiece.

A very interesting centerpiece is a tall, crystal, clear, vase filled with water and a brightly colored beta fish swimming in it. Add more color by topping it with a fern that thrives in water. I would avoid using this centerpiece for your annual fish fry—but then on the other hand, it might just be the thing if you use a brightly colored fish theme to decorate your dinner party.

## Candles

Candles are a basic decoration for tables. They are very versatile and can be used any time of the day. Candles are appropriate during formal or informal meals coupling them with other centerpieces or placed at individual settings

---

[7] Peggy Post, 426.

to serve as light during a candlelight dinner. Candles can be reused, but when you are serving guests the ones you use on the table should be new. They should be lighted before your  guests come to the table and remain so throughout the entire meal. It is wise to purchase drip-less candles so you won't soil the table linen. Drip-less candles are a little more expensive, but they are worth the time saved trying to remove candle wax out of a tablecloth or from an intricately carved candleholder.

### Fruit Centerpieces

A large bowl filled with fruit can be a colorful centerpiece. Use a sugar glaze for a crystallized look. For a luncheon, or casual dinner, scoop out a watermelon and carve it in the shape of a basket or bowl and fill it with melon balls for an eatable centerpiece. A fruit platter placed in the center of the table makes a nice centerpiece. Use the top of a fresh pineapple in the center of your platter for added beauty.

Any centerpiece you use will add beauty and personality to an otherwise ordinary setting. Suit your personality or the celebration from simple to extravagant. Centerpieces may not be a priority for every occasion, however, they add a gracious touch to any meal.

## Notes

# *46*

## *Napkin Folding*

Napkin folding is an art that adds special effects to your table, whether you are serving a casual meal or a formal dinner. Cloth napkins are economical because they can be washed and used again. If the napkins become limp after washing, starch and iron them to maintain their shape better.

### Formal Napkins

There are many ways to fold napkins. For the formal table, simplicity is the most appropriate. The napkins used for formal folds are large, measuring twenty-four inches square.

**Dramatized Monogram**

1. Fold napkin into quarters, top to bottom then side to side. The fold of the napkin will form the point of a triangle.

2. Next fold over the point to form a small triangle above the monogram.

3. Now fold under the other two side points. Lay flat on the dinner plate with the monogram facing you.

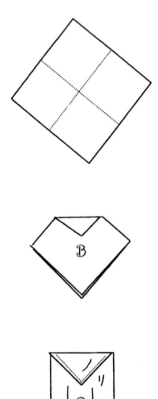

**Basic Three-fold**

1.  Lay napkin flat. If it has a monogram, place it face down in the right-hand corner, and fold into quarters, left edge to the right edge, then, top to bottom.

2.  Fold one more time, right to left, forming a rectangle. The top edge should have only two folds if folded correctly.

3.  Place in the center of the dinner plate. It does not matter whether the fold is either on the left or the right, as long as all the place settings are consistent and the monogram is facing you.

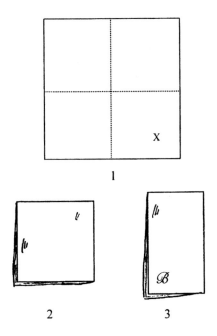

**Tiered Point**

1.  Fold napkin into quarters, top to bottom, then side to side.

2.  Take the open-ended bottom corner and fold the first layer back diagonally, about 1" from the opposite corner.

3.  Repeat with the next three layers, folding each one about 1" from the previous corner.

4.  Fold side-corners back so they overlap behind the napkin.

Center on dinner plate.

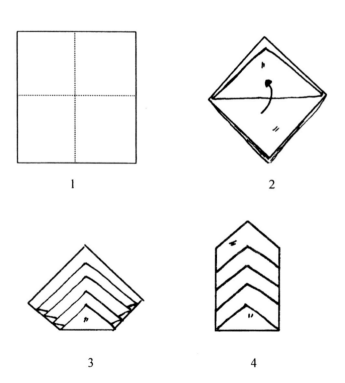

## Informal Napkins

### Side Stripes

1. Fold napkin into quarters with open corners at upper right.

2. Fold one open corner over three times to form diagonal across center.

3. Fold over next corner and tuck into the first fold to make a strip of equal width.

4. Turn under top and bottom.

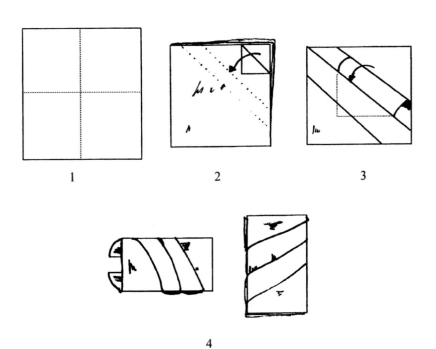

## Fleur-de-lis

A large napkin works best for this fold.

1. Fold napkin into quarters.

2. With open points up, pleat each side as shown, leaving a wider space at the bottom.

3. Turn bottom point up as shown.

4. Turn over, pleat and insert into wineglass.

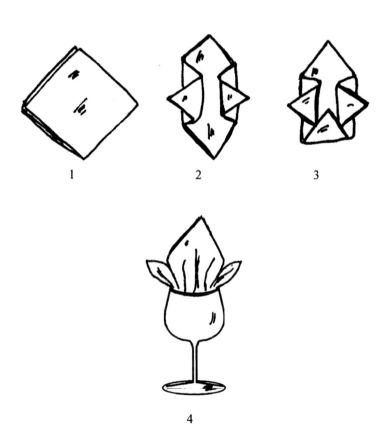

1          2          3

4

**Candle fold**

1. Fold napkin in half diagonally.

2. Fold back bottom of napkin two inches or more to get a candle that is not too tall.

3. Starting at one end, roll napkin fairly tight.

4. Tuck remaining flap into bottom fold.

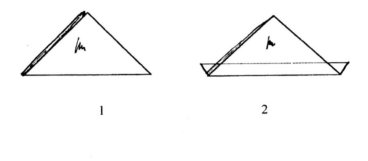

1                    2

3

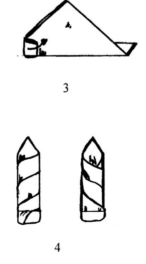

4

**The Fan**

1. Fold napkin in half.

2. Accordion pleat, creasing firmly.

3. Slip through a napkin ring and fan out top.

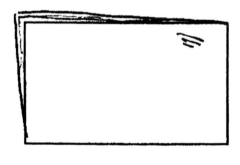

1

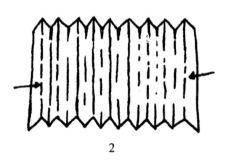

2

3

# 47

# *The Guest Quarters*

A guesthouse would be nice, but few of us have one. You are probably housing guests right in your own home. So your house, like many others is the guesthouse. Many guests will return where they are welcomed in earnest sincerity. The secret is making your guests feel like non-guests, actually making them feel as though they are home. Little touches of personal attention make your guests feel warm and welcome.

An antique pitcher filled with fresh flowers on a nightstand is a welcome sight to an overnight guest. There is something about the beauty of real flowers that touches the heart. It draws a little springtime into the room.

Leave room in the closet and a few drawers empty for your guests to put their things in. This will help them feel more at home, rather than living out of a suitcase. Have extra blankets handy in case they need extra covering during the night or a small fan for warm evenings.

Try to anticipate every need your guests may have. Speaking of comfort, Bonnie Markham suggests sleeping on the bed one night before you offer it to guests.[8] If there is something you can do to make it more comfortable before they arrive, that would be great. For a quick-fix you can purchase an egg-crate type piece of foam to put under the

---

[8] Bonnie Jean Markham, *The Nitty-Gritty for Ministers' Wives* (Hazelwood, MO: Pentecostal Publishing House, 1988), 105, 106.

mattress pad. They are very comfortable and will camouflage lumps and bumps. Also, if the mattress is old and sags in the middle, a board slipped between the mattress and box springs helps (caution, it makes a very firm mattress).

When making beds, place the flat sheet facing the fitted sheet. Leave the top sheet with enough margin to turn down over the blanket exposing the lovely design.

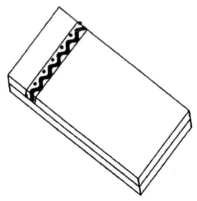

If your guests come in the evening, turn the blankets down on one side and lay a silk rose or a few mints on the pillow. They will surely have "sweet" dreams.

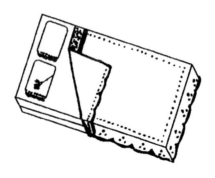

A basket of trial-size shampoos, conditioners, and lotions make a nice addition to the guest bath. Add a razor, trial size bath oil, *Rolaids* and other necessities for the convenience of your guests. Then attach a note that lets your company know they can be used, possibly saving a trip to the store. Make sure there are plenty of clean towels and wash clothes in a convenient place. Don't forget extra rolls of toilet paper (its very embarrassing to ask for them), air fresheners, and feminine napkins for emergencies.

If you house your guests in a trailer or motor home on the premises, stock the refrigerator with filtered water, a few soft drinks and a small carton of milk. Leave a basket of crisp crackers, fruit, and other items for a midnight snack. Supply your guests with individual boxes of cereal on the cabinet for an early breakfast.

ৡৣ **Grace Notes** ৡৣ

*Save a little money. Don't use the small amenities when you go to a motel. Take them home with you. They are small enough to fit in the special guest basket you have in your guest bathroom at home. Use the money you saved for other purchased items.*

# *48*

# *The Extended Guest*

Not often are you asked to open your home to someone for over a week or two, but on occasion you will. If you open your arms of hospitality to a young girl in need of shelter, a couple between homes, or your own married children, it can get pretty hair-raising after about three weeks. Usually, the extended guest will be a relative or close family member for just a few weeks during the holidays but on rare occasions it may be otherwise.

Occasionally, a daughter will find that when her father passes away, her mother will "make the rounds," staying with each sibling for a period of time each year. Having your mother in your home may sound wonderful at first, but no matter how well you may get along, you are both adults now, and times can become difficult. The old saying, "No house is big enough for two women," is an understatement, to say the least! God made you the keeper at home, and no one can do it as well as you—at least not in your own home. These times can be wonderful times of making memories, or miserable times making regrets. A few helpful suggestions may keep the pressure from mounting and help you feel better about your role as the hostess.

First of all, you must remember that this is your home. You are responsible for keeping it a safe, pleasant environment for your family. When the normal schedule and structure of doing things is interrupted with an added tenant, it is the hostess that preserves sanity. You are the one who follows situations around and patches them back together when they explode or fall to pieces. Sound like an impossible job? Well, it can seem that way sometimes. Anything you can do to make life easier on everyone living in your home the better.

➤ Make schedules and tape them to the refrigerator. In as much as possible, keep the same schedule you had before your guests arrived. Other members of the family will adjust easier if their lives are not turned "topsy-turvy." It will be much easier for your extended guests to adjust to your schedule than it will be for your whole family to adjust to theirs. This may not always be possible, during holidays, weddings, or funerals, which is understandable.

➤ Have frequent "family talks" to clear the air and vent frustrations on neutral ground. By "neutral ground," I mean a time when all those present can say what is on their mind provided they remain respectful and in control. They can speak their mind without any rebuke or correction from anyone else. Once the meeting is over, a fresh start has begun and no ill feelings are carried away from there. Always end with prayer, holding hands, and sharing a time of appreciation for each other.

➤ Share the responsibilities and chores. It is not fair for your guest to expect maid service. Neither is it appropriate for you to allow a guest to do your housework while you rest (unless of course you are convalescing). It is fair to expect an offer of help when one is staying for awhile. If the woman guest does not offer to help with the vacuuming and dusting, it is acceptable for you to ask. You may include this in one of your meetings and work out a schedule of weekly chores. Some people are reluctant to offer to help with house cleaning, not because they are lazy, but because they are shy about infringing upon your territory. The same may apply when you are fixing a meal. They may feel uncomfortable offering to help; afraid they will get "under foot." A courteous suggestion could take care of their misconceptions and make them feel free to "jump right in" and help. Perhaps you would like to offer the kitchen once a week for them to cook their specialty. Let them know that they will have complete liberty in the kitchen and you will be the helper, assisting the chef.

➢ Take a night off. That's right, a night off—just you and your husband. Once a week you need to get in the car and go away from the house for awhile. Go on a weekly "date." You don't have to spend a lot of money at an expensive restaurant, but you can find something you both enjoy for a few hours each week. If you can spend the night somewhere, plan to do that periodically. This will help you come back feeling refreshed and ready to face another round with extended guests in the home (and it does wonders for your marriage).

➢ Give your guests their privacy. Whether you have offered visitors the guestroom, or one of your children's rooms, it is good to respect the guests' privacy as long as they are staying with you. Instruct the rest of the family to knock before entering. Ask permission before going into the room to look for something in the closet or under the bed. Make it clear to the household that a door closed means "do not disturb," while an open door means "come on in." This allows every member of the household to know that each one is privileged to have private time and will be left undisturbed by the others.

➢ Keep smiling. Nothing is more miserable than a grouchy hostess. A smile can smooth out many oncoming disagreements or misunderstandings. If you want to feel better when you don't, smile, it does wonders for the spirit.

*A merry heart does good, like medicine, But a broken spirit dries the bones* (Proverbs 17:22).

# Part Eight

# The Gracious
# Guest

# *49*

# *The Dinner Guest*

I believe as Pentecostals, one of our favorite pastimes is eating out. I'm not sure why we like to socialize around the table so much, but it seems to be the most obvious place to fellowship. Perhaps it is because we have Jesus as our example. He often had fellowship with His disciples while dining in someone's home. John 12:2 records Him eating at the home of Lazarus, Mary and Martha. In Mark 2:16 He ate with the sinners and tax collectors; in Luke 7:36 He ate with a Pharisee. He chose the dinner table to explain to His disciples the curse of betrayal and the hope of a new covenant. According to Mark 8:19-20, He was the host, breaking bread for a crowd of five thousand hungry people one time and four thousand another.

Have you ever wondered how it would feel to be the guest of Jesus Christ? Do you wonder what it would be like to sit at the same table with Jesus and listen to His teachings? It won't be long before you will realize that dream. He has arranged the marriage supper of the Lamb for us when we get to Heaven (Revelation 19:9). Accept every dinner invitation you are able to attend. Practice using your best manners at every meal. Just think of all the experience you are receiving in preparation for the ultimate dinner invitation of your life. Now is a good time to brush up on some of those long-forgotten table manners.

Table manners should be observed whether you have been invited to dine at a fine restaurant, go on a picnic, or be a guest in someone's home.[1]

## Dining Out As a Guest

Women probably have the opportunity to be the guest while dining out more often than men. After all, where does a Christian gentleman take a young lady to get better acquainted with her? He takes her to dinner, of course. Dining manners may vary with the type of restaurant or dinner you attend.

Nowadays, you have a wide range of dining options, from the exotic restaurant overlooking a lake to the simple park vendor or the mall kiosk. With the popularity of casual dining on the rise, formal manners are rapidly being forgotten, but the chivalry of courting a young woman has not lost its magic. The formal date may have changed, but the "I want to impress you" attitude has not.

I am frequently amazed at young people I see hanging around the college lunchroom. The guys are dressed in faded old jeans and worn-out tee shirts. The girls often wear straight skirts with shirts so over-sized they hang almost to their knees. When I become disillusioned and think the world is going to pot, a Valentine or Christmas Banquet rolls around. Some of these same young men are now dressed in suits, ties, and newly shined shoes. They are escorting the same young ladies, now beautiful, their hair meticulously fashioned in the latest style carrying a fresh

---

[1] Basic dining etiquette is covered in Chapter 41, "Mealtime Manners." If you are an evangelist's wife, the section, "Dining with the Pastor" on page 347 may interest you.

bouquet of flowers. My faith in youth is renewed as I observe their careful actions. Many times I am surprisingly rewarded with the observance of meticulous manners and proper etiquette. Hooray! You haven't lost it! That just reinforces my theory that when people want to be on their best behavior, they thrive on manners.

Most of the time you may head to the nearest fast-food restaurant after church. In a group, a person is not considered anyone else's date unless it is made clear before ordering. Fast-food restaurants are considered casual dining. Manners are always in order, but the etiquette in this atmosphere is much more relaxed and free. Manners are not meant to make mealtime a difficult regime with the sole purpose of making life miserable. Rather, manners are suggestions to remind us to be polite and respectful to each other.

**Formal Dining**

In a formal setting, you are expected to be on your best behavior, observing a few more rules of etiquette. It is a miserable feeling to find yourself at a formal dinner or banquet, wishing you knew what to do next.

After someone prays for the food, wait for the host or hostess to unfold his or her napkin. Then you may remove your napkin from the table, gently shaking it unfolded. Place the napkin on your lap, completely unfolded if it is a small one or folded in half if it is larger. Never tuck it in your neck collar. This looks like you are about to tackle the meal rather than simply enjoy it. If the host or hostess forgets about his or her napkin, feel free to go ahead. Perhaps others will follow suit.

Usually, the napkin is unfolded as soon as you are seated, unless you are at a banquet or meeting where the meal is served after the preliminaries. In this case, follow the head table, or keep an eye on the servers. When the servers are ready to bring the first course to the tables, remove the napkin from the table at that time.

At a restaurant, if you forget to unfold your napkin, often the waiter or waitress will offer to do it for you. This is common, just sit politely and let them pamper you. Remove your hands from your lap and remember to reward the waiter with a gracious "thank you" and smile. The napkin should remain on your lap throughout the entire meal. If you need to leave the table during the meal, excuse yourself, fold the napkin, and place it either on your chair or beside your plate. Once the meal is over, you should place the unfolded napkin to the right of your dinner plate.[2] An unfolded napkin at the side of your plate signals the hostess or waiter that you have finished your meal.

**Ordering**

The person who asks you out to dinner will usually suggest that your order be taken first. Sometimes, however, the server will decide how the ordering will proceed, often taking women's orders before that of the men. When couples dine, some women enjoy having the man place their order with the server. This does not mean you have no preferences. After you have made your choices, your host will recite your wishes to the server as a gentleman's gesture.

As the guest, you should not order one of the most expensive items on the menu unless your host or hostess makes a suggestion, indicating that it is all right. You may put them at a disadvantage if you order an expensive entrée and an appetizer. He or she may not have the money to cover the expenses. If the host says something like, "I think you

---

[2] Ball State University Career Center, Muncie, Indiana , *Dining Etiquette,* on-line, accessed 10 March 2001, available at http://www.bsu.edu/careers/manners.html.

would enjoy the filet mignon. It is the specialty here," or "I'm going to have cheesecake. Would you like dessert too?" It is then all right to order that item. Sensitivity to the financial needs of your host is a gracious gesture that will be well rewarded with extended friendships. If you have the selfish opinion that this is just a free meal with a "get what you can while you can," attitude, take care lest you are saddled with guests of the same mind-set.

**Using the Silverware**

At a formal dinner you may become overwhelmed at the scores of implements and utensils on the table. Rather than succumb to an anxiety attack, take a deep breath and remember this simple rule. **Work from the outside in**. *(See Chapter 42 for details on place settings.)* If the table is set correctly you can't go wrong looking at the utensil that is farthest from the plate and starting there. Your napkin is on your left. Your silverware should be arranged in order as the courses are served. On your left, look for at least two forks, a smaller salad fork and a meat fork. If the salad is served, before the meat, the smaller fork is placed on the outside. If the meat is served first, then the larger fork will be on the outside. Many fine-dining restaurants are serving salad as a separate entrée, making it more common to see the salad fork on the outside. If they are both the same size, you won't have to worry. Just use the outer fork with the first thing served. On your far right there will either be a small fork (which indicates an appetizer of shrimp or oysters will be served) and/or a soupspoon farthest from the plate. Sometimes the soupspoon is used for a fruit cup. Your teaspoon is to the right of your knife. If steak is served, a steak knife will be placed to the right of the dinner knife which is closest to the plate. If you see a fork and/or spoon above your plate, they are the dessert utensils. A goblet of water is toward the upper right of your setting. If the table is set with a coffee cup and saucer, it is placed on your right, above the spoons. It should have a spoon resting on the saucer. If anything is missing, you may ask a server or hostess politely for the utensil you need. *(See illustration on pages 290 & 292.)*

There are occasions when the table is not set exactly right. I attended a Minister's Wives Luncheon at a conference recently and was quite amused to see that the napkin was placed in the coffee cup between each place setting. The tables were round and quite crowded. We had a difficult time figuring out whose cup belonged to whom. If we were to follow the general rule, I would have plucked my napkin from my neighbor's cup, all in good sport, of course. Such as it was, we were so confused, the lady on the farthest side of the table was wondering where in the world her napkin went. After we found it in an abandoned cup, we settled down to a very delicious lunch. If you find yourself in a situation like this, you may have to smile and go with the flow. Realizing that everyone else is just as confused as you are is a great consolation.

## Casual Dining

Casual dining has become more and more popular. This is probably because people are eating out more and making choices that are easier on their pocket books. Also, we live in such a fast-paced society, many just eat and run, finding fast-food more convenient. What do you do when you are headed down to the nearest fast-food restaurant? Well, I wouldn't suggest forsaking all manners just because you have to stand in line to get your food and fill your own paper cup with soda.

Casual dining does not require any special attire. In most eating establishments, men must wear shirts and everyone are required to wear shoes. This doesn't seem to be a problem with Christians, since our men usually wear shirts in public anyway. Shoes or sandals should be worn anytime you go out in public (unless you are wading in the ocean or lake).

Being courteous to others while waiting line probably comes naturally. If you are the guest of someone else, as you approach the cashier, stand aside a little to make sure they intend to pay for your meal. There is nothing more embarrassing than someone who presumes to be on your bill, when you don't have the money to cover the expenses. Usually your host or hostess will encourage you to order first, or they may go ahead and then say, "Please order what you like," or "Go ahead, I'm treating today." It is good to say, "Thank you," and then order. When the meal is finished, you can thank them again.

Many fast-food restaurants allow you to wait on yourself for the condiments. Unless the person you are with offers to get your condiments, you will be expected to wait on yourself.

Let your host pick a place to sit, or ask if he or she has a preference. You can decide where to sit when you are the one who pays. Being courteous and mindful of other's needs makes you a popular guest no matter what type of dining you are engaged in.

Another type of casual dining is the picnic. As a guest invited for a picnic, it is perfectly in order to ask your host if you may bring something to contribute to the meal. Many times you may be able to supply the ice and cold drinks, or a bag of chips, with a few different kinds of dip. Usually your host will supply the tablecloth, napkins, utensils, plates, and cups. If your host is a single man, he may not have thought of these necessities and it would be safe to ask if he needs any of them. It would be a challenge to eat potato salad on a napkin, or worse yet, in your hands!

## Dining in Someone's Home

Casual dining in someone's home is usually very relaxed. Often the food is served on paper plates with a serve-yourself type meal. As the guest in this situation, you may offer to help with any part of the meal the hostess agrees to. This type of dining is usually done when several friends get together and go to a particular home after church. Casual dining is excellent for a holiday barbecue, or an informal get-together to introduce and meet new friends. Whatever the reason, it can be a wonderful time of fun, relaxation, and fellowship.

Semi-formal meals served in someone's home are more formal occasions. The host and hostess will provide the entire meal, and many times will refuse to let you help with the clean up. It is proper etiquette for the hostess to refuse the guest's offer to help at a semi-formal or formal meal. However, this could develop into a very difficult situation. I have experienced hostesses refusing my help at the beginning of the meal, insisting I relax after the meal with an obvious undercurrent of resentment. Being ignorant of proper etiquette, I was taught to **always** help clean up, so I would insist on helping. I never knew what to do. Some hostesses would let me help, while others were offended if I insisted.

After several uncomfortable experiences, I tried to understand the hostess's true intentions. If the hostess begins to clean up before you leave, it is a good indication that she doesn't mean what she says and she really does want some help cleaning up. A hostess who does not want any help will usually go with you to the living room where you can visit and she will do the chores after you are gone.

If the hostess declines your help after a semi-formal dinner, do not feel guilty. This is an opportunity to be a gracious receiver when another is giving you the gift of hospitality. A thank you note should be sent after an evening of relaxation in someone's home always within a few days after the dinner.

Pentecostal etiquette allows for another style of dining. Although the traditional rules for semi-formal dining are more formal than casual, there is another style that may be situated between the two. This is when two families want to get together, share expenses, and have a semi-formal meal. In this setting, it is perfectly acceptable for the guest to offer to help shoulder the set-up and clean-up responsibilities. This may explain some of the confusing messages coming from a hostess when declining an offer of assistance with the meal.

*Notes*

# 50

## *The Extended Stay*

We have talked about being the hostess and how to treat guests in your home, but what if you are the guest? If you are in a situation where you will be staying in someone's home for more than a couple of weeks, consider yourself an extended guest. A review of some common courtesies will help your visit be extremely enjoyable, with the guarantee you will be invited to come again.

➤ Remember they have a schedule. Try to adjust your plans with your host and hostess' daily routine. If you don't have your own vehicle and you need a ride to the store, make a list and go when someone else is going.

➤ Offer to help with chores right away. Help lighten the load by offering to do the dusting or vacuuming. It is not a good idea to offer to wash their clothes unless you are familiar with their machines and have received instructions for garments that need special care from the hostess.

➤ Remember, you are not the lady of the house. This is her domain, let her be the queen. Help lighten her load, but try to do things her way. When she comes to your house, she should do the same for you.

➤ Be sensitive. If your hostess needs a few moments to rest after a day of work, give her time to relax before offering to start the salad for supper. It is not appropriate for a woman to allow a guest to work around her while she rests (unless of course she is convalescing). If you understand this, you will know that if you start puttering around in the kitchen, she will be obligated to get up and assist you.

➢ If your host and hostess are invited to go to a dinner party and you are not included, graciously let them know that you will be fine for a few hours alone. Take the time to read that new book you brought along, do some mending, or work on a craft you have been eager to start.

➢ When you leave, offer to change the bed linens. If your hostess refuses, you may remove them, pull the spread up over the mattress cover and lay the soiled sheets at the foot of the bed.

➢ If you are there over two weeks, offer to help with the groceries, unless you are in the home to perform a requested duty (nursing the sick, preaching a revival, or baby-sitting the children while the parents are away).

➢ Be sure to send a thank you note to express your gratitude and let them know how much you enjoyed your visit.

# 51
# *The Evangelist's Wife*

Many times the evangelist's wife finds herself the proverbial *man without a country*. She is tossed from pillar to post, from hotel room to evangelist's quarters, to pastor's home, etc. She may not know what kind of lodgings she will be subjected to next. Hopefully, it will be clean and warm (or cool in the summer)!

## The Calling

If you are the type of person who thrives in the midst of a new adventure and loves to meet new people, evangelizing may be the next thing to Heaven for you. Called to be an Evangelist's wife? **No Problem!** On the other hand, if you are the wife that adjusts poorly to new surroundings, evangelizing can be nothing short of a nightmare at its best. How far does *the calling* expect you to go? Doesn't the Bible say somewhere that God wouldn't put more on us than we could bear? Are you wondering how much more you can bear? Are you ready to break under the load?

If you have asked yourself these questions with a feeling of despair, what you need is a shot in the arm of confidence—not confidence in yourself—confidence in God. He has brought you right here, right now for a purpose. No matter how "unqualified" you may feel, God chooses the right tools for the job. When a carpenter builds a house, he carries a pouch filled with tools. "Why so many?" one may ask. Because each tool is tailored to do a specific job—he needs each one! God has chosen you to do what you are doing because you are the perfect tool!

Let's establish what your calling is. You may say that you were never called to travel. God never prepared you for this! That sweet man you married is the one who was called to evangelize! And, well—this just isn't fair!

> *And He answered and said to them, "Have you not read that He who made them at the beginning 'made them male and female,' and said, 'For this reason a man shall leave his father and mother and be joined to his wife, and the two shall become one flesh'? So then, they are no longer two but one flesh. Therefore what God has joined together, let not man separate (Matthew 19:4-6).*

When you vowed to honor, cherish, and obey "till death do us part," you promised to keep the commandments of the Lord. You became "one flesh" with your husband. There is no longer a separation of calling. Your ministry is one. Whatever God called your husband to do, you are a part of that flesh and will naturally be at his side. You wouldn't leave a leg at home when you go shopping just because it is tired! You would either stay home until the leg feels better or limp along to the mall! It is the same in marriage. Being one flesh means sharing the same calling.

Technically, your "calling" is sitting in the chair across the breakfast table from you, with his face buried in the newspaper. As the spiritual leader of your home it is natural for God to impress upon your husband the direction of His will. As the wife, you must learn to trust the decisions and direction your husband leads. This takes a lot of pressure off the wife and is very pleasing to God, not to mention pleasing to the husband.

The wife is the helpmeet or helper in the marriage. (See Genesis 2:18.) An embittered, angry evangelist's wife will destroy her husband's ministry, but a happy, contented, evangelist's wife will support her husband's ministry and help him be the successful minister God intended. Do you want to be married to a successful man? It just may be up to you to help him get there.

### Dealing with Shyness

The social aspect of traveling may be a fearful prospect. Is meeting new people difficult for you? Just like anything else, practice makes perfect. As you make the effort, it will get easier for you. Try taking it one person at a time.

Usually, you will have the opportunity to meet the pastor's wife before church. If you don't, she understands that you are the stranger and will usually be most congenial. When you go to church, find the pastor's wife and ask if you may sit with her. Many times she will ask first. This will give you a little more confidence because she will be able to introduce you to the others. Don't worry about remembering everyone's name the first night. You will catch on. Take one at a time, repeat their name after you are introduced. Be sweet and smile a lot. That's all you have to do. People are drawn to others who smile. I can't think of a better thing to hide behind.

My sister Jolene was very shy when she was young. In fact, when we had guests in our home, she would retreat to her room. I never knew until we were adults that many times she would sit on her bed alone and cry because she was too frightened to be around people. She had the fear of being ignored, or not being heard when she tried to speak, so she would never say anything. Many years she lived in misery.

The sad day came when Daddy excitedly announced that our family was going to go evangelizing as a gospel family band. All Jolene could think of was that her nightmare had only begun. She was mortified to think how she was going to deal with this. At first, she found refuge in our youngest sister and me. She would stay around us; two very talkative, outgoing personalities! She had it made! She never had to say a word, we did all the talking. But the time came when she was caught on the opposite side of the church and we were no where around. Then she had to do the talking. As time went on, after a lot of prayer and practice, it became a little easier for her. She was forced into a situation that cured her shyness.

Years later, Jolene began selling *Tupperware*. I was amazed to find out that she was doing great giving these parties from house to house! My, this was a different woman from that shy, scared little girl who was my sister! Today, you would never know she ever had a shy day of her life. She is a confidant, gracious woman who makes those around her feel comfortable. She has learned that she doesn't have to do all the talking—thank goodness! Many people just need an ear; and she is a great listener who has many, many friends.

## The Outgoing Person

The evangelist's wife who has no problem in this area may struggle on the opposite end of the spectrum. Staying in someone's home is easy for you. You love to meet new people and see new places. Being in a different environment challenges you to adapt for a moment or two, and then you have it down. You are indeed a blessed woman. You have the perfect personality for evangelizing. You have no problem chatting away after church with everyone. If these things come easy for you, your difficulty may be talking too much. You must be careful not to carry gossip from one pastor's home to another. Many times you will be told things that you are just *dying* to tell someone else. If it is going to hurt someone, or spread evil gossip, you had better keep it to yourself. Check these three things before you repeat anything about someone else.

➤ Does it edify the person you are talking about?

➤ Does it edify the person you are telling it to?

➤ Does it edify Christ?

> *Therefore let us pursue the things which make for peace and the things by which one may edify another (Romans 14:19).*

> *Therefore comfort each other and edify one another, just as you also are doing (1 Thessalonians 5:11).*

### Help! I'm in someone else's home!

The nature of your work calls for a more relaxed atmosphere when you stay in the pastor's home. Although you may only be in the pastor's home for a week, your responsibilities as a guest are the same as an extended guest. *(See The Extended Guest on page 335.)*

During the time you are staying in the minister's home, there are some responsibilities you can shoulder that will be a blessing to the pastor's wife. It is good to remember that the life of the pastor and his family goes on even during revival. Many have to work full-time jobs and pastor at the same time. This makes it difficult to entertain guests on a 24-7 (twenty-four hours, seven days a week) basis. Others pastor full-time and devote the days of the revival to the needs of the evangelist. The spectrum of diversity is wide. You will not be able to anticipate what any one pastor's family will do. A few basic rules will put you at ease and help establish a protocol with the pastor's wife.

## Dinner Help

As we have already mentioned, helping at dinnertime is a delicate area. Most people don't fellowship like we do. We spend more time together at each other's tables or at restaurants, than the average unchurched family member. Normally, (that is, according to etiquette books) when someone hosts a dinner party, the guests do not help with the meal or clean up. As an evangelist's wife, this situation is not necessarily a normal one, as the way normality goes in etiquette. Here is another example where "Pentecostal Etiquette" may differ from traditional.

You may attend a dinner in the pastor's home for five consecutive evenings, or be staying in their home for all the meals. The fact is, after the first dinner, you are more than a guest; you are now a fellow-partner with the pastor's wife in the role you both play for the success of a revival or crusade. You are a guest, but at the same time you are serving the pastor and his wife in a position of ministry.

When I was younger, our family evangelized, traveling all over the country singing and preaching. It was a wonderful time in my life. I will never forget my Dad drilling us girls to get up and offer to help the hostess with the dishes after a delicious meal. It became second nature to us. Several times we hustled the pastor's wife and my mother out of the kitchen after supper, to sit in the living room and relax. My sisters and I cleaned up the meal and did the dishes. I remember one pastor's wife exclaiming, "I've never been treated this good." We left her home feeling so good, as though we had given her something valuable. Little did we know the precious gift we had given her. Showing kindness to someone who sacrifices for your enjoyment is putting action to the words, "thank you."

Sometimes the Pastor's wife will decline help with fixing the dinner but welcome assistance after dinner. She often feels awkward accepting help with meal preparations. When this happens, it is good to find a few small tasks, like putting ice in the glasses, and take the initiative to see if she really does not want or need your help. After the meal, when you see the pastor's wife start clearing dishes from the table, it is an indication that you may begin to help also. Gather dishes close to you and carry them to the kitchen. That will give her the opportunity to either express appreciation or for her to choose to clean up later or alone. If you are staying in the pastor's home, never leave the kitchen a mess without offering to help clear the table and clean up the dirty dishes before leaving.

**Tips to Lighten the Load**

Set the pastor's wife at ease! Let her know that you will help with anything around the house during your stay. It is polite for you to offer, then it is her decision whether she accepts or declines. You may ask to vacuum if you get up one morning and see her dusting or doing laundry.

Try to keep your room neat and tidy, making your bed each morning. It is a challenge to live out of a suitcase, but if you practice some discipline such as putting your clothes away immediately after undressing, it will help keep your area clean.

Whether you share the main bathroom with others of the household or you have your own private one, it is good to be sensitive about keeping it clean also. Do not store your toiletries in a bathroom that others will be using also, unless the hostess insists or has a small storage area vacant for guests' things. Ask the lady of the house what to do with damp towels. Some wash each towel after a single use; others use a towel several times before washing it.

## Traveling With a Recreational Vehicle

If you are fortunate enough to have a travel trailer or motor home, count your blessings. Part of our traveling experience was without a trailer, but the majority of the time we had our own living quarters. When our children were small, the trailer was a real blessing.

### *Hermit Always* versus *Howdy Always*

Privacy is a wonderful commodity that comes with traveling in your own facility. It would be easy, however, to lock yourself away and deprive your host and hostess of your company. Refrain from enjoying your privacy so much that you forget to be a blessing to the pastor and his wife on a social level.

After service each night of the revival, many pastors invited us to go to a restaurant or to their home for a time of fellowship. Many times I was tired and my children were ready to go to bed, but my husband would lovingly remind me that this part of our ministry was as important as praying in the altar with sinners, or singing a special during the service. I knew his conviction was right. We were now moving into the most important part of our ministry—ministering to the ministry.

Many pastors and their wives live in remote cities that have no close churches with which to fellowship. These ministers and their wives need the fellowship of people of "like faith," and "like ministry." Being a pastor and wife can be a lonely life in these areas because of the caution needed in making casual friends with the congregation. The pastor and his wife need someone they can talk to and confide in. They have to be careful to shelter the flock God has given them. If a pastor or his wife were to confide in a member of the congregation or become too familiar with that person, it could cripple the confidence he/she has in the ministry, causing eternal damage to that precious saint. If they have no other ministers in their church with which they can let their hair down, so to speak, the evangelist is a refreshing friend they can laugh, cry, and fellowship with.

In contrast with pastors who need and welcome your fellowship long into the night, there are those who cannot spend the time with you for various reasons. A full-time job may keep a pastor busy during the day. By the time he gets home, has supper and attends church, he is exhausted and just wants to go to bed. By all means, honor this without offense. It is not because they don't *want* to spend the time with you; it is because they don't *have* the time to spend with you. If you are visiting after church over some coffee or small snack and you notice the pastor's wife nodding off, a simple suggestion of your wish to retire may be just the relief she needs. Their schedule does not change when you pull into town. Daily schedules, meetings, phone calls, school, and other responsibilities continue for the pastor and his wife in addition to the revival. Being sensitive to their lifestyle is a wonderful virtue.

**Grocery List**

If you have a recreational vehicle and love to cook, or if the pastor and his wife are unable to host you in their home, many times they will ask you to make out a grocery list of things you need. It is important to be sensitive to several things before indulging in a long list of items.

1. Take into consideration the kind of ***budget*** the pastor and his wife live under. Try not to be too extravagant, asking for expensive items or asking for more than you can use during the time of your stay. This is not a chance to restock your pantry. Take into consideration if you eat all the meals in your quarters or eat your main meal with the pastor and a few others in your own trailer. If you are only eating breakfast in your quarters, it is unfair to put grocery items for dinner on your list. An exception to this would be if the pastor or pastor's wife makes it clear that they want to bless you with groceries to use after your initial stay with them.

2. If there are a few "***name brand***" items you prefer, it is better not to include them on your list unless

the pastor's wife suggests you do so. This gives the appearance of a finicky, picky person, rather than a grateful guest.

## Dining Out with the Pastor

Many places you go, the pastor and his wife will take you and your husband out to eat. This may be on a daily basis at some churches and only occasionally at others. Because of the fact that dining out involves your husband as much as it does you, I have tried to include a few etiquette notes to help you both in difficult situations.

It is the pastor's responsibility as a host to invite you and pay for the meal. If you prefer to offer to pay for the meal or help, let the first experience set the precedent. If the pastor chooses to pay for the meal the first time and refuses your monetary help, it is no longer necessary for you to continue to offer in subsequent dinner engagements during the same revival. Do not feel resentment toward the pastor if he allows you to help pay for the dinner when you offer.

There is a certain amount of pride for a pastor to feel he is "taking care of the evangelist." It is gracious on your part to let him do so. Although it is a common practice, it is not proper etiquette to ask if you may pay the tip. A tip is hardly enough to justify "helping" with the meal and appears only as an insult to the graciousness of the host. If a pastor suggests you do so, it would be better to oblige, rather than educate him on the proper etiquette. Unless the suggestion going "Dutch" has been made clear, it is proper to assume your host or hostess is going to pick up the tab *(For more etiquette on dining out, see Chapter 41).*

On occasion, you will find a pastor that fails to make himself clear about your meals. In this situation, it is understandable that you will need to ask some questions to find out what your obligations are. At the time of ordering, if you will ask the waiter to put your order on a separate ticket, this will give the pastor a little time to get the hint that you are unsure of his intentions. If he does not intervene, you should cheerfully follow through with buying your own meal and leaving your own tip. The same principles apply when the pastor's wife invites the evangelist's wife out to lunch.

## Dining Out with Saints

When saints approach you offering to take you out to dinner or after church, you should ask if they have talked to the pastor. If they have, then you go to the pastor privately and ask how he feels about this. If they have invited the pastor to go along, that is the most comfortable situation. If the pastor has not been invited, you may suggest that they be invited. Kindly remind the people inviting you out, that you are here on the invitation of the pastor, therefore, you are his guest. Although you would love their company, you just could not go without the pastor also.

If you discover that an old friend is attending a church where you are ministering and she has asked to take you to lunch while you are there, the same rules apply. Many times the pastor has no problem with a saint taking out an old friend, but it is important to make sure before you accept.

If the pastor's wife is invited to go along, you can still have a wonderful time reminiscing about old times, but do not forget, she was not there when you were "pals, running around" back then. Keep her involved in the conversation by looking her way when you talk and asking questions. She may decline to accompany you, telling you to go ahead and have fun. If that is the case, do as she says!

Some pastors genuinely don't care if you go out with the saints. In larger churches, the pastor may designate different families to entertain you during the revival. In this case, have a good time with old friends and also new ones that ask you out. Listed below are some important points to keep in mind when dealing with other people's saints, whether they are your personal friends or not.

1. Never talk against the pastor or his pastoring philosophies.

2. Avoid discussing theological controversies that may conflict with the pastor's teachings.

3. Never accept money from saints without the pastor's knowledge.

4. Do not invite the saints to your next revival. If they suggest coming, encourage them to ask their pastor first.

## What Do I Do In Church?

### The Musician

If you play the piano, organ, tambourine, or another instrument, it is best to wait to be asked before presuming to

play during the service. Some smaller churches love to have the evangelist's wife play for the service. This can be very tiring, but if you feel it would give the regular pianist a break and she would enjoy the revival more, the Lord will bless you for it. Granted, everything usually runs more smoothly when they continue in the same manner in which they are accustomed, but if they insist, be gracious and try to do your best.

It is never appropriate to suggest playing for the song service just because you are a more experienced musician. Enjoy the service, worship the Lord and when your time comes to play for a special, or for your husband, try to be humble, reverencing the Lord in your talents. A proud spirit can be spotted a mile off when it comes from a musician on the platform. It is very important not to participate in the spirit of competition that plagues many Christian musicians in our churches today. The effectiveness of your ministry in the church will be compromised if others sense a condescending spirit of superiority. A woman with an humble attitude, offering her talents to the Lord in an effort to propel His purpose in every service will be rewarded with the dividend of many souls.

If you are the type of person that feels inferior to other musicians, playing is a chore and your "plunking" may be hindering the spirit, you may be surprised to learn how valuable you really are. When my husband and I were evangelizing, I played the keyboard or piano and sang. Before his sermon, I would play the keyboard; after his sermon, I would play the organ. I was not as good on the organ, because I had not played it as long as the keyboard, but my husband liked it during the altar services.

Many times I would play for hours, watching wonderful things happen in the altar. But I felt detached, unconnected, and very unsure that I was contributing anything to the real cause of the Kingdom of God. I never had the chance to pray anyone through to the Holy Ghost because I was stuck on the organ. I never had the opportunity to shout all over the front of the church with a backslider finding her way back home. I was a prisoner of the music needed at the altar service. I had a great pity party for many months, all by myself.

Nobody seemed to understand, until one revival we were in Oklahoma City, preaching for Pastor R. D. Whalen. Their daughter, Patty, was the church organist, and she could make that thing talk! Really! In my opinion, she is absolutely the best organist I have ever heard.

My husband always wanted me to play after he preached. I was horrified to think I would be sitting at the organ, plodding through my simple chords while Patty stood on the side and had to suffer listening! "Please," I begged, "don't make me play. Just let me pray in the altar. That's what I've wanted to do! I want to really be a blessing." My husband was not sympathetic at all. "If you don't play, I don't preach," he stubbornly stated. Needless to say, I reluctantly shuffled to the organ that night and began playing my simple little songs. I felt humiliated! This poor congregation was used to the best and now they had to listen to me—for hours!

As I sat mulling over my dilemma, Sister Whalen quietly slipped beside me on the bench. I was afraid she was going to give me some tips on how to improve my playing, but to my relief she didn't; I should have known better. Instead she said, "Sister Baughman, I want to thank you for being such a blessing to my daughter, Patty." I looked to the left. I looked to the right. I could not see Patty anywhere. Where was she?

Before I could form the question Sister Whalen pointed to a group of girls pouring their little hearts out to God; Patty was in the middle of them. "That is her Sunday school class. She never gets to pray with them because she is always playing the organ. Thank you so much for giving her this opportunity. It means so much to her."

Sister Whalen had no idea the blessing she was to me, thanking me for being a blessing to someone else. I have learned to thank the Lord for using me even with my limited talents. When you give what little you have to Him, He multiplies it and makes it a great blessing to someone else! Keep singing; keep smiling; keep praying; keep playing. Some day the results of your meager efforts will be unveiled and the reward will be in the shape of a crown.

**The Musically Challenged**

It would be easy to feel that if you do not play an instrument or sing, that you are just a "bench warmer" during each revival. If you choose to, you may be just that. But if you don't, the rewards and dividends are limitless. The evangelists' wives that have impressed me the most over the years were not necessarily the ones used in the area of music.

When I was a young girl, Cleveland Becton came to Idaho to preach our camp meeting several times. His wife, Margie Becton was the most exuberant, delightful preacher's wife. She would sit on the front pew, or close to it, and cheer her husband on! She was his number one fan! Every song he played was the best! She cried as she was moved when he played the beautiful songs "I Must Tell Jesus" and "What a Friend" on the accordion. Every sermon he preached was the best. From the first pew her voice was the loudest "amen." Then as the altar call was given, she was ministering and prayed for those responding to God's message through her husband. What an example!

Aaron and Nadine Thames pastored in Arizona and Texas for many years. In his later years, they evangelized, blessing churches with their seasoned ministry. Nadine Thames wrote a book of poems and prose. She was gifted with inspirational recitation. Before her husband spoke, she would go to the platform, recite one of her memorized pieces, leaving us in tears or raptured wonder. What a wonderful alternative she was to the "special song" before the sermon.

Music is only a small part of the larger ministry picture. Many ministers' wives find themselves among the musically challenged. This does not mean they cannot be greatly used in the ministry. There are many other things to do in the kingdom of God outside the music field.

➢*The artist's touch.* If you are an artist, offer to draw a poster or banner for the upcoming revival.

➢*Prepare a testimony or learn some beautiful poetry.* Talk it over with your husband and ask him to give you a few moments before his sermon to share a special writing or testimony. If you don't feel comfortable standing behind the pulpit, you can stand at your place. You can preach a mini-sermon through a poem or a thoughtfully prepared testimony that will stir the hearts of the people.

➢*Be a fire starter.* Every service needs a person who will be the lighter fluid for the fire. You've seen them. They are the first ones on their feet, the first ones to clap their hands, the first one to run the aisles. Why can't that be the evangelist's wife? Why can't that be you? You could be so sensitive to the moving of the Spirit that when a small spark flies, you catch it and **ignite!**

➢*Be an example of true worship.* As the service proceeds become a participator rather than a spectator. Show new converts how to worship. You may have had the Holy Ghost many more years than they, but don't let them out shout you.

➢*Work in the altar.* There is a need for experienced altar workers in every service from the hometown revival to the conference in a coliseum. There is no better place to feel the pulse of God's heart for revival than in an altar. Just as He walked among the sinners, forgiving them, you become the link, walking among them to help put their hand in Jesus' hand.

Think about what your talent is. Tailor the gift God has given you to a ministry. Ask yourself, "How can I use this for the kingdom of God?" Are you an artist, a musician, or a singer? Are you good at recitation? Has God given you the talent to be a good listener or to be a "people person?" Every talent has a place in the kingdom of God, and every one is vital, working together to create a complete effort. Begin to pray for an open door and look for opportunities to use that talent. You will be surprised at the unique way God can use you and your talent. Let Him give you ideas that come from Heaven!

# Part Nine

# The Pastor's Wife

# 52

# *The Roller Coaster Ride*

Did you ever dream you would be where you are today? Does the life you are living now even resemble the ideal life you had envisioned when you were single? Usually the answer to these questions is "no." Some pastors' wives knew the road they would travel at a young age. Others married young men, safe from the clutches of "the call," only to enter the ministry years later. Some feared going into the ministry while others wanted to be a part of it. Some had no clue what they wanted and it caught them off guard. Others were raised in ministers' homes so they were comfortable with the prospect. Whatever category you find yourself in, the reality of the road you are traveling may be quite different from the picture you imagined.

Not all our dreams turn out less than idealistic. Perhaps you can think of a few things that are going on in your life right now that are better than you could have ever imagined.

However, there are situations that turn your nice little drive into a roller coaster! You suddenly experience some ups and downs, good days and bad. You learn that life throws curves to the ministry just as to the laity, and you don't have any idea what may lie around the next corner. The problem is, you did not choose to get on this ride. You happened to marry this guy, and once you were connected,

357

or handcuffed together, he pulled you on the ministry roller coaster.

You are along for the ride, so hold on! It doesn't matter how much you kick and fuss, or cry and complain. You better stay put if you don't want to get hurt. If you plan to stay connected to that dreamboat husband of yours, you will buckle your seat belt and ride the bumps with him. You will go it together. Together—that sounds better. At least you don't have to go alone.

Now that we have established the fact that you didn't have a choice, whether you like the ride or not is up to you. You can choose to be miserable, making the trip unbearable for everyone around you, or you can choose to be happy. Happiness is a choice but be aware, it is very contagious. If your desire is to be effective, to touch lives, and to make a difference, it starts with a happy you. Let's face it, disappointment comes—so does failure, but failure is a teacher. In mathematical terms, the formula for success when the first equation results in failure is: (Try + Inexperience = Failure) X (Try again + Learned Experience) = **Success**.

$$(T + I = F) \times (TA + LE) = SUCCESS$$

If you never try again after failing, then you are a failure, but if you keep trying, you are learning—you will eventually succeed! Mark a failed project down to experience and move on. Many have failed before you and survived; you can too. Resolve yourself to happiness even after failure. If you cannot resolve yourself to happiness, every other area of your life will be affected.

## Happiness is a Choice

Happiness bubbles from within. It builds an exuberant pressure spilling out like an over-boiling saucepan onto the lives of those you come in contact with. It affects your children, your husband, your saints, and your community. Your children will be contented preacher's kids if your attitude about the ministry is presented in a positive light. They will learn to hate the ministry (and some saints) if your attitude is one of resentment. They will learn to love the ministry and the people it involves, if they can see that even through the rough times you have not lost your love and compassion for the work of God. Your saints will love the work of God if you can rejoice during adversity as well as blessing. The community will want to be a part of the Gospel because of the peace and happiness they see you represent.

> *"...counselors of peace have joy"*
> *(Proverbs 12:20b).*

You are a counselor of peace, a bearer of good tidings, spreading the Gospel to a lost world. Proverbs 12:19 says that if you proclaim truth your words will be established forever. No wonder you will have joy when you proclaim the Gospel. It is the good news that will help a hurting world. It is the only thing that offers hope in a world of hopelessness, life in a world of death and destruction, and joy in a world of sorrow and pain. In John 16:24 Jesus said to ask and receive, that your joy may be full. Ask God today for whatever you need to perform at your greatest potential. When you ask and receive, it increases your faith. Then your joy is multiplied over and over again until it is completely full! Ask the Lord to help you be a happy pastor's wife making a difference in the lives around you. He will answer your prayer and *fill* you with joy at the same time.

> *"...for the joy of the LORD is your strength"(Nehemiah 8:10b).*

Even when things don't go as smoothly as you wish and the roller coaster gets a little fast for your comfort, you will find that the joy of the Lord will be constant. Joy is the inner source from which you draw your strength. When you realize the joy of the Lord, happiness becomes the expression that reveals that joy to others. It makes them want what you have. They will listen more attentively to what you say, and they will watch more closely the way you live. They will glean everything they can from you because you have found the source of happiness—**Joy**!.

# *53*

# *Family Comes First*

## Your children

Life does get wild on this roller coaster. Sometimes the going gets so fast that you forget you have a family. It's like, who is that young man walking through the door? Just yesterday he was a toddler pulling at your dress hem. Or,

who is that beautiful young lady receiving her high school diploma or getting married? Just yesterday she was pretending to be a mommy, holding a doll in her arms. Time flies. Make the most of the time you have with your family. They come first. They are your closest mission field. If you reach out to the community and overlook your children, you are missing the rare opportunity to win a soul God has literally put smack-dab in your lap.

*Spend time with them* – All those projects at the church will wait. They will be there after you have spent the valuable time you need with your family. Your children need a mommy first, then a pastor's wife. Your husband needs a wife first, then a pastor's wife. Don't feel guilty saying, "I'm sorry, that is our family night," or "Thank you for the invitation, but I have reserved that time to be with my son or my daughter."

A pastor's wife shared an interesting perspective on the mess children make in the living room. One day, not long after her only daughter was married, she walked into the tidy living room. Everything was in place, it was as neat as a pin. Suddenly, an instant picture of toys strewn across the carpet flashed into her mind, stinging her eyes with tears. Oh, how she wished those toys were there now! Why had she wished away the clutter as though she wished away the years with it? If only she could buy more time to spend with her little girl. If she had it to do over again, she would sit in the floor and play with those same toys. She would spend more time playing "Mommy" with her baby. I've heard that hindsight is always twenty-twenty vision. Learning from someone else's experience is valued education for your present performance.

The next time you see a cluttered floor remember the lesson from this mother. Put her *past* experience in your *now* performance. Tell yourself, "Someday I will wish my child hadn't grown up so fast. I will make the most of each moment with her or him now." The next time you have to pick up a baby doll from the floor, allow the nasal-monotone, "mah-mah" be a memory-maker as it lands in the toy box. Remind yourself that exercise is good for your heart as you are bending over to retrieve a wooden block from underneath the couch. As you tiptoe precariously through a maze of tiny cars and brightly wrapped crayons that look like construction in rush hour traffic, thank God you're home and not out in it!

My husband and I started having mother-daughter and father-son days with our children when they were very young. I was not really sure how our children felt about this until one day my son came up to me and said, "Mommy, aren't we ever going to have a mother-son day?" I realized he wanted some time alone with me. From that time on, we started mother-son and father-daughter days also. One of these very special times was when my daughter went on her first date. Her sixteenth birthday date was with her daddy.

You will never regret the quality time you spend with your children. You may not have an entire day you can devote to them on a consistent basis, but the time you set aside for them will reap dividends all the money in the world cannot buy. The busier you are, the more valuable your time with your children will be. They know when you are busy, and they will analyze their importance to you by the time you sacrifice for them. Your children's self-acceptance is affected by the value you place on their company.

Sometimes children misbehave because they want attention, any kind of attention. If you will give them the attention they need, they will not try to attract your attention with bad behavior. I do not agree with the old adage, "Children are to be seen and not heard." If children are not heard, they will do something to be heard. Children should be treated with respect, just as an adult. If a child is used to being treated with respect, he will learn how to treat others the same way.

*Approve, Support, and Compliment them* – When children are young, a mother is the most important person in their lives. They need her approval, support, and public recognition. A balance of praise and instruction is most effective for perceptive learning. A child will even accept the bitter pill of correction when it is mixed with loving praise. Children need to know that whatever they do, whether right or wrong, they have your approval as a person. When they do something right, watch their little faces light up after a word of praise. Even when they do something wrong, a reassuring word will help remind them that your love and acceptance is not based on their performance. Your approval is of utmost importance to them.

Your children need your support. Heaven knows they get pressure from the saints. Without anyone saying anything, they feel pressure being the pastor's kids. They may not hear it from you, but someone is expecting them to be an example to the other children at church. After all, they are the pastor's kids. If you reassure them that you don't expect them to be perfect, they will be able to deal with the other pressures better. They need to know that it is all right to be normal, and normal kids make mistakes.

Children need to know when they make you proud. It is all right to compliment them in public. They may appear a little embarrassed, but knowing they have made you a proud parent is worth a few seconds of embarrassment. Older children love receiving cards and notes commending them on a job well done, or a reminder that you are proud they are part of the family and they are special to you. This should not take the place of verbal affirmation. Good kids need to hear that they are good.

*Feed them a balanced diet* – Many children are grabbing food on the run. You may need to set up a schedule so they will know when to sit down and have a meal with you and your husband. Sickness, lethargy, and other symptoms can be avoided with a balanced diet.

Children need a good breakfast to start their day. It helps them think better and perform better in school. Giving them a balanced diet starts good eating habits that will carry them through their older years. I worry about young people that never eat fruit and vegetables. These foods are a great source of vitamins and minerals. Without these important nutrients, our bodies cannot perform correctly. Eventually their lack will show up either in sickness, or low energy levels. There has been the suggestion that various fruit and vegetables may even help prevent some long-term diseases. Supplying your children with the correct nutrition from all the food groups may be all they need in the way of minerals and vitamins *(see page 42)*. If they are not getting a balanced diet you may want to supplement their diet with a multi-vitamin and mineral preparation with no more than 100% of the recommended daily allowances (RDAs) for healthy children.[1]

*Teach them respect* – I have heard saints complain about pastor's children lacking respectful attitudes toward other adults. (This is not to say that saints' children don't have the same problem.) It is never acceptable for children to treat adults with disrespect. I think all parents want their children to be liked and accepted. Disrespect among preachers' kids may not be the result of faulty teaching. Neglect in the area of observation may be the culprit. Paying attention to how your children treat others may be a great revelation. Always encourage them to answer in a respectful way even if they disagree. Being respectful is a lost art for many in our worldly society.

Children need to be respected by their parents. Many children were not even wanted at birth, let alone respected. When children feel no respect, the base to build reciprocation of respect is gone. In other words, treat your children with respect in order to teach your children to respect. You are the example, you are the base they will pattern after. Whatever happened to, "Yes ma'am, no sir, thank you and please?" These are not old-fashioned words. They are valuable tools to exercise respect for each other.

---

[1] *The American Medical Association New Family Medical Guide*, Charles B. Clayman, MD. Ed., (Random House, New York: 1994), 532-537.

Remind your child that he is special because he is God's child, not because he is the pastor's child. If he has the concept that he is on the same level as the saints' children, it will remove much of the pressure he may feel from critical saints. It will also nip a prideful, superior attitude in an extroverted over-confident child.

*Shelter them from church trouble* – There may be times when it is very difficult to hide church problems from your children. They will sense an undercurrent of dissension without you saying a word. If you uphold the saints in their eyes, there will probably never be a justifiable need for your children to become bitter or angry at the people you minister to.

Many preachers lose their young teenagers because of unfair small talk against the saints. It breeds a spirit of gossip, dissension, and disunity in a child that sprouts rebellion in the teen years. Do you wonder where that rebellion came from? It was born out of all the garbage and trash that was planted in his or her heart as a child. You will do your child the best service by sheltering him from anything that would cripple his faith in the people of God. Just as you would shelter saints from trouble, your children should also be spared the worry of church problems.

**Your Husband**

Society has robbed us of the privilege of taking care of our husbands. In this fast-paced world, women are involved in careers and are away from home as much as the man. Because of this, many men have had to do menial tasks that, in the past, women have taken pride in doing. One of these areas is helping with the laundry, another the cooking. Some men are very helpful, but others don't know the first thing about loading a washer or ironing a shirt.

366

Many suffer because they need women to look after them. (Of course, they don't know it yet!)

*Keep him looking good* – There are some husbands who wash and iron as well as the wife, but they are few and far between. Most men don't know the difference between a steam iron and a waffle iron. Have you ever gone to church and seen a husband's shirt wrinkled? Of course you would notice, you're a woman. He probably doesn't even notice. Our husbands need us. They need us to keep their shirts clean and pressed. If you cannot find the time to press your husband's shirts, send them to a laundry. They do a great job. Keeping his shirts white can be done easily with a little bleach. If they are real dingy, there is a product that whitens clothes beautifully. It is in a box just like fabric dye, but it removes color rather than dyes it. This works great for shirts that have been neglected or washed in hard water several times.

My husband can iron and wash as well as I can. But when I anticipate his need, and iron his shirt before he gets a chance to, I usually get a little extra attention later on. Don't

ask me how, but a woman is more appealing to her husband after she has ironed a shirt, cleaned the house or cooked a meal. Try this, iron several shirts the next day you have off and fix a nice meal. Notice how your husband treats you afterward. Your name may even be mentioned in the prayer before he eats. JOY!

Before your husband goes out the door, check to make sure he matches. Men have a tendency to think blue looks great with brown, and on rare occasions, it does. Be sure to compliment him when he makes a good choice.

Let him know when his hair is getting a little shaggy. If your husband looks good, you will too! The woman in Proverbs 31 knew how to take care of her husband. In fact, he was known in the gates. Do you think he would have dared go to this busy important place with a wrinkled, dirty shirt? I think not!

*Keep him eating right* – You may have some help preparing the meal, but be sure to take note of how your husband is eating. If you take the responsibility of caring for his nutritional needs, he will probably eat what you fix. Low fat, high fiber diets are more healthy for the heart, tending to lower cholesterol. With the stress of being a pastor, there is plenty of pressure on your husband's heart without added cholesterol pressure. If you want to keep him around, help him eat healthier meals.

*Let him be the pastor* – You and your husband are a team, it is true, but there are some things he should handle alone. Some pastors' wives make everybody's business their own. They take pride in the fact that there are no secrets between them and their husbands. There are times when a pastor *should* keep a secret, even from his wife. When he is told something in confidence, it is important that he honor that confidence. Only a meddling wife will pressure her husband to break a confidence. I admire the pastor that can be trusted, one who is worthy of confidence.

When you are asked to be present during counseling, spend some time laying groundwork that will be consistent with your husband's counsel. For example, you would not want to contradict your husband in front of someone he is counseling. For that matter, you should never contradict your husband in public. It demeans him as a person, and it lowers the standard of his position as pastor. In public, it is vital that you uphold your husband at all times. Never argue, bicker, or raise your voice at him in public.

When you are in church, it is easy to let your feelings be read on your facial expressions. An immature teenager will do this to get a message across. But a mature adult need not revert to such immature tactics. Be careful to keep a sweet, kind expression no matter what the situation. If you want to express yourself to your husband in the privacy of your home later, that is your prerogative.

I watched in horror as a pastor and his wife argued on the platform in front of an entire congregation. I was embarrassed and felt sorry for the congregation. It put us all in a very awkward situation. If the wife had closed her mouth, smiled, and given in to her husband, it would have accomplished two things. One, it would have shortened the misery for everyone and two, it would have been a visual lesson in submission to the women observing. Whether she was right or wrong, she was an example to all the women in the church. Unfortunately, she was not an example of submission. God will bless the pastor's wife who will uphold her husband in public with no thought of her own feelings.

# Notes

# 54

# *Entertaining Responsibilities*

We have covered many general areas of social graces while entertaining. I will not reiterate what I have covered in previous chapters, but the following are some areas that are relevant specifically for the pastor's wife.

Hospitality plays a major part in the life of a pastor's wife whether or not she feels comfortable with it. After you have organized a Sunday "dinner on the ground," entertained  an evangelist for two weeks, served refreshments after thirteen home Bible studies, and baked four pies for the bake sale, you may become a little overwhelmed; suffering fatigue and possible burn out. Don't panic. It is normal to have those feelings when you find yourself in a whirlwind of activities.

You need to re-fuel. If you continue to run on the energy you have, it will soon run out and you will be exhausted. Just like a car needs fuel, you need to find a time when you just sit back, relax, and let the Lord fill you up. A car won't run if it is empty; neither can you give of yourself if you are empty. When you stop long enough for God to replenish your spirit, you can return with fresh, new vitality.

Take a little time and relax away from home if you can. Ask your husband to take you to the next town and get a motel. Go somewhere away from the phone, the children, and the saints. You will feel much more refreshed and ready to face the next entourage of guests.

### The Visiting Minister's Wife

Do you feel like you are running a Bed and Breakfast rather than just a normal home? If you are sitting in the recliner reading a magazine and a stranger walks through the house, fear not, your husband probably just invited the neighboring pastor's evangelist home with him. You may not feel too gracious at that moment, but you can gracefully acknowledge his presence and make him feel at home. Attempt to hide your surprise at him being there. The Bible does not command minister's wives to be instant in season or out, but many times we have to be just that.

First-time visiting ministers may be reserved at first. There is a possibility that their wives may feel apprehensive as though they are "barging in" on you. You can make them feel wanted or unwanted by your initial reaction to their presence. Greet them with a warm smile and a friendly attitude. If you meet them for the first time just before church, ask the evangelist's wife to sit with you. This will make her feel more comfortable, especially if she is a stranger to your church. If she has a child, you may ask if she needs someone to watch him or her while she participates on the platform. You may offer your services, or find a kind person who loves children, to help her during services.

I wish you could meet my mother. Traveling ministers seem to migrate toward her home when they have nowhere else to go. Mama always has a place for them. They must feel at home, because many of them call her "Mom" or their children call her "Grandma." When my parents were pastoring, I remember Mama referring to young evangelist couples as "my kids," making them feel like part of the family.

Mama has always had a talent with people. I have tried to observe the things she does to pass them along to others. Mama is not a gourmet cook, nor is she the most meticulous housekeeper. Her talent is the loving, gentle way she deals with people. She is unselfish with her time and her possessions. She spends quality time with people. When someone approaches her after church, Mama stops and gives that person her full attention. If someone walks up during a conversation with another, she will reach out and touch the newcomer's arm or some other gesture to acknowledge her and let her know she is next.

Mama is free with compliments. If she thinks something nice, she usually says it. She is unselfish with her home. She always has a house full. It doesn't bother her to be saddled with overnight company at the last minute. She will have a room ready, with fresh linen before she needs it. She is unselfish with her food. She does not get offended if her guests go to the refrigerator and make themselves at home; she encourages them to do so.

Over the years, her warm hospitality has been a welcome homecoming for young evangelists and their wives that had no home. They found a place in her home with a sense of belonging; a major need for couples living out of suitcases.

You may be able to do all the right things: cook a delicious meal, set the table perfectly, and serve dinner on time, but helping your guests feel at home is the most important element of hospitality. A guest can detect almost immediately if you are uncomfortable with people in your home. Company will feel only as comfortable as you do. They will relax if you are relaxed, and they will come back if you welcome them.

Working a full-time job and fixing meals for an evangelist family during revival can be quite stressful. The ideal situation would be to solicit help from the ladies in the church. Each day a different lady could bring pre-cooked food to your home and stay to help with pre-dinner duties. Many women in the church enjoy contributing to the revival in this way. A woman with an unsaved-husband may not be able to support the revival in offerings, but may view this as a wonderful opportunity to contribute. Of course, this will need to be planned ahead of time.

Many times the evangelist's wife will offer to help you with something. There is nothing wrong with accepting the invitation of assistance. An evangelist's wife is in your home for several consecutive meals, so mealtime help is appropriate. It is up to you whether you choose to accept or not, but don't be offended when she goes to the living room to read a magazine if you decline. Also, don't be surprised if she does not offer again. If you would prefer to have help with the clean up you could say something like, "I don't need any help right now, but I may need some assistance after dinner so we can be on time for church." This leaves the option open for help later. If you prefer to do the preparation of the meal and clean up by yourself, make it clear that she is free to sit down, read, or pull up a chair and talk to you while you work. At the end of the meal, do not start washing the dishes unless you are willing to accept help from your guest. If she has a baby and an emergency comes up, let her know that you understand her baby comes first.

 Many times, larger churches are able to afford luxury accommodations for an evangelist in a nice hotel arranging meals in a nearby restaurant. This lifts much of the burden of entertaining from the shoulders of the pastor's wife. If this is your situation, although it may save a lot of stress, you must be careful to avoid the possibilities of the evangelist and his wife feeling detached or isolated. A "hospitality basket" is a good suggestion to help make them feel welcome. Arrange to have a large decorated fruit basket waiting for them in the room when they arrive. A variety of healthy snacks, bottled water, and fruit are among some of the suggestions for a "hospitality basket."

If you feel comfortable inviting an evangelist and his wife to your home, either for dinner before church or for a snack afterward, that is acceptable. If not, dining together at a restaurant gives them an opportunity to get to know you better. You are not obligated to have them over every evening, but you must make your intentions known right away so they will know what is expected of them.

**Forsaking Your Privacy**

I'm sure you have heard before that since you are married to a pastor, you live in a glass house. Everything you do will be broadcast on the public address system of neighbors' and friends' word of mouth. You may feel that you live in a see-through house, but being a pastor's family does not require that you forsake all privacy. You must preserve as much privacy as you possibly can.

Involvement in home missions is the most difficult situation to preserve privacy, especially if you are having services in your home. Draw some boundaries and limits. Let the people attending services in your home know where the boundaries are. Reminders are usually only necessary with small children. Most adults won't go wandering into your bedroom or pantry. If you have a designated area where you have your meetings each time, they will get used to the area dedicated to the church.

Living in a parsonage next door to the church is the next challenge to privacy. Many times people will ask for things that are not available at the church. You may or may not feel comfortable letting people use the telephone, get drinks, or warm their hamburgers in your microwave. This will have to be determined by individual preference. You may want to sit down with your husband and decide where to draw the line. Another consideration is to be careful not to get something started that will be a problem later on. A few guidelines are:

➢ Does it infringe upon your private life?
➢ Does it interrupt your meals?
➢ Does it keep you up, depriving you from sleep? (i.e., after service or on Sunday afternoons.)
➢ Can it be taken care of somewhere else? (i.e., restroom facilities, telephone, refrigerator, garden hose, ladder, etc.)
➢ Is it becoming a habit?
➢ Do you feel you are losing control of your home?
➢ Is it causing problems with your children? (i.e., nap time for babies and toddlers; children inviting friends over without permission.)
➢ Is it an unnecessary added expense? (i.e., water, electricity, food.)

**Lower your stress level**
Many pastor's wives suffer anxiety attacks and have great difficulty dealing with stress. Your ability to function will be challenged if you succumb to stress. You will find

that you can't think straight, make rational decisions, and many times become physically sick.

Save your heart and reduce your stress level. Anxiety, fear and worry rob you of your peace. Many times, fear of what the future holds causes anxiety. Taking one minute at a time will help lighten the load. Here are a few creative ways to reduce your stress level and rid yourself of anxiety.

1. *Be yourself* – trying to play the role of someone you are not creates more stress because you are not being yourself.

2. *Take one project at a time* – Start with the most important or most difficult task and continue from there. Make a list and cross each completed task off for a feeling of accomplishment.

3. *Be realistic* – Some things you can change and others you cannot. Accept the fact that you are not expected to change things you cannot.

4. *Don't procrastinate* – Putting off a necessary or unpleasant task will only prolong your misery. Make a positive decision to take care of the problem and move on to the next project on your list.

5. *Choose your friends wisely* – Seek out people who are pleasant, and affirmative. True friends are those who love you even when you are wrong, but will not hesitate to let you know how to get back on the right track.

6. *Admit your fears* – Find out what your fears are and try to reason through their origin. Talk to a trusted friend and ask God to help you overcome these fears.

7. *Work on a realistic self-image* – You have both weak and strong points. Admit your weaknesses and ask God to help you overcome them. As you work through your weaknesses, realize that you will not be able to do everything well—no one can. Accept your strengths and build on them. Allow God to use your strengths to help you excel in these areas.

8. *Be willing to compromise* – Be flexible with situations that can be compromised. Rigid refusal to give in only causes stress.

9. *Reach for balance in your life* – Try to balance work with pleasure, physical exercise with relaxation, and spending with saving.

10. *Reach out to others* – It is easier to forget about your problems when you are helping someone else.

11. *Slow down* – Make yourself slow down physically. Walk slower, talk slower, and eat slower. You will feel less pressure.

12. *Talk it through* – Take time to talk to your husband or a trusted friend. Talk about things that are unclear to you. Many times just having a sounding board helps to clear the air and your mind.

13. *Get away* – Take a few moments each day to be alone. Relax and think about your day. Make time for this even if you have to get up a little earlier to find time without interruptions.

14. *Find an activity that reduces stress* – Swimming, biking, listening to music, and reading are just a few of the things you can do to reduce tension.

Make time to include one in each day, even if it is for a short time.

15. *Have coffee or tea with the Lord* – Take a few moments each day to have devotions. Rise a few moments earlier to have a cup of coffee with God. Save the newspaper for later in the day. Start your busy activities with the Word of God rather than the problems of the world.

## *Notes*

# *55*

# *In the Church*

**The First Lady**

You are the *First Lady* of the church. On various occasions different saints will honor you with special tribute. Accept such gifts as compliments on your leadership. Let them treat you like the first lady. Fill the role proudly and honorably. Of course you know it is not all honor, for there is some grit and grime that goes with serving others. In fact, you don't have just one person to answer to, but you have a whole group of ladies to whom you are responsible.

**Big "I's"**

You may be honored at times, but the minute you expect it, you have lost honor with the One who is most important—God. Humility is the virtue that brings honor to God. I'm sure you have heard, "There are no big 'I's' or little 'you's' in the kingdom of God." This is very true. The only big "I's," a pastor's wife should seek after are:

*Influence* – Use your influence to care for the women God has placed under you. Impart to them the values you have been given.

*Impact* – Make an impact on every life you come in contact with. Don't limit yourself just to the saints. Challenge yourself to touch the life of the bank teller, the postal clerk, and the bag boy at the grocery store or your child's teacher.

*Impartial* – Show the same love and concern to each lady in your congregation. Never show "favorites" among them. This will only cripple your influence with them as a whole. At times, it is a great challenge to be impartial when you feel lonely. Seek out another pastor's wife in the district to make friends with. This will help meet the need of a close friend in your life.

*Involved* – Stay involved in as much activity surrounding the church as you can. Balance your involvement with family responsibilities. As the church grows, you may not be able to attend every social event sponsored by your church, but at the same time, you don't want to be so absent that you become unapproachable. Being involved is being accessible and available whenever you are needed.

# 56

# *In the Community*

There are things the pastor's wife can do to put your church in the mind of the community. This is not your sole responsibility, but you can become involved. You may also encourage your ladies to get involved.

Community projects such as parades, voting booths, fairs, craft sessions and other activities can be fun and double as an outreach. Doing a bake sale at a fair may be a more profitable than sitting in front of your church entrance and selling exclusively to your people.

If your children are in public school, get involved in the Parent-Teacher Association or a similar program. Not only will your voice be heard as a parent, but also you will be valued as a conservative citizen.

Attend a prayer breakfast, or organize one yourself and invite the other pastors' wives in your community. Create a bond in your community with the other churches. Although they may not teach the truth as you do, your contact with them will give others the opportunity to see what Pentecost is and remove pre-conceived ideas about what you believe.

Go to the library, community center, and other community sponsored events whenever possible. The greatest advantage of community involvement is to meet people by becoming a friend, gaining their confidence, and leading them to faith in Christ.

**Times and Seasons**

Before you go out and volunteer at your local hospital, you should first consider your season of life. If you are a young mother, or if you have small children, it is the season of your life to nurture your community at home. Your young children need you home with them (if you are privileged to stay home). If you have children and work outside the home, you probably have little time for anything else but working and raising children. That is okay. You are in the child-rearing season.

The next season of your life is when your youngest child goes away to school. This will give you some liberty during the day. Now you may want to become involved in other projects. This is the perfect time for the PTA or other educational programs. The benefits your children receive from the educational system are incentives to help you stay on the cutting edge of what is happening in the local schools, community, and even the state and federal governments.

The next season of your life is when your family is gone. Some call this the *empty nest syndrome*. This is a time when you **need** to find some things to help fill the void left after the children are gone. Sitting in a rocker pining and whining, the laughter and hustle and bustle of a house full of children will only make your life miserable. Step outside, drink in the sunshine and embark on some new adventures. Pick up a hobby, or do some long-term projects around the church and home. Keeping your hands busy will help keep your mind sharp. Idle hands create idle minds; working hands create working minds. The woman in Proverbs 31 works willingly with her hands.

There are so many areas of pastoring that could be discussed; hopefully these recommendations are helpful. Some things come naturally and need not be covered again and again. About the time you think you have it all figured out, someone comes along with a unique need or challenging situation and it's back to the books. None of us have arrived, but we can share ideas and learn from each other.

I pray for you, pastor's wife! You are part of a mighty army in the Kingdom of God. May you live in prosperity, serve in humility, and reap in abundance!

# *Notes*

# Part Ten

# The Layman's Wife

# 57

# *The Privilege*

The honor to be among the great collection of laymen's wives is a great one. This is an opportunity to rise to every occasion God puts in your path with strength and support. Be the best saint you can be. Don't settle for being just ordinarily good, be the best. Some may say, "I don't have time to be a maid to the pastor's wife." I'm not suggesting you do anything you probably don't already do. Being the best you can be with the time you have and the talent God has given you is living life at its best.

Every pastor's wife needs a friend among the laity. In other words, she needs someone who is mindful of her needs as she meets the needs of everyone else.

When we pioneered a church in Peoria, Arizona, the Lord sent along a couple to help us. Janice was soon to become my friend. Having been in the ministry herself, she anticipated my needs and made herself available to lighten my load whenever possible. She could sense when I was under a heavy load or burden. She would put her arms around me in a great big hug and say, "Sister Baughman, I was praying for you this week." There was nothing more valuable she could have given me than the gift of concern.

## The gift of concern

To be a friend to the minister and his wife is to minister to them. Many saints do not understand the ethical guidelines that pastors and their wives have to follow in regard to their relationship with the saints. To a certain extent, they are your best friends and are disposed to be at your service whenever you need them. On the other hand, however, if they are too casual with you, it is difficult to retain a respect for their position. Thus, they have to hold themselves away to a certain degree to prevent the pastorate from becoming too common. Be patient with them and understand this delicate sacrifice. It is not always easy to do.

On the other hand, you are not required to attempt to hold yourself in a leadership position in relation to the pastor and wife. You can pour yourself into their lives meeting a need in them whether or not they can return it. To help you further understand the role you may fulfil, here are some areas you may want to consider:

➤*Be faithful* to your commitment to God. The ministry is greatly encouraged by a Christian who does not constantly need care and encouragement.

➤*Be sensitive*, not only to the needs of the pastor's family, but also to the other members of the church. By bearing the burden of another member you may lighten the load of the pastor and leaders.

➤*Be compassionate* toward others. Refuse to allow an insensitive and grumpy sister to rob you of the gift of compassion, and a heart after God.

➤*Be passionate* toward the things of God and feel after the heartbeat of the pastor. To have his vision is to see what God wants to do in your community.

➤*Take initiative* wherever you go to find things to do to make life easier for others. Pull up the slack in others to lessen the load on leadership.

# 58

# *Your Relationship to the Pastor's Wife*

To avoid jealousy and multiple other problems in the church, the pastor's wife may not be able to count you verbally as her best friend. As the laymen, deacons, and other men of the church are under the pastor, so it is with their wives. First they are under the authority of their husbands, who are in turn under the authority of the shepherd who is under God.[1] This puts the pastor's wife in a position of ministry over the ladies in the congregation. She does not take the place of her husband, but as his helper, she can minister more uniquely to the ladies' needs because she can identify with them. As the pastor gives her the authority, you are subject to be as mindful of her leadership as you would the pastor.

Expecting the pastor's wife to spend all her time with you and no other lady in the church is unfair and selfish. She has to divide her time among all the ladies in the church, which, at any rate, is a challenge. If you haven't noticed already, the new converts will require more of your pastor and his wife's time than other members will. Just like natural babies, these spiritual babies need special attention, which is

---

[1] 1 Corinthians 11:3; Ephesians 5:22-26; Colossians 3:18; 1 Peter 5:1-5, Titus 2:4-5

very time consuming. It would be better to share the responsibility with the pastor's wife and help care for the new converts than to demand hours of her attention yourself. In doing so, you will find a close place in her heart.

The pastor's wife has a plate full of responsibilities in the church, but her first one is to her family. If she insists on staying home with her children rather than taking a day out with the ladies, be understanding of her devotion to her family. Her family must always come first.

The pastor's wife has added responsibilities when a revival is scheduled. Many times the evangelist and his family will eat one or more meals at the pastor's home. If she does not ask for the help of the ladies in the congregation, it would be a thoughtful gesture to offer to organize a group of ladies to help during this time. You may feel a little unfamiliar with organizing something like this, so I have offered some suggestions to help you.

➢First, ask the pastor's wife how many meals she will be serving. Will they be taking the evangelist out to dinner and when?

➢Would she like to make the menus and the ladies cook them? Or would she like you to make the menus and go from there.

➢Would she prefer to cook the main dish and the ladies bring in side dishes and dessert?

➢Ask her what she prefers in the way of food. Are there any things either family cannot eat for health reasons? Would they prefer a full meal or a few snacks for after church?

➢Would she like one lady each night to stay and serve the meal? (This is a *very* unselfish offer!)

➢Finally, assure her if there is anything she or the evangelists need to let you know. Then follow through to meet this need.

Now you are ready to approach the church ladies. Ask the pastor to announce a short meeting after church a few weeks before the revival. At the meeting, you will first express how the ladies can get involved in this revival. Encourage them to sacrifice one evening for the revival for service unto the Lord.

Explain to the ladies that it is your burden to help the pastor's wife entertain the evangelist and lighten her load. Assign volunteers to cook different dishes and others to deliver the meals. The ladies delivering the meals may stay and serve if that is in the plans. Let them know that when they all work together the load will not fall on anyone in particular. Divide the main and side dishes up evenly among the ladies.

Each evening meal should include a main dish, vegetables, salad, dessert, and drinks. Keep an open mind to those volunteering and be considerate of the women that work outside the home. You may suggest a meal be served at the church. The people in the congregation would enjoy the opportunity to interact with the evangelist and his family one evening.

If you offer to organize a project like this during revival and the pastor's wife declines any help, do not be discouraged. She may be the type that *loves* to entertain. You may ask her if you can bring in some desserts to help with the budget, or offer to do anything else and let her decide what she needs.

This is not a suggestion to put more unnecessary responsibility on you or the other church ladies, but to give you the chance to participate in ministry. This is another facet of the *ministry of Christian hospitality.*

The Bible says, *"you do not have because you do not ask" (James 4:2).* This is not only true in our relationship with God, but it is also true with each other. If you want the blessing of serving, you have to ask what is needed. After you do it the first time, you will feel like an old pro, and it will be easier the next time.

If you do not feel comfortable organizing something like this, suggest it to the Ladies Leader of your church. She can organize it and you could offer to assist her in the project. This way, you are not in charge, but able to be a large part comfortably working behind the scene.

# 59

# *Other Relationships*

## Your Relationship with the Evangelist

When your pastor announces there is going to be a revival, don't you feel a little over excited sometimes? If you are from a small church in a small town, just knowing company is coming is great news. Even if the pastor invites your very favorite evangelist, there are some guidelines you need to keep in mind. These guidelines probably fall under the category of ethics rather than etiquette, but as you have already discovered, often there is a close relationship between the two.

➤Never offer the evangelist money without the pastor's knowledge. This puts the evangelist in a very awkward position. He does not know if you may have just paid him the tithes you withheld from your church.

➤Conversations that include dissatisfaction with any part of the ministry or your pastor should be avoided. If you have a problem with your pastor, go to him first, not someone else.

➤If the evangelist and his wife have a recreational vehicle parked on the church property, or they are staying in the evangelist's quarters, it is not a good idea to "drop in" for a visit. Many times the evangelists have schooling for their children, prayer and preparation time, or other private matters to take care of during the day. If they are outside when you are at the church, it is fine to visit, but do not invite yourself into their private quarters.

## Your Relationship with Others in the Church

The joy of Christian fellowship when handled correctly cannot be measured. Getting together with others who share your faith can provide spiritual encouragement and be a major source of happiness. Proper fellowship involves gossip-free visits that edify and encourage each other. Barbecue picnics, dinner parties, potlucks, afternoon teas, and other eating activities are popular among Pentecostal friends.

Christian fellowship need not be limited to eating activities. Craft fairs, state parks, science fairs, museums, and other educational opportunities are fun things to do together. Many times a local mall will sponsor antique and craft shows. Other special events that travel through your town are fun to share with friends.

Social activities that include county fairs, theme parks, rodeos, concerts, and dinner theaters should be carefully considered before attending. Some pastors would rather you not attend some or all of these places. It is a good idea to check with him before inviting someone else in the congregation to go with you, especially a new convert.

Improper fellowship would include anything that does not lift each other up. Gossip is never appropriate whether among close friends or casual acquaintances. Talking about others can be hurtful and cause irreparable damage. On occasion, I have left a simple conversation and felt it was not edifying, so I had to repent and ask the person I was with for forgiveness.

We are all a part of the body of Christ. If we had been at the cross, when Jesus' body was removed, we would have handled his fleshly body with the utmost care and respect. We would not have let his head drop to one side or drag his legs in the dirt. Why do we handle his body differently now? We must treat each other with care and respect for we are the body of Christ.

God will help you know when you have participated in fellowship that is not pleasing to him. Be sensitive to the Lord and obedient to your pastor and God will truly bless your fellowship.

# Notes

_____
_____
_____
_____
_____
_____
_____
_____
_____
_____
_____
_____
_____
_____
_____
_____
_____
_____
_____
_____
_____
_____
_____
_____
_____
_____

# Resources

## Self & Social-Image

Fischer-Mirkin, Toby. *Dress Code.* Clarkson Potter Publishers, New York.

Gillham, Anabel. *The Confident Woman.* Eugene: Harvest House Publishers, 1993.

Jackson, Carole. *Color Me Beautiful.* New York: Ballantine Books, 1980.

Littauer, Florence. *It Takes So Little To Be Above Average.* Eugene: Harvest House Publishers, 1983.

Lush, Jean. *Emotional Phases of a Woman's Life.* New Jersey: Fleming H. Percell Company.

Maxwell, John C. *Your Attitude Key to Success.* San Bernardino: Here's Life Publishers, Inc., 1984.

McDowell, Josh. *Building Your Self-Image.* Wheaton: Living Books, 1998.

McQuay, Chris. *Behold Thy Handmaid.* Hazelwood: Pentecostal Publishing House, 1991.

Ortlund, Anne. *Disciplines of the Beautiful Woman.* Waco, TX.: Word Books, 1977.

Price, Eugenia. *Woman to Woman.* Grand Rapids:
    Zondervan Publishing House.

Trobisch, Walter. *Love Yourself: Self-Acceptance &
    Depression.* Downers Grove, IL: Inter-Varsity Press.


### Hospitality

Greig, Doris W. *We Didn't Know They Were Angels.*
    Ventura, CA: Regal Books, 1987.

Stewart, Martha. *Entertaining.* New York: Clarkson N.
    Potter, Inc., 1982.


### Wedding Etiquette

Bride's Magazine. *Bride's Wedding Planner.* New York:
    Fawcett Columbine, 1990.

Chase, Deborah. *Every Bride is Beautiful.* New York:
    William Morrow and Company, 1999.

Lalli, Cele Goldsmith. *Modern Bride Guide to Etiquette.*
    New York: John Wiley & Sons, Inc.

Loots, Barbara. *The Bride's Book of Beautiful Ideas.* Kansas
    City: Hallmark Cards Inc.

McBride-Mellinger, Maria. *The Perfect Wedding.* New
    York: Collins, 1997.

Piljac, Pamela A. *The Bride to Bride Book, A Complete Wedding Planner For the Bride* Chicago: Chicago Review Press, Inc., 1983.

Post, Elizabeth L. *Emily Post on Weddings-Revised Edition.* New York: Harper Perennial, 1994.

Roberts, Cookie. *The Creative Wedding Guide.* Valrico, Florida: Heartstrings, 1989.

Williamson, Martha. *Inviting God to Your Wedding.* New York: Harmony Books, 2000.

## Communication Etiquette

Feinberg, Steven L., ed., *Crane's Blue Book of Stationery; The Styles and Etiquette of Letters, Notes, and Invitations.* New York: Doubleday, 1989.

Isaacs, Florence, *Just a Note to Say.* New York: Clarkson Potter/Publishers, 1995.

Mandel, Thomas and Gerard Van der Leun. *Rules of the Net: Online Operating Instructions for Human Beings.* New York: Hyperion, 1996.

Martin, Judith. *Miss Manners Basic Training: Communication.* New York: Crown Publishers. 1997.

Phillips, Linda, and Wayne Price. *The Concise Guide to Executive Etiquette.* New York: Doubleday, 1990.

## General

Baldrige, Letitia. *The Amy Vanderbilt Complete Book of Etiquette*. Garden City, New York: Doubleday & Company, Inc., 1978.

Baldrige, Letitia. *Letitia Baldrige's New Complete Guide to Executive Manners*. New York: Rawson Associates, 1993.

Markham, Bonnie Jean. *The Nitty-Gritty for Ministers' Wives*. Hazelwood: Pentecostal Publishing House, 1988.

Martin, Judith. *Miss Manners Basic Training: Communications*. New York: Crown Publishers, Inc., 1997.

Martin, Judith. *Miss Manners Basic Training: Eating*. New York: Crown Publishers, Inc., 1997.

Phillips, Linda and Wayne. *The Concise Guide to Executive Etiquette*. New York: Doubleday, 1990.

Post, Elizabeth L. *Emily Post on Etiquette*. New York: Harper Perennial, 1995.

Post, Elizabeth L. *Emily Post's Etiquette,* 15th ed., New York: Harper & Row, Publishers, 1984.

Post, Peggy. *Emily Post's Etiquette*, 16th ed., New York: Harper Collins, 1997.

Roosevelt, Eleanor. *Book of Common Sense Etiquette*. New York: Macmillan, 1962.

Tuleja, Tad. *Curious Customs*. New York: Harmony Books, 1987.

# *Other Books Available*

## *Let's Go!* An Autobiography of Mark Baughman, with Terry R. Baughman

The story of a pioneer preacher, his conversion to Christ during depression years and the strong call of God on his life that led him from raising crops on an isolated Oklahoma farm, to labor in another harvest field across the country; the field of souls. He candidly reveals his personal struggles to fulfill God's call in the face of obstacles. You will sympathize with the struggles and rejoice in the victories as you journey through the pages of the lives of Mark and Zealous Baughman as they raise four children in evangelistic work and labor to build seven churches throughout the Southwest. (196 pages, softcover, 5½ x 8½)

**Item 1-08524-563-2**                    **USD        $11.00**

---

## MYSTERIES OF THE KINGDOM, Terry R. Baughman

Jesus promised to reveal the "mysteries of the kingdom" to those that hear and believe his teaching in the parables. Jesus explained that an understanding of the mysteries of the kingdom of heaven was given to the disciples but concealed from those who rejected his message. *Mysteries of the Kingdom* is a study of the parables of Matthew 13 and what they reveal concerning the inclusion of Gentiles in the kingdom of heaven. (129 pages, softcover, 8½ x 11)

**Item 1-08524-563-6**                    **USD        $12.00**

**Terry R. Baughman** is the Academic Dean at *Christian Life College*, Stockton, California, where he teaches a number of Bible courses as well as courses in practical ministry. He earned a Bachelor of Arts in Bible and Theology from *Christian Life College* in 1977 and received his Master of Arts in Exegetical Theology in 1999 from *Western Seminary* in San Jose, California. A minister for over twenty-five years, he has evangelized extensively, pastored *Truth Center* in Canyon, Texas, and founded *Worship & Word-the Northwest Church* in Peoria, Arizona.

**Gayla Baughman**, songwriter and musician, is an instructor and Academic Assistant at *Christian Life College* where she received a Bachelor of Arts in Christian Music. During her musical career she has recorded four projects with her family, *The Bible Singing Bibb Family,* two choir projects with *Abundant Life Temple* in Gladewater, Texas, as well as three recordings with her husband in their twenty-two plus years of marriage. Terry, Gayla, and their children, Marenda and Terry Robert comprise *the Baughman Group.* They are involved in various singing and ministry projects.

*Order additional copies of:*

## Christian Social Graces, A Guide for the Pentecostal Woman, by Gayla M. Baughman

*C hristian Social Graces* is an etiquette book tailored for the Christian woman. Author Gayla Baughman stresses the importance of who you are and how to conduct yourself socially in areas of communication and hospitality etiquette, such as manners and the setting of a table. She also includes the proper etiquette involved in planning weddings and showers, as well as how to act as a guest in someone else's home and tips on being a proper hostess. The reader will be entertained and educated in the areas of various social graces as Gayla shares personal experiences mixed with traditional etiquette designed for Pentecostal women of all ages. (415 pages, softcover, 5½ x 8½)

**ISBN 0-9710411-0-5**　　　　　　　**USD**　　**$14.00**

---

***Clip, copy, or transfer all information to another sheet:***

___ copies of *Christian Social Graces* @ $14.00 ea. $_____

___ copies of *Let's Go!* @ $11.00 ea. $_____

___ copies of *Mysteries of the Kingdom* @ $12.00 ea. $_____

___ CD(s) *Is that love in your Eyes?* @ $15.00 ea. $_____

___ cassette(s)*Is that love in your Eyes?* @ $10.00 ea. $_____

10% Shipping & Handing (20% Canadian/30% Foreign) $_____

Total amount enclosed  $_____

***Ship to:*** (Please Print)

| **Name** | | |
|---|---|---|
| **Address** | | |
| **City** | **St** | **Zip** |
| **Phone** | | |
| **Email** | | |

### Make Checks payable and mail to:
### Baughman Group Ministries
914 Shadow Creek Dr. • Stockton, CA 95209
209.956.2692 • email: trbaughman@baughmangroup.org
Visit our website: www.baughmangroup.org